PERGAMON INTERNATIONAL LIBRARY
of Science, Technology, Engineering and Social Studies

*The 1000-volume original paperback library in aid of education,
industrial training and the enjoyment of leisure*

Publisher: Robert Maxwell, M.C.

Adult Cognition and Aging
(PGPS-139)

87- 723

Pergamon Titles of Related Interest

Carstensen/Edelstein HANDBOOK OF CLINICAL GERONTOLOGY
Lewinsohn/Teri CLINICAL GEROPSYCHOLOGY: New Directions in Assessment and Treatment
Pinkston/Linsk CARE OF THE ELDERLY: A Family Approach
Tamir COMMUNICATION AND THE AGING PROCESS: Interaction Throughout the Life Cycle
Yost et al. GROUP COGNITIVE THERAPY: A Treatment Method for Depressed Older Adults

Related Journals
(Free sample copies available upon request)

LANGUAGE AND COMMUNICATION
EXPERIMENTAL GERONTOLOGY

PERGAMON GENERAL PSYCHOLOGY SERIES
EDITORS
Arnold P. Goldstein, Syracuse University
Leonard Krasner, SUNY at Stony Brook

Adult Cognition and Aging
Developmental Changes in Processing, Knowing and Thinking

JOHN M. RYBASH
Mohawk Valley Community College

WILLIAM J. HOYER
Syracuse University

PAUL A. ROODIN
State University of New York College at Oswego

87-723

PERGAMON PRESS
New York   Oxford   Beijing   Frankfurt
São Paulo   Sydney   Tokyo   Toronto

Pergamon Press Offices:

U.S.A.	Pergamon Press, Maxwell House, Fairview Park, Elmsford, New York 10523, U.S.A.
U.K.	Pergamon Press, Headington Hill Hall, Oxford OX3 0BW, England
PEOPLE'S REPUBLIC OF CHINA	Pergamon Press, Qianmen Hotel, Beijing, People's Republic of China
FEDERAL REPUBLIC OF GERMANY	Pergamon Press, Hammerweg 6, D-6242 Kronberg, Federal Republic of Germany
BRAZIL	Pergamon Editora, Rua Eça de Queiros, 346, CEP 04011, São Paulo, Brazil
AUSTRALIA	Pergamon Press (Aust.) Pty., P.O. Box 544, Potts Point, NSW 2011, Australia
JAPAN	Pergamon Press, 8th Floor, Matsuoka Central Building, 1-7-1 Nishishinjuku, Shinjuku-ku, Tokyo 160, Japan
CANADA	Pergamon Press Canada, Suite 104, 150 Consumers Road, Willowdale, Ontario M2J 1P9, Canada

---

Copyright © 1986 Pergamon Books, Inc.

First printing 1986

Library of Congress Cataloging in Publication Data

Rybash, John M.
  Adult cognition and aging.

  (Pergamon general psychology series ; 139)
  Bibliography: p.
  Includes indexes.
    1. Cognition--Age factors. 2. Aging--Psychological aspects. I. Hoyer, William J. II. Roodin, Paul.
  III. Title. IV. Series. [DNLM: 1. Aging.
  2. Cognition--in adulthood. 3. Cognition--physiology.
  4. Models, Psychological. BF 311 R989a]
  BF724.55.C63R93   1986   155.67   86-4939
  ISBN 0-08-033166-1
  ISBN 0-08-033165-3 (pbk.)

Printed in the United States of America

We dedicate this book to our wives, Vinnie, Joan, and Marlene, and to our families for their continued patience, understanding, inspiration, and love.

Contents

Preface

A wide range of theories and research concerning the nature of adult cognitive functioning emerged during the late 1970s and early 1980s. This work was an outgrowth of several distinct traditions in the study of cognition and cognitive development (e.g., information processing, psychometric, genetic-epistemological, cognitive science). In *Adult Cognition and Aging* we review and critique these theoretical perspectives and empirical findings. In this text, we also present an Encapsulation Model of adult cognitive development. This model integrates and expands the traditional approaches to the study of adult cognition.

The Encapsulation Model addresses itself to the analysis of age-related changes in the three dominant strands of cognition: *processing, knowing* and *thinking*. Specifically, the Encapsulation Model suggests that: (a) there are age-related losses in the basic mental processes that allow adults the opportunity to acquire, organize, and retain new information; (b) there are self-constructed domains of knowledge within which adults do not evidence decline or reduced efficiency of function until very late in life; (c) within these domains of expertise, adults employ extant knowledge systems and sophisticated styles of thinking in order to compensate for losses in cognitive hardware; and (d) the continued refinement or evolution of domain-specific, cognitive specializations is characteristic of development throughout the life course, but occurs most commonly during adulthood. Thus, the Encapsulation Model simultaneously addresses the declines that take place in the *processing* aspects of cognition and the advances that may occur in the *knowing* and *thinking* dimensions of cognition.

Adult Cognition and Aging is intended to meet the needs of advanced students and professionals in the fields of developmental psychology, cognitive psychology, and aging. As a text, it is intended for upper-level undergraduate and graduate-level courses and seminars in adult cognition and aging as well as general courses in cognitive development. Students will benefit from the emphasis on new conceptualizations of developmental change and cognitive aging. As a professional reference, it is intended to serve as a resource for academicians and researchers in the fields of life-span cognitive developmental psychology and cognitive aging. Professionals in the field of adult cognition will value our scholarly and comprehensive approach.

We acknowledge Jerome B. Frank from Pergamon Press for his assistance and cooperation during all of the phases of this project. We are also very grateful to Dr. Andrew Coyne and other colleagues and reviewers for their insightful comments on an earlier version of this manuscript.

Finally, we hope our text will stimulate interest in the study of adult cognition and help to clarify important research issues that need to be addressed. We caution our readers, however, that *Adult Cognition and Aging* represents one relatively frozen moment in our developing awareness of the parameters and meanings of adult cognitive change. As students who are witnessing the continual growth and evolution of the field of cognitive aging, it would be wise to heed the words of Jacob Bronowski from the *Ascent of Man*: "It is important that students bring a certain ragamuffin, barefoot irreverence to their studies; they are not here to worship what is known but to question it" (p. 360).

1

Introduction

The message of [William] James for psychology today is this: Narrow consistency can neither bring salvation to your science, nor help to mankind. Let your approaches be diverse, but let them in the aggregate do full justice to the heroic qualities in man. If you find yourselves tangled in paradoxes, what of that? Who can say that the universe shall not contain paradoxes simply because they are unpalatable?

G. Allport
The Person in Psychology: Selected Essays

The revival of psychological interest in the study of cognition has been underway for some time now. Simultaneously, the study of the cognitive psychology of adulthood and aging can no longer be thought of as a neglected topic of inquiry as it once was, given the amount of research published in this area in the past decade (Abrahams, Hoyer, Elias, & Bradigan, 1975; Hoyer, Raskind, & Abrahams, 1984; Poon, 1980). However, the research accumulates in a piecemeal fashion, and there are few, if any, comprehensive and integrative treatments of this field.

This book offers an integrative approach to the study of the organization and function of cognition during adulthood. We attempt to bridge gaps between research and theory in information processing, cognitive science, psychometric intelligence, and genetic–epistemology. Although there has been a proliferation of research on adult age differences in information processing, the results of these studies generally are not meant to address the emergence of more sophisticated styles of thinking during the adult years. It may be that these higher level aspects of thinking are among the most interesting and typical characteristics of adult cognition. Research conducted from a cognitive science viewpoint has exhibited substantial progress in recent years, in part by placing emphasis on the structure and function of knowledge in cognition. Most cognitive scientists, however, have not addressed the question of what happens to knowledge during adulthood.

Psychometric research is differential and multidimensional in its approach, but it does not tell us much about the processes and operations that account for cognition and its development. Genetic–epistemological theory has a sound developmental basis, but it falls short when evaluated by strict empirical criteria. Another problem for genetic–epistemological theory has to do with the manner in which cognition is conceptualized. That is, Piagetian theory is focused on the development of logical–mathematical thinking, and other domains and types of thought are subsumed by this type of reasoning.

In this book, we highlight the strengths and weaknesses of these various perspectives in reviewing research and theory bearing on cognition and cognitive development during the adult years. We attempt a synthesis of theory and research on cognition with the developmental study of cognitive functioning. We identify and discuss issues in the study of cognitive development and aging with the aim of sparking the interest of cognitive scientists in the problems of cognitive development across the adult years. We also hope to show developmental psychologists how some of the current research and theory in cognitive science contributes to the understanding of age-related cognitive change.

THE DEVELOPMENT, REPRESENTATION, AND ORGANIZATION OF KNOWLEDGE

In this chapter we address questions concerning the nature, development, representation, and organization of knowledge. We take the view that human cognition involves the representation and use of substantive knowledge. Knowledge is roughly organized into categories called domains. Domain-specific knowledge systems, we argue, structure the acquisition of new information and the application of old information. We see the need for pluralism in the study of cognitive development during the adult years and present a framework for integrating research and theory in the areas of information processing, cognitive science, psychometric intelligence, and genetic–epistemology.

Questions about the nature and organization of knowledge domains are fundamental to the concerns of psychologists, philosophers, computer scientists, biologists, and others. Recent debate regarding the organization and development of knowledge has been stimulated by Fodor's (1983) discussion of modularity. Fodor, along with Chomsky, has taken a strong nativist position, arguing that there are biologically pre-formed faculties of knowledge. In contrast, many researchers in the area of artificial intelligence, information processing, and psychometric intelligence take an empiricist or "tabula rasa" position. They make no assumptions about the underlying structure and organization of cognition. Few, if any, developmental psychologists are represented by either of these polarized positions regarding the organization and development of knowledge. Notably, Piaget identified himself as a constructivist or interactionist rather than as either a nativist or empiricist. Similarly, many contemporary developmental psychologists are interested in the developmental and maturational boundaries of learning. They recognize the operation of both environmental and maturational forces throughout the life span and do not adhere to either a purely empiricist or nativist conception.

Many researchers have neglected to take into account the dynamics of knowledge in the developmental study of cognition. This omission has limited the understanding of cognition in adulthood because knowledge affects and constrains cognitive functioning, and knowledge changes with development (Keil, 1981, 1986). We mean by knowledge that there is a representation in the mind of experience about the world. This representation of experience is cumulative, and it is recorded and successively integrated with existing knowledge. This growing and changing knowledge system affects how the person thinks about new information. The processes of information acquisition are not static, but are affected by the kind of information being processed and what the individual already "knows" about this kind of information. Of course, it is also important to recognize that the information processes associated with knowledge acquisition may change in speed and efficiency with age. There are many studies showing age-related declines in such processes during the adult years (Botwinick, 1984; Kausler, 1982; Salthouse, 1982). However, recent work (Labouvie-Vief, 1985) has questioned the practical meaning of these age-related decrements.

We propose a description of adult cognitive development, which we have termed the Encapsulation Model. This model is based on the emergence and increased differentiation of domain-ordered knowledge specializations. Although, there has been recent emphasis given to the importance of knowledge in the development of memory and thought in childhood (Carey, 1982; Chi, 1983; Keil, 1981,1986), we argue that the organization of substantive domains plays a distinct role in adult development due to: (a) the relative lack of age-ordered, biologically programmed development; (b) the emergence of a unique differentiated cognitive system based on experience and incorporating various affective and motivational variables; (c) the increased encapsulation of input analyzers and other aspects of the information-processing system (e.g., memory access) with age and experience within specific domains; and (d) environmental press factors that encourage experience-based cognitive differentiation through the development of specializations within prescribed knowledge domains (e.g., careers). This differentiation can contribute to the emergence of unique hierarchical integrations across domains of knowledge.

Our position is that cognition changes in overall organization and form with consequent changes in knowledge acquisition. We suggest that development in adulthood is unidirectional (i.e., toward increased and differentiated complexity) and increasingly resistant to modification and/or revision. A mature or final form of human knowledge systems and organization is *a priori* unspecifiable, because it is dependent on characteristics of particular knowledge domains and age-related interindividual differences in mastery/competency in selected domains.

We suggest that the antecedents and consequences of pre-adult cognitive development are distinct from those associated with adulthood. Unlike cognitive development during the early years, which is relatively morphogenetic, inevitable, momentous, and uniform, no such underlying processes constrain and direct cognitive development in adulthood. That is, adult cognition can be characterized as largely experiential, irreversible, nonuniversal, and directed toward domain-specific mastery. To the extent that there are uniform aspects of cognitive development in adulthood, such uniformities can be attributed to commonalities in the experience of adulthood.

Our functional view of knowledge acquisition, representation, and organization suggests that the number and content of the domains of cognition cannot be specified *a priori*. The degree of compartmentalization of cognition is a function of the individual being represented. In contrast to Gardner's (1983) viewpoint that individuals possess multiple, hard-wired intelligences, a functional view suggests that individuals create unique domains of knowledge. Wide individual differences can be seen in the number and types of domains constructed by adults. People seem to build their own knowledge systems to forms (or foundations) that represent how they use their mental resources. In this sense, domains are representations of different areas of cognitive involvement on the part of individuals. Although there is some naturalness or universality to the domains developed, attributable to cultural commonalities and species factors, there are also unique environmental and person-based factors involved in the evolution and structure of adult cognition.

We stress, therefore, the active role played by the individual in the construction of knowledge domains and the allocation of psychological resources. The developing individual actively organizes and monitors what is known, what needs to be known, and intentionally determines how to utilize what is known. The active, constructive quality of individuals, as well as the knowledge structures that they create, may be most readily apprehended within the domain of personal knowledge, a domain within which self-representations and self-schemata have become encapsulated. It is not surprising, for example, to find that age-related changes in adult cognitive development are related to parallel changes in adult self-representation (cf. Broughton, 1978; Edelstein & Noam, 1982; Kegan 1982). Thus, there is a need to integrate theory and research in cognitive psychology with that in the area of social–emotional growth. Adult cognitive functioning, in our opinion, may be described and explicated only if we adopt such an integrative perspective.

Before elaborating on our approach, we discuss various meanings of the term *development*. We contrast different viewpoints regarding the nature of cognitive competence versus performance. And, we describe alternative conceptualizations of the growth and representation of knowledge.

THE MEANING AND NATURE OF DEVELOPMENT

There are several contrasting definitions of the term *development* vis-à-vis cognition and knowledge organization in adulthood. To Werner (1957), development was defined as increasing differentiation and hierarchic integration. To Nagel (1957), the term applied to a system possessing a definite structure and a definite set of pre-existing capacities. Development involved age-ordered changes in the system, yielding relatively permanent but novel increments not only in its structure but in its modes of operation. Schneirla (1957) contrasted the terms *growth*, *differentiation*, and *development*. The concept of growth, he argued, involved change by means of tissue accretion; differentiation emphasized variation in the changing structural aspects of the organism with age; and development referred to progressive changes in the organization of a functional, adaptive system (i.e., an individual) throughout its life history. Furthermore, Schneirla (1957) proposed that the processes of growth and differentiation are subsumed within the process of development. He also cautioned that a science of behavioral development should *not* be based on fully formed theories and principles from other sciences.

Recently, Baltes and his associates (Baltes & Willis, 1979, 1982; Dittmann-Kohli & Baltes, 1986; Willis & Baltes, 1980) have suggested that four different concepts need to be considered when interpreting cognitive development, especially as it relates to psychometrically defined intelligence, during the adult years. These four concepts were termed: multidimensionality, multidirectionality, interindividual variability, and intraindividual plasticity.

Multidimensionality refers to the notion that cognition is not a unitary construct or ability. Cognition is best conceptualized as a multiplicity of abilities and/or knowledge structures that are organized into a coherent whole.

Multidirectionality suggests that different aspects of cognition do not develop in the same (i.e., unidirectional) manner over the adult years. Instead, different cognitive abilities are expected to manifest different trajectories during adulthood.

Interindividual variability refers to the idea that there are differences between adults in the directionality and patterning of cognitive change. Within any single cohort and for any specific cognitive ability, some adults display an age-related increase in their level of cognitive sophistication, some evidence little or no change, and others manifest decremental patterns of change.

Intraindividual plasticity refers to the wide range within which particular cognitive abilities may manifest themselves. The notion of plasticity stresses the modifiability of cognitive abilities, as well as the role played by the context within which an individual exists in determining the level, directionality, and patterning of his/her cognitive development. Dittmann-Kohli and Baltes (1986) have summarized this position in the following manner:

> It is stated . . . that any comprehensive interpretation of adult and aging intelligence needs to include multidimensionality, multidirectionality, interindividual variability, and plasticity as salient features requiring integration. Together, the concepts emphasize a dynamic view of intelligence, a position that permits growth and decline to occur at the same time in the same individual and in persons of the same age. (pp. 8–9)

We agree with the list of descriptors elaborated upon by Baltes and his colleagues. However, we view these four concepts as just as descriptive of development as a "whole" as they are of any one strand of development (i.e., cognitive development). Furthermore, we add that the developing person is active in the construction and development of his/her own knowledge system. Our position is similar to the one expressed by the proponents of action theory (cf. Chapman, 1984; Eckensberger & Meacham, 1984). Action theorists suggest that all knowledge is acquired and synthesized within the context of intentional, self-regulated human activities and that knowledge can only acquire meaning within the context of an individual's direct relationship with the material world. Therefore, the person, his/her knowledge, and the environment are inextricably linked within the context of activity.

Our multidimensional/constructive viewpoint concerning the nature of human beings, human development, and human knowledge structures may be used to illustrate what Kegan (1982) has referred to as the dialectic relationship between entities (i.e., things) and processes (i.e., activities). For example, it is common to view development as a *process* that changes the *things* (i.e., the person as well as the knowledge he/she possesses) that develop. It may be just as meaningful, however, to conceptualize the person as well as the knowledge he/she possesses as *processes* that create the thing we call development. To paraphrase Kegan (1982), the subject of our book is the development of knowledge, where knowledge refers just as much to an activity as a thing—"an ever progressive motion giving itself new form" (p. 8).

COMPETENCE, PERFORMANCE, AND COGNITIVE DEVELOPMENT

The attainment of a relatively full range of competencies in adulthood is considered by some theorists to be the hallmark of mature development. With regard to specific theories of cognitive competence in adulthood, the main issues seem to be: how various competencies emerge, the extent to which these competencies are organized independently from each other, and the extent to which new competencies replace previous competencies.

It is important to distinguish between the concepts of competence and performance as they apply to the study of cognition. Stone and Day (1980) suggested that the competence/performance issue may be illustrated within the context of Chomsky's (1965, 1968) theory of psycholinguistics and Piaget's stage theory of cognitive development. Competence, for Chomsky, referred to a speaker-hearer's tacit knowledge of the idealized rules that allow for the association of sound and meaning within the context of his/her language system. Performance, on the other hand, was regarded as the actual production and comprehension of utterances. Chomsky argued that the linguistic performance of an individual does not approach the linguistic competence of an individual. Linguistic performance is typically imperfect and ungrammatical, whereas linguistic competence represents an intuitive understanding of those rules that should lead to the production of perfect grammatical utterances.

A similar distinction between competence and performance is readily apparent within Piagetian theory. Stone and Day (1980) observed that it is common for researchers working with Piagetian tasks to discover *horizontal décalage* (i.e., differential performance on tasks that differ with regard to the abstractness and familiarity of both instructions and materials but which nevertheless have the same structural/logical basis). For example, it has been reported (Brainerd, 1978, Keating, 1980; Neimark, 1975, 1979) that a relatively small percentage of adolescents are capable of solving formal-operational thinking tasks and that successful performance on some formal tasks is unrelated to performance on other formal tasks. These findings have led several researchers to suggest that all adolescents possess formal operational *competence* (i.e., a logical–mathematical thought structure that combines the 16 binary operations of propositional logic with the functions of the INRC Group), but their *performance* (i.e., their actual problem-solving behavior) rarely measures up to their competence. This gap between competence and performance has been attributed to characteristics of the task (e.g., abstractness, familiarity) and to a variety of nonstructural characteristics of the subjects' cognitive system (e.g., attention, memory span, cognitive style).

Stone and Day (1980) have maintained that psycholinguists and genetic epistemologists have an erroneous conceptualization of the competence/performance issue, that has given rise to a form of *negative rationalism* (cf. Rommetveit, 1978). Negative rationalism, a viewpoint that pervades the cognitive sciences, refers to the position that a person's thought is understood via its deviation from some idealized inner mental structure or rule system. More specifically, Stone and Day (1980) commented:

What has happened in cognitive developmental psychology is similar to what happened in psycholinguistics. The term competence has often been used to refer to a specific and integrated set of operations "in the head" of the individual, i.e., it has been used to refer to a mental structure that is empirically real. . . . These structures have been separated from performance factors or automation processes (psychological processes such as memory and attention) that are thought to determine whether competence is revealed in behavior. . . . (p. 333)

Stone and Day (1980) further argued that negative rationalism gives rise to a fragmented view of cognition. For example, knowledge structures come to be viewed as separate from attention, memory, and cognitive style. Consistent with this outlook, many research studies have as their goal an analysis of how performance factors block the expression of certain competencies. Negative rationalism also leads researchers to make too many competency-based assumptions about what individuals *must* be doing as they solve problems and tasks. Consequently, Stone and Day (1980) have suggested that theoreticians and researchers place a greater emphasis on the construction and evaluation of performance models. Performance models have as their goal an understanding of how the individual's knowledge structures, memory capacity, attentional mechanisms, and so on become integrated during the process of problem solving.

Stone and Day (1980) also suggested that psychologists who seek to develop performance theories would be wise to take into account the basic tenets of Soviet-based action theory (cf. Vygotsky, 1962, 1978). As previously mentioned, the focal point of action theory is an analysis of the goal-directed activity of the individual within his/her particular social and historical context. Action theorists are interested in determining the meaning that people attach to the problems they face in the everyday world and the goals that underlie problem definition and problem solution vis-à-vis the cognitive skills and processes that are deployed within the defined problem space. Thus, action theorists have developed a viewpoint about cognitive activity that has focused on concrete performance.

In addressing these issues, we believe that it is important to recognize that adults may perform in a dramatically different fashion on similar tasks from one occasion to the next. Clearly, much of everyday cognition involves cognitive activity that does not approach an individual's level of maximal or optimal performance on the problems to be solved. Yet theory in the cognitive sciences needs to describe the characteristics and boundaries of cognition by representing the types of mental activities that individuals are capable of performing in some situations some of the time. Thus, we see the need to embed cognition and all of its facets within the goal-related, intentional activity of the individual.

CONTRASTING VIEWS OF THE GROWTH AND REPRESENTATION OF KNOWLEDGE

There are several contrasting positions regarding the growth of knowledge. These general views differ with regard to the nature and nurture of knowledge structures, universality, constitutiveness, and descriptive properties.

The Pre-Formist View

The pre-formist or nativist position is that all knowledge is generated on the basis of already achieved or pre-existing knowledge. Chomsky (1965, 1979, 1980), Fodor (1965, 1975, 1979, 1983), and Quine (1953) are identified with this position, because they imply that there are innate similarity standards and knowledge dispositions. Chomsky, for example, makes the case that language and other domains represent innate "mental organs." Caplan and Chomsky (1982) proposed that language acquisition depends on environmental input only to the extent that a few basic parameters must be set. Once a particular direction to language development is established, language unfolds according to a genetically determined blueprint. The pre-formist claim with regard to language is supported by the proposition that it could not be acquired otherwise. That is, environmental input is too inadequate and the inductive abilities of the developing child are simply too weak to account for such acquisition.

In tracing his heritage in linguistics to Descartes, Chomsky (1966) overlooked his epistemological descendance from Plato. The pre-formist position can be traced to Plato's *Meno*, in which it was argued that the emergence of knowledge out of ignorance was incomprehensible. Plato's doctrine of *anamnesis* (recollections) posited that all knowledge or learning is actually remembering. Popper (1959) categorized Platonic epistemology as *essentialism*, because it was presumed that true knowledge is an exact description of the ultimate nature or essence of things. Quine (1969) discussed how even the simplest learning of a conditioned response always presupposes prior knowledge. To quote Peirce in Hartshorne and Weiss (1960):

> You cannot seriously think that every little chicken that is hatched has to rummage through all possible theories until it lights upon the good idea of picking up something and eating it. On the contrary, you think the chicken has an innate idea of doing this. . . . The chicken you say, pecks by instinct. But if you are going to think every poor chicken is endowed with an innate instinct toward a positive truth, why should you think that to man alone this gift is denied. . . . I am quite sure that you must be brought to acknowledge that man's mind has a natural adaptation to imagine correct theories of some kinds. (pp. 414–415)

Several new variations of the pre-formist viewpoint have recently emerged. One of these variations has been termed the *modularity* viewpoint. The modularity perspective suggests that the mind is organized in terms of a number of relatively specific, autonomous, and impenetrable cognitive subsystems or modules (Chomsky, 1975; Fodor, 1975, 1983; Gardner, 1983; Gazzaniga, 1985). Fodor (1975) suggested that different cognitive modules have different formal properties. In contrast to Piaget, Fodor (1975) argued that a child's thinking does not develop in terms of logical power. Rather, there is a progressive extension of the contents to which specific computations can be applied. Development is an increasing expansion of cognitive processes to various domains of thought, rather than an increase in logical power.

Chomsky's presupposition is that cognitive structures are in principle *explicable* in terms of a genetic program universal to the human species, even though this program remains to be explained or specified. Chomsky has described the process that is responsible for the attainment of language structures as a mapping function. Mapping involves imposing a lawful point-to-point correspondence between patterns belonging to "real" space and "image" space. That is, experience maps onto the developing knowledge state according to universal rules enacted by the person. From this view, mapping, or the learning or acquisition process, is a gradual "selective stabilization of functioning synapses" (Piattelli-Palmarini, 1979).

Empiricist Views of Knowledge Differentiation

The empiricist view is that knowledge develops out of experience and learning. Current empiricist views differ from each other with regard to their focus and level of analysis (or explanation). Information processing models emphasize the subprocesses that constitute intelligence or cognition. Researchers in the cognitive sciences frequently study performance in singular domains, or even a relatively singular process such as selective attention, without examining the overall organization of cognitive abilities. There is a large body of research on age differences in information processing abilities that does not provide an integrated framework for representing the nature of adult cognition.

Psychometric research on the structure of human intelligence is generally considered to be in the empiricist tradition. In recent years there has been much work on the nature of ability change during adulthood and on the patterns of change. Some of the models that have been proposed are multidimensional and describe a pattern of differential change along various dimensions of human abilities (see Baltes & Nesselroade, 1972; Cunningham, 1980, 1982; Garrett, 1946; Horn, 1982; Reinert, 1970; Schaie, 1983). In addition to psychometrically derived conceptions of the multidimensionality of intelligence, Gardner's (1983) theory of multiple intelligences suggests that there may be a neurobehavioral basis to the organization of human abilities. He suggested that there are at least seven natural modules or "frames," such as mathematics and music, into which we encode and organize the world. The artificial intelligence view is that knowledge is a representational system. Work on artificial intelligence and computer simulations of thought can be identified with the empiricist tradition, because generally no assumptions are made about innateness of knowledge. Questions about the developmental construction of knowledge are simply not addressed. A representational system is an evolving, self-updating collection of knowledge structures. It can be designed or organized to reflect the developing individual's experiences. In discussing the shortcomings of the artificial intelligence and computational models, Hofstadter (1981) noted that no matter how accurately a painting or a photograph captures some aspect of the world, it is not representative of how knowledge of that worldly object is organized, because it is static. He noted also that a mirror is not an accurate metaphor of the human representational system, even though it provides an immediate and continuously up-to-date reflection, because it only reflects. In other words, pictures and mirrors are inadequate cognitive or computational metaphors because they do not represent the functions of categorization, construction, and anticipation of knowledge. In addition, human representational systems represent aspects of the world even in the absence of contact with those objects, and the representations undergo time-related change.

Piaget's Constructivist View

In contrast to the pre-formist view, Piaget has argued that the functional invariants of cognition (i.e., assimilation and accommodation) are innate, but there are no innate cognitive structures. In contrast to an empiricist view, Piaget argued that knowledge cannot result from the mere recording of observations. According to Piaget, cognition is constructed by the person through successive actions performed on objects and information. Cognitive structures come about through the dynamic interplay of assimilation, accommodation, and equilibration. There is continual elaboration of new structures and operations (i.e., constructivism). No knowledge is based on experience alone (i.e., the empiricist view), because perception is always directed by schemes of action. Knowledge proceeds from action, and schemes develop as actions are repeated, internalized, and generalized. Piaget (1971) has expressed this viewpoint in the following way:

> No form of knowledge, not even perceptual knowledge, constitutes a simple copy of reality, because it always includes a process of assimilation to previous structure. (p. 4)

The importance of the concept of assimilation is twofold. On the one hand . . . it implies meaning, an essential notion because all knowledge has a bearing on meaning. . . . On the other hand, this concept expresses the fundamental fact that any piece of knowledge is connected with an action and that to know an object or a happening is to make use of it by assimilation into an action schema. (pp. 5-6)

Piaget's concept of decalage, or time lag, is related to the question of how knowledge domains develop in adulthood. More specifically, Piaget (1972) suggested that mature thought structures (i.e., formal operations) become contextualized within particular fields of specialization. This position seems consistent with the results of several empirical studies, which suggest that: (a) all of the structures characterizing a particular stage of cognitive development do not exhibit themselves at the same time; and (b) adults display differential levels of performance on experimental tasks whose solutions are dependent on the same cognitive structures (Brainerd, 1978; Keating, 1980; Niemark, 1979).

Maturational, Ethological Views

Rozin's (1976) position takes into account an ethological perspective. He suggested that cognitive development involves specialization along preformed, ethologically selected lines. Cognition is organized in a hierarchical manner, based on component, biologically pre-wired subprograms. These subprograms, which he called *adaptive specializations*, originate as specific solutions to specific problems in adaptation and development. Adaptive specializations can be functionally defined as simple programs or neural circuits (Ebbesson, 1984) or as clusters of programs and circuitry, and may contain both plastic and pre-wired aspects. Adaptive specializations become the building blocks or elements of complex cognitive function and its development. Initially, or at the time of their origin, these adaptive specializations are dedicated to serve a particular function and are inaccessible for other purposes. With development, experience or practice, and evolution, these programs may become more accessible for other functions and may become integrated within complex actions.

Some writers (Brent, 1978, 1984; Mergler & Goldstein, 1983) have recently suggested that adult cognition is characterized by cognitive integration and specialization. From this perspective, it may be largely adaptive for adults to attenuate the goal of seeking new information with age. It becomes increasingly age-inappropriate to evaluate adult mastery in terms of the efficiency and rate of such processes as encoding, learning, and memorizing.

Of course, one implication of this view is that researchers should cease comparing old and young along measures based on the cognitive strengths of the young. Older adults themselves should avoid the temptation to self-evaluate such cognitive skills as acquisition efficiency in terms of earlier skill levels. The skills of acquisition and memory storage may be replaced by a style of thinking that places emphasis on knowing and on affect, value, and meaning in experience. The cognitive concerns of older adults are likely to be different than those of younger adults. Older adults may pay more attention to new information in the context of extant knowledge than younger adults, who focus more on acquisition per se. Although all information may be processed in terms of existing knowledge, there may be an increased effect of established knowledge on the filtering and interpretation of new knowledge with aging. It may be that the past becomes a greater resource for interpreting the present with age (Boden & Bielby, 1983).

Rate of learning and access to acquired information are typically measured in studies of cognition. Such measures generally yield age-related deficiencies. One explanation for such findings is that individuals may not be equipped or prepared to be "ideal learning machines" throughout their life span. From an ethological perspective, early development can be characterized as a time of massive acquisition. In contrast, producing and knowing may be the predominant concerns of mature adults — to carry out the acquired knowledge mastered earlier in development (Labouvie-Vief, 1982a; Lerner & Bosnagle, 1981; Mergler & Goldstein, 1983; Schaie, 1977).

EVALUATION OF TRADITIONAL VIEWS OF THE GROWTH AND REPRESENTATION OF KNOWLEDGE

We have reviewed several domain-ordered conceptions of knowledge and cognitive development. All of the viewpoints mentioned above place different amounts of emphasis on the function and structure of knowledge representation. For example, a strong (i.e., nativist) position asserts that pre-formed knowledge representations determine the selection of particular sorts of incoming information, and a weak (i.e., empiricist) position presumes little or nothing more than the formation of knowledge categories as a function of input. Also, note that there is a difference in choice or breadth of inquiry among the various views we are considering. Piaget's constructive view, for example, chooses to explore those linguistic and cognitive properties that are also common to other cognitive domains, whereas Chomsky's "Cartesian" view chooses to examine linguistic properties that have no counterpart elsewhere in the cognitive repertoire.

There is a wide range of positions regarding domain-ordered cognition from hard-wired and pre-formed, on the one hand, to a differentiated system of knowledge organization based on learning, on the other. However, the most important point of convergence between the varieties of constructivism and innatism discussed previously is the rejection of the empiricist view. This convergence suggests that nothing is knowable unless a cognitive organization of some kind is present from the outset and unless the subject acts on the environment in some way.

Despite the diversity inherent in the above-mentioned models of knowledge representation, we believe that these models do *not* capture the observable strengths and dynamic characteristics of adult thought and/or adult knowledge structures. For example, most of the research conducted within the nativist/modularity framework has focused on animals and young children, while the data bearing on adult cognition have been gleaned from a most atypical population (i.e., brain-injured and/or stroke patients). Evidence that supports the validity of the hard-wired, modularity position comes most frequently from research involving infrahuman subjects. Human children, however, seem to possess a nervous system that is marked by plasticity and the nonspecific localization of various cognitive functions. Brain-injured adults display what appear to be different hard-wired cognitive modules. However, it should be noted that: (a) there seems to be a great deal of interindividual variability concerning where these functions are localized — even Gardner (1983) has pointed out the different ways in which *musical intelligence* is localized; and (b) proponents of the modularity or preformist model seem to be more concerned with the innate nature of general forms of cognition rather than specific knowledge systems. With regard to this last point, Gardner (1983) has argued for the existence of a hard-wired brand of *linguistic intelligence*, but he offers no specific explanation of how individuals develop particular knowledge systems or skills within this frame of intelligence (e.g., how does one individual become an accomplished poet but a mediocre playright, whereas another individual evidences the opposite profile of literary skills?).

Several writers within the genetic–epistemological camp have recognized the inadequacy of Piaget's formal operational description of adult cognition (Commons, Richards, & Armon, 1984) and have argued for the existence of postformal modes of reasoning unique to adulthood. This certainly represents a significant redirection in genetic–epistemological research. However, investigators working within this perspective have placed too much emphasis on the development of general thought structures and too little emphasis on the growth of expert, domain-specific knowledge representations.

Other researchers have offered new conceptualizations of existing psychometric models. Horn (1980, 1982), for example, recently proposed a modification of his earlier crystallized–fluid model (see also Cattell & Horn, 1978; Horn & Cattell, 1966). According to Horn (1980), the two broad sets of abilities known as crystallized and fluid intelligence can be hierarchically arranged and influenced. Dittmann-Kohli and Baltes (1986) have also expanded on Horn's (1970) model of fluid and crystallized abilities. They argued that adult cognition represents the emergence and elaboration of synthetic abilities (i.e., crystallized intelligence) and that more emphasis should be given to the crystallized aspects of cognition in our conceptions of adult intelligence. Further, crystallized abilities serve as the primary basis for adult wisdom and competence (see also Clayton & Birren, 1980). Similarly, Hoyer (1985) has proposed a three-factor model of cognitive aging based on the domain-specific nature of knowledge and: (a) the efficiency of various component or elementary information processes, (b) the efficiency of the control processes responsible for activating and integrating appropriate component processes and knowledge stores, and (c) the applicability of acquired knowledge structures in the form of rules, scripts, or schemas to the cognitive task at hand. However, the research bearing on psychometric intelligence and expert cognition has not taken into account the unique, qualitative characteristics of adult thought that have been recognized by postformal theorists (cf. Commons, Richards, & Armon, 1984).

TOWARD AN INTEGRATIVE APPROACH
TO ADULT COGNITION

Despite recent theoretical and conceptual advances and the emergence of new directions in empirical studies, we do not yet have a comprehensive picture of what happens to cognition during the adult years. Studies of cognitive processing differences between younger and older adults yield a narrow, pessimistic conceptualization of adult cognitive function. Such studies taken together suggest an irreversible decrement view of cognitive aging (Schaie, 1973). There is a scrapbook-type collection of findings showing losses in a wide variety of cognitive functions, but the results are not representative of real-life cognitive performance. In the area of memory, for example, which is probably the most researched aspect of cognitive aging, there is not an integrated theory of memory aging.

The psychometric studies of adult intelligence collectively yield an equally scattered catalogue of changes and differences, one that is unrepresentative of what is observed in the workplace and other real-life contexts. The postformal frameworks, in contrast, seem comprehensive and representative, but these conceptions fail to take into account what is known about age-related declines in cognitive processing abilities. Their intent is to highlight the positive and unique aspects of adult thinking, but they do so without reference to empirical evidence. We think that there are important aspects to be considered from the postformal views and that the data on age differences in cognitive processing should also be considered. Hence an integrative approach that describes several dimensions of change is useful and needed. Developmental change (and regularity) in adulthood arises out of transformations in thought structures and knowledge representations, as well as from age-related changes in fundamental or elementary information processes.

The Encapsulation Model

We have developed a model that draws together the divergent and fragmented theoretical arguments and empirical findings that surround the topic
of adult cognitive development. This model, which we have termed the
Encapsulation Model, will be fully elaborated upon in chapters 6 and 8 of
this text. At this point, however, we believe it useful to offer a brief sketch
of our Encapsulation Model.

We conceptualize cognition as consisting of three interrelated dimensions:
processing, knowing, and thinking. These dimensions, unfortunately, have
been examined in relative isolation from each other by those psychologists
interested in the study of adult cognitive development. Processing has been
explored by adherents of the information-processing and psychometric
approaches. In general, researchers working within these traditions have concluded that adults (a) become less adept at general problem solving, and (b)
process reduced amounts of information in a progressively less efficient
manner.

Developmental changes in thinking have been the focus of theory and
research within the genetic–epistemological framework. The predominant
emphasis has been on the description of qualitatively unique styles of postformal thinking that emerge during the adult years. These styles of thinking, which predispose adults to view reality in relativistic and dialectical
terms, provide the necessary basis for the solution of both well-defined and
ill-defined problems and the discovery of new perspectives from which new
problems may be identified.

The cognitive science framework (see Gardner, 1985), which has emerged
from a blending of recent work in the areas of artificial intelligence and
expert cognition, focuses attention on the dimension of knowing. The primary concern within this tradition has been the growth and representation
of expert knowledge systems. Research conducted within the context of this
approach suggests that, during the adult years, knowledge is more likely to
become expert, intuitive, and domain-specific.

Our Encapsulation Model integrates and extends the three dominant
strands of adult cognition: processing, knowing, and thinking. Processing
refers to the manner by which various mental abilities and psychological
resources are used to process (i.e., intake) environmental information.
Knowing refers to the manner by which information is represented, stored,
accessed, and used. Thinking refers to the manner by which individuals
develop an understanding or a perspective on their knowledge. Specifically,
we suggest that information control processes and fluid mental abilities
become increasingly dedicated to and encapsulated within particular representations of knowledge (i.e., domains) throughout adult development. As

general processes and abilities become encapsulated within the parameters of domain-ordered knowledge systems, extant knowledge becomes more differentiated, accessible, usable, and "expert" in nature.

The acquisition of new knowledge (i.e., knowledge that is *unrelated* to that already encapsulated in specific domains) may become increasingly less efficent with advances in age. The reduced capacity to acquire new knowledge, however, may be compensated for by the development of expert knowledge within existing domains and the development of a postformal perspective on that knowledge. Once adults conceptualize their domain-specific knowledge in a relativistic, dialectic, and open-ended manner, they become capable of: (a) solving the ill-defined problems characteristic of real life, (b) finding new problems and new perspectives from which they may be solved and, (c) producing creative and sophisticated works within defined areas of expertise.

We argue that the encapsulation of thinking and knowing within specific domains represents a necessary and adaptive feature of adult cognitive development. Thus, the age-related loss of the general abilities as reported in psychometric and information-processing research may have little functional significance for most adults in most situations. Assessments of cognitive functioning should emphasize the forms of knowing and the styles of thinking that a person uses to create and resolve the problems of everyday life. The frequently reported age-related declines in fluid abilities are the result of the practice of assessing mental processes apart from the domains in which they have become encapsulated.

Individuals, we propose, construct unique domains of knowledge via the encapsulation process. From this functional perspective, domains are acquired representations of different areas of cognitive involvement. Thus, we suggest that the developing organism is relatively self-organizing with regard to the number and nature of domains.

In summary, the major points of our Encapsulation Model are as follows:

1. Processing, knowing, and thinking are the three dimensions of cognition that must be addressed in any comprehensive theory of adult cognitive development.

2. The processes associated with the acquisition, utilization, and representation of knowledge become encapsulated within particular domains as one grows older.

3. Fluid abilities and control processes appear to decline with age when assessed as general abilities, but they may show less age-related decline when assessed within encapsulated domains.

4. The products of adult cognitive development are the growth of expert knowledge and the emergence of postformal styles of thought. Adult styles of thinking and forms of knowing are the end result of the process of encapsulation.

OVERVIEW OF THE BOOK

Piaget's emphasis on the growth of logical competence, interiorized action schemas, and organism–environment interaction has clearly had a major impact on our understanding of cognitive development. Piagetian theory, therefore, is our point of departure. Its focus on formal operations as the endpoint of mature intellectual development has a long-lived tradition in developmental theory. Critics (Arlin, 1975, 1984; Basseches, 1980, 1984a; Commons, Richards, & Armon, 1984; Dulit, 1972; Labouvie-Vief, 1980, 1982, 1984; Riegel, 1976; Sinnott, 1984) have argued, however, that Piaget's theory of formal operations is an unsatisfactory description of adult thought. They have suggested the need to develop a postformal account of cognitive functioning in adulthood. In chapter 2 we provide a detailed description of the essential characteristics of formal operations and point out the immature qualities of formal thinking. In chapter 3, we present an in-depth examination of several models of postformal thought, and we review research bearing on the formal/postformal distinction. In chapter 4 we focus on several models that attempt to explicate the growth of postformal styles of thinking within specific knowledge domains.

Although postformal models represent an advance over formal operational descriptions of adult cognitive functioning, these models are limited, in that they do not take account of age-related changes in basic cognitive abilities. Therefore, in chapter 5 we present a review of current theory and research within the psychometric and information-processing traditions that identifies age-related changes in various control processes and fluid mental abilities. In chapter 6, we present the cognitive science view that cognitive performance is dependent on the application of domain-specific knowledge structures rather than generalized mental abilities. Furthermore, we outline our Encapsulation Model, which integrates: (a) the three dominant strands of cognition: processing, knowing, and thinking, and (b) the extant theory and research on adult cognition from the genetic–epistemological, information-processing, psychometric, and cognitive science perspectives. In chapter 7 we illustrate the basic features of our Encapsulation Model within the context of real-life cognitive performance. More specifically, we show that with increasing age, adults are more likely to view intelligence (i.e., cognition) within a social or interpersonal context. We also show how adults employ domain-specific "personal knowledge" and postformal styles of thinking in order to help them adapt to the personally meaningful problems of daily life. In chapter 8, we provide a final integrative synthesis of research and theory on processing, knowing, and thinking. We also comment on the significance of our Encapsulation Model and indicate a number of salient research issues that arise from our model. Finally, we present a critique and evaluation of our Encapsulation Model.

2

Formal Operations: Scope and Status

This general form of equilibrium (formal operations) can be conceived of as
final in the sense that it is not modified during the life span of the individual.
B. Inhelder and J. Piaget
The Growth of Logical Thinking from Childhood to Adolescence

In this chapter we contrast Piaget's implicit theory regarding the nature of cognition and knowledge with his theory of formal operations. We point out the "immature" qualities of formal operational thinking and suggest that formal operations is neither an end state of cognitive development nor a fully accurate representation of mature cognition. We suggest that adult thinking about the physical and social world is more usefully represented by descriptions provided by theories of postformal thought (see Commons, Richards, & Armon, 1984).

PIAGET AND KNOWLEDGE

Jean Piaget devoted much of his professional life to the study of cognitive growth. He was specifically interested in ascertaining the means by which individuals acquire a "scientific" understanding of the physical world. It was Piaget's view that knowledge of the physical world gradually evolves through the formation of logical–mathematical thought structures. The primacy that Piaget attached to logical–mathematical thinking is expressed in the following passage from his text, *Biology and Knowledge (1971)*:

How, in fact, are we to explain the harmony that exists between mathematics and the real world? First, we must remember that this harmony is a real fact . . . the entire world of reality can be expressed in logico–mathematico terms and, a fortiori, in logical terms. There is no known physical phenomenon which has defied expression in mathematical form, and attempts to prove the contrary . . . have come to nothing. (p. 339)

Gardner (1973) noted that this emphasis on the logical, mathematical, and purely rational properties of human thought was consistent with Piaget's training within the French intellectual tradition.

Once Piaget decided to place special emphasis on logical–mathematical thought structures, his next task was to identify the means by which logical–mathematical thought structures give rise to logical–mathematical knowledge. Piaget examined the validity of two widely accepted epistemological positions: *empiricism* and *nativism*. He rejected the empiricist view for two reasons. First, it views the human knower as a passive organism responding to a changing, dynamic external world. Second, Piaget argued, knowledge could not take the form of a copy of the external world because "only a copy could supply us with the knowledge of the model of the copy being made, and, moreover, such knowledge is necessary for the copy of the model" (1971, p. 361). Piaget discarded the nativist perspective because of its pre-formist (and consequently nondevelopmental) conception of knowledge as well as its ignorance of the role played by experiential/environmental factors in the acquisition of knowledge.

Both empiricism and nativism created a *subject* (i.e., the human knower) and an *object* (i.e., the thing to be known), which were construed as separate and independent of one another. What was necessary, Piaget maintained, was to view knowledge as a subject–object *relationship* in which both subject and object mutually transform one another and are interdependent of one another. Knowledge, therefore, is best understood as an active construction that evolves over time and has its source in the dynamic relationship between the individual's present way of structuring the world and those aspects of the world to which the individual is sensitive (Gardner, 1978).

This position expresses Piaget's constructivist point of view. However, Piaget has been interpreted by many developmentalists as a structuralist. They have viewed structuralism as a position which argues that the structural characteristics of an individual's knowledge system determines the manner by which the individual experiences the objects that comprise the external world (i.e., a subject actively structures a passive environment in a progressively more coherent manner). This viewpoint of structuralism is mistaken. It fails to consider that if: (a) knowledge is constructed by the individual as a result of the individual's interactions with the external world; and (b) the individual becomes sensitive to different aspects of the external world at different times in development (i.e., the fabric and composition of the environment change over time); then (c) it is the changing complexion of the external world that actively structures the individual's knowledge system.

Piaget claimed, then, that the individual actively structures the external world to the same extent that the external world actively structures the individual! Piaget suggested, therefore, that the individual and his/her environment form an interdependent, evolving whole. For example, when asked the question, "Can the external world exist independently of and prior to our knowledge of it?" Piaget replied: "The instruments of our knowledge form part of our organism, which forms part of the external world" (quoted in Inhelder, 1962, pp. 18–19).

Piaget's early professional training in the biological sciences provided the basis for his structural/constructivist theory of knowledge. One of the basic hypotheses that guided his epistemological approach was that "cognitive functions constitute a specialized organ for regulating exchanges with the external world, although the instruments by which they do so are drawn from the general forms of living organization" (Piaget, 1971, p. 361). This hypothesized isomorphism is readily apparent when one examines the mechanisms that Piaget viewed as responsible for growth and autoregulation on both an embryological and cognitive level.

Following Waddington (1957), Piaget (1970, 1971) proposed that two complementary processes account for organic embryogenesis: *homeostasis* and *homeorhesis*. Homeostasis refers to a form of self-regulation by which an organism orchestrates its exchanges within itself, and between itself and the environment, in order to preserve its stability. Homeorhesis refers to a form of self-regulation by which the organism actively changes its structure and dynamics in order to pursue its epigenic pathway and to compensate for environmental coercion that might result in a deviation from its channeled, perhaps canalized, course. Thus, embryonic growth seems to occur within a dialectic context, because homeorhesis enjoins the organism into change, differentiation, and growth; whereas homeostasis ensures that growth, differentiation, and change occur within a framework marked by order and stability.

Cognitive ontogenesis is characterized by equivalent processes that share the same dialectic relationship. Piaget's (1971) notion of equilibration corresponds to the organic process of homeorhesis. Equilibration has been conceptualized as a process designed to bring the functional invariants of assimilation and accommodation into balanced coordination. It must be emphasized that such a balance can only be achieved if the organism searches for environmental interactions that are typified by novelty and unfamiliarity (i.e., equilibration implies a continuous need for change). Consistent with this viewpoint, Furth (1969) has argued that Piaget viewed cognitive structures as being

> in a state of dynamic equilibration, a state that is not the static equilibrium of an unchanging, rigid balance which needs an outside pull to make it move. The living equilibration of a biological organization is ever in a state of flux, if not growing, at least interacting with new elements of the environment, always exercising previously acquired structures. (p. 81)

Furth (1969; see also Koplowitz, 1984) suggested that Piaget viewed the human cognizer in a manner that is consistent with the general systems theory of von Bertalanffy (1968). A general systems thinker will not see a boundary between the ending of one event and the beginning of another, nor a clear boundary in time between cause and effect. Piaget and von Bertalanffy both regarded the human mind as an open, active, and self-regulating system.

Equilibration, however, only occurs within the context of the psychological counterpart of homeostasis — equilibrium. Equilibrium has been conceptualized as a cognitive system's need for order and stability along with its reticence for structural change due to alterations in input. The various equilibrium states (i.e., *stages*) within Piagetian theory owe their emergence, stabilization, and destruction to the continuous process of equilibration.

In summary, it may be argued that Piaget viewed human beings (as well as human minds) as open, self-transforming systems that actively construct logical–mathematical systems of thought and knowledge. Knowledge was not something that purely existed within the human mind. Knowledge, he contended, was another name for the continuous relationship between the mind's attempt to structure its environment and the environment's attempt to structure the mind. Thus, Piaget's view of knowledge was dialectical, structural, and constructive (Basseches, 1984b; Rybash, 1981). Piaget (1970) stated this position as follows:

> Structuralism has always been linked with a constructivism from which the epithet "dialectic" can hardly be withheld. The emphasis upon historical development, opposition between contraries and "Aufhebungen" (depassements) is surely just as characteristic of constructivism as of dialecticism, and that the idea of wholeness figures centrally in structuralist as in dialectic modes of thought is obvious. (p. 121)

How did Piaget develop his relativistic, dialectic, and constructivistic conception of knowledge? Would the thought structures that he argued were descriptive of the terminal stage of cognitive development (i.e., formal operations) have allowed him to construct Piagetian theory? Is Piaget's conceptualization of knowledge a product of a form of thought more advanced than formal operations? In order to propose answers to these questions, we present a description of the stages that comprise Piaget's theory of cognitive development. We place special emphasis on explicating the strengths and limitations of formal operational thought structures.

PIAGET AND THE STAGES OF KNOWLEDGE

Piaget envisioned cognitive development as consisting of a number of structural stages. The stages are descriptions of the changing forms of the knower–known relationship in which both the knower (the active human subject) and the known (the active environmental object) mutually transform one another. On a collective basis, the various stages form a developmental sequence that is characterized by: (a) qualitative re-structuring; (b) hierarchical integration; (c) structured wholeness; and (d) invariant, universal progression.

The unique characteristics of each stage depend on several factors. First, one must consider the nature of the *operations* through which one comprehends the objects of one's knowledge. Operations refer to *actions* that may be internal/external, reversible/irreversible, and coordinated/uncoordinated. The significance of action in the development of knowledge is seen in Inhelder's (1964) description of Piaget's response to the question, "Do you think that an object exists prior to any knowledge of it?" Piaget replied, "As a psychologist, I have no idea; I only know an object to the extent that I can act on it; I can affirm nothing about it prior to such action" (p. 18). Second, one must consider the objects of knowledge toward which one's operations are directed. These objects (i.e., the aspects of the world to which the knower is sensitive) constantly change over time. Third, of prime importance to Piaget were the types of egocentrism (Elkind, 1967; Kegan, 1982), conservation, and equilibrium that are manifest at each particular stage. Table 2.1 provides an overview of the characteristics that correspond to each Piagetian stage. An example of the specific content of knowledge at each Piagetian stage is given in Table 2.2.

Significance of Formal Operations

The stage of formal operations, which according to Piaget emerges between 11 to 16 years of age, has occupied a central position in the study of adult cognition. The importance of formal operations lies in the fact that because it is the final stage in the cognitive developmental sequence, it must represent Piaget's conceptualization of the nature of mature cognition.

In general, there are three special characteristics associated with formal operational thinking (Inhelder & Piaget, 1958; Piaget & Inhelder, 1969). First, formal thinkers are capable of hypothetico–deductive thought. In other words, formal thinkers reason like scientists, in that they are capable of testing abstract hypotheses by observing the occurrence or nonoccurrence of specific outcomes. That is, they construct theories that can be tested by experimentation. Second, formal thinkers are able to reverse the relationship between reality and possibility. They envision reality as an actualized possibility within an infinite set of potential possibilities. It is this reversal, accordingly, that allows the formal reasoner to generate the hypotheses that are tested in the real world. Third, the formal thinker is capable of thinking about thinking. This may manifest itself in the tendency to become introspectively aware of oneself as the object of one's thought, to engage in

TABLE 2.1. The Traditional Piagetian Stages: An Overview

STAGE	NATURE OF OPERATIONS	OBJECTS OF OPERATIONS	TYPE OF EGOCENTRISM	TYPE OF CONSERVATION	TYPE OF EQUILIBRIUM
Sensori-Motor	Operations are external actions which tend toward reversibility.	Operations are directed to objects in the external world.	Objects cannot be disassociated from the actions and the sensations directed to them.	None. The self as well as the objects which comprise its environment cannot be differentiated from one another.	Overt actions are organized into systems of reversible actions.
Preoperations	Operations are irreversible, internal mental activities.	Operations are directed to the symbols and images which represent objects in the external world.	Objects in the external world cannot be separated from the symbols and images used to represent them.	Conservation of the permanent object, the self as well as the objects that comprise its world are understood as permanent and stable; but the properties of these objects as well as the relations between these objects are understood as transient and impermanent.	Preoperations does not have a specific equilibrium state because preoperations is essentially a "preparatory" period for concrete operations.

24

Concrete Operations	Operations are first-order, reversible, mental activities.	Operations are directed to the properties of concrete objects as well as the relations that exist both within and between concrete objects.	The real properties and relations of objects cannot be separated from the possible properties and relations of objects.	Conservation of the properties of permanent objects as well as conservation of the relation both within and between concrete objects.	Overt actions are internalized in the form of reversible activities which can compensate for apparent changes in reality. Two forms of reversibility are identified: (a) reciprocity, which operates on relations, and (b) negation which operates on properties.
Formal Operations	Operations are second-order, reversible mental activities.	Operations are directed to verbal propositions that need not have a basis in concrete reality.	None	Conservation of specific abstract laws, principles and rules that are seen as having absolute and universal qualities.	The twin forms of reversibility acquired during the concrete operations stage are co-ordinated within a single, more all-encompassing system: the INRC Group.

TABLE 2.2. The Content of Intelligence at Each Piagetian Stage: What a Person
Would "Know" About a Ball of Clay and Its Characteristics

STAGE	MODE OF UNDERSTANDING AND CONTENT OF THOUGHT
Sensori-Motor	The ball of clay's existence cannot be separated from the infant's actions towards it, and his perceptions of it. The infant cannot differentiate himself from the ball, both the infant and the ball are impermanent and unstable. If the infant could think in symbolic terms he would say, "I'm not "me" and the ball is not the "ball," we are indistinguishable from one another. Why can't I live in a world where I can differentiate "me" from "not me"? Why aren't the objects in my world (myself included) stable, permanent and real?"
Preoperations	The ball of clay's existence is now viewed as separate and permanent from the child's existence. But the characteristics of the ball (e.g., its weight) cannot be separated from the child's symbolic representation of the ball. Therefore, as the appearance of the ball changes, the characteristics of the ball change, because the internal symbolic representation of the ball changes. The child thinks, "I know the ball continues to exist even if I don't look at it and hold it in my hand. But, why does the ball get heavier or lighter every time it changes its shape?"
Concrete Operations	The ball as well as its characteristics are viewed as stable, permanent and real. The child thinks, "The only possible world is the real world. Aren't I lucky to live in a real world where real objects have invariant characteristics. The weight of the clay doesn't depend on the shape of the clay."
Formal Operations	The ball is viewed as stable and permanent. The observable characteristics of the ball (e.g., its weight), however, are viewed within the framework of the abstract relationships. The adolescent thinks, "If I took the ball of clay to the moon it would weigh less. Therefore, the weight of an object is best understood as an abstract, invariant relationship between its mass and gravity, not as the apparent heaviness of the object."

Source: Adapted from Gardner, H. (1979). Getting acquainted with Piaget. *New York Times*, January 16.

various metacognitive thinking, and to become increasingly capable of performing mental operations upon other mental operations.

In contrast to formal operations, concrete thinking is directed toward either the properties of concrete objects or the relations that exist between and/or within concrete objects. Specifically, the concrete thinker understands properties and relations by virtue of the implementation of two distinct forms of reversibility: negation and reciprocity. Negation is a mental activity that "undoes" another related mental activity. For example, subtracting is an activity that undoes adding, such that if: Apples + Oranges = Fruit, then: Fruit − Apples = Oranges. In a conservation task, a child can negate the action of pouring water from glass A to glass B by mentally pouring the water from B to A and thus establish the equivalence of $A = B$. Reciprocity is an activity that can compensate for the changing nature of the relationship that exists within objects or between objects. For example, a concrete thinker knows that when water is poured from a tall, narrow glass to a short, wide glass changes in height $(H' > H'')$ are compensated for by changes in width $(W' < W'')$. Or, when asked to solve a transitivity task that employs three sticks $(A, B,$ and $C)$ as stimuli, the child understands that if: $B > A$, and $B < C$, then: $A < C$. Despite the concrete reasoner's ability to classify, conserve, and seriate objects, concrete operations is a limited mode of thought because: (a) concrete thinking can only be directed to properties and relations that are abstracted from concrete or real objects and events; and (b) the twin forms of reversibility (i.e., negation and reciprocity) are not coordinated or integrated.

Formal operational thought, in contrast, is directed toward verbal *propositions*. Propositions are essentially statements about "what could be possible." Statements about what could be possible may be contrary to fact, purely hypothetical, abstract, and have no basis whatsoever in concrete reality. Consequently, the truth value of propositions depends on the logical relationships that propositions have to one another. It is logical to assume, for example, that heating water will make it freeze, if one is given the working assumption that cooling water will make it boil (Berzonsky, 1978). Understanding something at the level of formal–operations, therefore, is characterized by the ability to: (a) generate all of the possible propositions that could characterize a phenomenon that is to be understood—Piaget calls this ability the *Combinatorial Scheme*, and (b) understand the various logical relationships that could exist between all of the propositions that could possibly characterize a phenomenon under investigation—Piaget describes this ability via reference to the *INRC Group*.

The functions of the combinatorial scheme and the INRC Group may be seen in the following illustration adapted from Piaget and Inhelder (1969). Imagine an individual who is brought before a table top on which is located a light bulb and an object. The light bulb is either "on" (i.e., it is shining) or it is "not on"; and, the object either "stops moving" or "keeps moving." By observing the light bulb and the object, the person is asked to determine the nature of the relationship between the light and the object (e.g, Does the shining of the light cause the cessation of the object's movement?).

The Concrete Operational Approach

The concrete thinker can deal with property combinations and can therefore generate the four classes of events he or she observes while watching this display. These combinations may be seen by inspecting the matrix that appears in Figure 2.1.

Status of Light

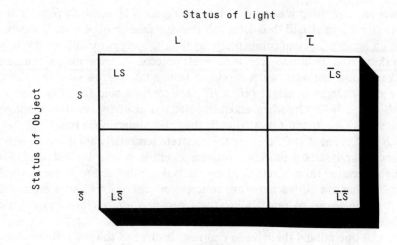

S- Object Stops Moving; S̄- Object Keeps Moving
L- Light Is Shining; L̄- Light Is Not Shining

FIGURE 2.1. Matrix of property combinations.

The Formal Operational Approach

The formal thinker can take a giant step beyond the concrete thinker by using the combinatorial scheme to "generate possibility." This means that the formal thinker is capable of constructing all of the possible combinations of the elements on the above-mentioned matrix. And, via the contemplation of each possibility, the formal thinker can deduce the logical relationship between the object and the light. See Table 2.3 for an example of the working of the combinatorial scheme. The observation listed in line 11 of Table 2.3, for example, would lead to the logical conclusion that the onset of the light is a *necessary cause* for the cessation of the object's movement. The observation indicated in line 13, however, would suggest that the onset of the light is a *sufficient cause* for the cessation of the object's movement (i.e., in the terms of formal logic, the onset of the light *implies* the cessation of the object's movement).

Furthermore, through the efforts of the INRC Group, the formal thinker can understand the logical relationships that exist between all of the possible logical relationships. Allow us to explain: The INRC Group consists of four different transformations that may be applied to propositions. The power of these transformations derives from the notion that they are trans-

TABLE 2.3. The Combinatorial Scheme

POSSIBLE OBSERVATION*	LOGICAL SYMBOL**	LOGICAL RELATIONSHIP
1. 0	(∅)	Negation
2. LS	(p·q)	Conjunction
3. L̄S̄	(p̄·q̄)	Conjunctive Negation
4. LS̄	(p·q̄)	Nonimplication
5. L̄S	(p̄·q)	Negation of Reciprocal Implication
6. L̄S + LS̄	(p ∨∨ q)	Reciprocal Exclusion
7. L̄S + L̄S̄	p̄ (q)	Negation of p
8. LS̄ + L̄S̄	q̄ (p)	Negation of q
9. LS + L̄S	q (p)	Affirmation of q
10. LS + LS̄	p (q)	Affirmation of p
11. LS + L̄S̄	(p ⊃ᶜ q)	Equivalence
12. LS + LS̄ + L̄S̄	(q ⊃ p)	Reciprocal Implication
13. LS + L̄S + L̄S̄	(p ⊃ q)	Implication
14. LS + L̄S + LS̄	(p ∨ q)	Disjunction
15. L̄S + LS̄ + L̄S̄	(p / q)	Incompatibility
16. LS + L̄S + LS̄ + L̄S̄	(p * q)	Tautology

Source: Adapted from Neimark, E.D. (1975). Intellectual development during adolescence. In F.D. Horowitz (Ed.), *Review of child development research* (Vol. 4, pp. 541–594). Chicago: University of Chicago Press.
*Every possible occurrence of a combination implies the nonoccurrence of its complement (observing LS + LS in line 11 implies that L̄S + LS̄ is not observed).
**L = p, L̄ = p̄; S = q, S̄ = q̄.

formations of each other, they are logically and consistently related to each other, and they form an integrated whole that possesses the qualities of a mathematical structure called a group. The four transformations are:

Identity = I. A transformation that leaves the proposition to which it is applied unchanged.

Negation = N. A transformation that completely denies the relationship between the elements of a proposition (e.g., the denial of the proposition, "The presence of X implies the presence of Y," is: "The presence of X does not imply the presence of Y").

Reciprocal = R. A transformation that reverses the relationship between the elements of a proposition (e.g., the reversal of the proposition, "The presence of X implies the presence of Y", is: "The presence of Y implies the presence of X").

Correlative = C. A transformation that reverses the denial (or denies the reversal) of the relationship between the elements of a proposition (e.g., the denial of the proposition, "The presence of X implies the presence of Y", is: "The presence of X does not imply the presence of Y". The reversal of this denial takes the form of: "The presence of Y does not imply the presence of X", which is the correlative of the original proposition).

Paraphrasing Piaget and Inhelder (1969), we suggest that an individual who employs the INRC Group might approach the "light and object" problem in the following manner. The person may wonder if the onset of the light implies the cessation of the object's movement (p ⊃ q). This hypothesis may be confirmed by discovering if the light ever goes on without an accompanying cessation of the object's movement (p·q̄); where: (p·q̄) is the *negation* of (p ⊃ q). But the person may then wonder if it is the cessation of the object's movement that implies the onset of the light (q ⊃ p); where (q ⊃ p) is the *reciprocal* of (p ⊃ q). This hypothesis may be confirmed by looking for the opposite case that would disconfirm it. Namely, does the object ever stop without the accompanying onset of the light (p̄·q); where (p̄·q) is the *correlative* of (p ⊃ q), which is also the *reciprocal* of the *negation* (i.e., (p·q̄) becomes (p̄·q)). See Figure 2.2 for an illustration of the interrelationship between all of these transformations.

Because all of these transformations are related to one another, the for-

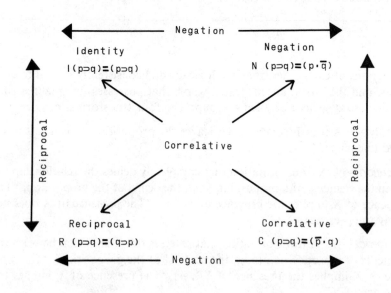

FIGURE 2.2. The interrelationship between the components of the INRC group [Adapted from Niemark, E.D. (1975). Intellectual development during adolescence. In F.D. Horowitz (Ed.), *Review of child development research* (Vol. 4, pp. 541–594). Chicago: University of Chicago Press.]

mal thinker, according to Piaget, has achieved the highest level of stability and mobility in his/her thought. Given a problem to deal with, the formal thinker can generate all of the possibilities and all of the interrelationships among the possibilities that comprise the problem. Therefore, because formal thinkers are capable of considering all possible propositions as well as their interrelationships, there could be nothing that could upset their cognitive equilibrium! According to Piaget and Inhelder (1969), the Combinatorial Scheme and the INRC Group are the basis for the formal thinker's understanding of proportionality, double systems of reference, mechanical equilibrium, probability, correlation and causation, and forms of conservation that are not casually verified (e.g., inertia).

Critique of Formal Operations

Formal operational thinking provides a powerful but nevertheless limited basis from which to understand the physical and social world. In this section, we discuss several limitations of formal thinking and the view of reality that it generates.

First, formal operational thought emphasizes the power of pure logic in problem solving (Labouvie-Vief, 1984; Perry, 1968). The formal thinker uses logical, rational analysis to provide the one correct solution to a problem, regardless of the domain within which the problem is embedded. This limitation is expressed in the following passage:

> Reason reveals relations within any given context. . . . But there is a limit. In the end, reason itself remains reflexively relativistic, a property which turns reason back upon reason's own findings. In even its farthest reaches, then, reason will leave the thinker with several legitimate contexts and no way of choosing among them—no way at least that can be justified through reason alone. If he still is to honor reason he must now also transcend it; he must affirm his own position from within himself in full awareness that reason can never completely justify him or assure him. (Perry, 1968, pp. 135-136)

Second, formal operational thinking places an overemphasis on possibility and abstraction, along with a corresponding underemphasis on the pragmatics of everyday life. The formal thinker is infatuated with ideas, abstractions, and absolutes. In fact, the formal reasoner may mistakenly assume that the goal of mature thought is to construct a set of purified, absolute principles that apply to problems-in-living. In late adolescence or adulthood, individuals become aware of this overemphasis on abstraction, absolutism, and logic. As individuals enter adulthood they realize that

> the categories of their reason cannot encompass the facts of their experience. This is the time in cognitive development that Inhelder and Piaget (1958) have described as "the return to reality," the shift from a metaphysical to an empirical truth that charts the "path from adolescence to the true beginnings of

adulthood" (1958, p. 346). The contradictory pulls of logic and affect, and the difficulty of their integration, call into question the equation of reason with logic. . . . (Gilligan & Murphy, 1979, p. 86)

Labouvie-Vief also emphasized this point when she argued that upon entry into adulthood

> there is a concern with the concrete constraints of real life or the refusal to sever cognition from its affective, social, and pragmatic ties. It is not only a more conscious, reflective awareness of the concrete constraints of real life, it is also an awareness that is closely integrated with action. (1984, p. 159)

Third, formal thinking places an overemphasis on problems within the realm of "physical reality" that are to be addressed via scientific thinking and logical–mathematical analysis. Piaget neglected the means by which mature cognition is directed to personally meaningful real-life problems — especially problems that are social and interpersonal in nature. The importance of such real-life problems vis-à-vis human cognition has been underscored by Flavell (1977), who maintained that

> Real problems with meaningful content are obviously more important in everyday human adaptation (than abstract, wholly logical problems), and it is possible that these are the kinds of problems our cognitive apparatus has evolved to solve. (p. 117)

Fourth, formal operations is suited to the contemplation of "closed system" problems (Basseches, 1984a, 1984b; Koplowitz, 1984). A closed system problem is one in which a number of finite and knowable variables produce a specific and reliable outcome. Furthermore, the outcome of a closed system problem, as well as the variables that affect the outcome, are not capable of being influenced by the context within which the problem is embedded. Inhelder's and Piaget's pendulum task is an example of a closed system problem. In this task a subject is required to develop a series of miniexperiments to determine the manner by which two variables, the weight of a pendulum and the length of a pendulum string, influence the oscillation of a pendulum.

Real-life problems, in contrast, are "open" to the extent that there are no clear boundaries between the elements of a problem and the context within which it occurs. For example, there may be an infinite number of variables, which emerge from the concrete contexts and circumstances of a woman's life, that she may consider in a decision about whether to have a child. As these different variables emerge from the changing circumstances of her life, the question of whether or not she should have a child may take on many different personal meanings, which will influence her ultimate decision. Thus, when we examine any real-life problem we see that the variables that surround it are essentially unbounded and dynamic because they are contextual. Therefore, as the person ponders an open problem, the nature of the problem itself (i.e., "What are the issues that define the problem?") along with the resolution of the problem (i.e., "How can this problem best be solved, if it can be solved at all?") may be regarded as both flexible and dynamic. This issue is related to points two and three. That is, formal thinking is geared to closed system problems, and real-life problems are frequently open-ended problems.

Fifth, formal thinking places an overemphasis on "separating and analyzing" the relationships among the variables within closed system problems. Koplowitz (1984) has referred to this aspect of formal thinking as "analysis of variance thinking." Thus, the formal thinker assumes that the finite number of variables that influence a given outcome can be separated from one another, analyzed independently of one another, and then viewed in interaction with one another. Such thinking may help to solve the pendulum problem, but this mode of thought may be of limited value in other contexts. In many instances it may be adaptive to consider variables as interdependent and inseparable. Reality may be viewed as a meshing of variables and experiences that defy separation. Could it be possible, for example, for a woman contemplating a decision to have a child, to determine the extent to which such factors as her religious convictions, yearly income, and her husband's attitudes about having children determine the outcome of her decision? Such a determination seems unlikely if we consider that the woman's religious convictions are influenced, in part, by the job she chooses, her yearly salary, and the man she marries. Furthermore, the type of man she marries will probably influence the course of her religious convictions and the nature of her employment. And the amount of money she makes could potentially influence her trust and faith in God as well as determine her husband's attitudes about whether it is wise to have a child.

Sixth, formal operations seems to place a greater emphasis on problem solving than on problem finding. This issue has been elaborated by Arlin (1975, 1984). The term *problem finding* implies that formal thought is best suited for generating and testing hypotheses that aid in the solution of given, well-defined problems. The formal thinker conceives of his or her cognitive apparatus as a resource that is to be used to solve the problems that spontaneously occur in the world, especially those that seem to be clear-cut and closed in nature. Problem finding, in contrast, represents the ability to raise general questions from many ill-defined problems (Mackworth, 1965). It refers to adults' abilities to ask generative questions of themselves, their life's work, and of the phenomena that surround them. Arlin (1984) observed that the essence of problem finding is to be found in the writing of Wertheimer (1945), who suggested that

the function of thinking is not just solving an actual problem but discovering, envisaging, and going into deeper questions. Often in great discovery the most important thing is that a certain question is found. (p. 46)

Arlin also observed that problem finding is dependent on the recognition and coordination of multiple frames of reference, a type of cognitive skill beyond the reach of the formal reasoner.

The notion of problem solving seems to have been captured by Thomas Kuhn's (1970) conceptualization of "normal science." From this perspective, science is viewed as a mop-up operation in which scores of investigators engage in research studies that fill in the gaps (i.e., solve all of the problems) raised by the dominant paradigm of the day. Instances of problem finding, on the other hand, may be seen in periods of "scientific revolution," when paradigms shifted because innovative thinkers (e.g., Darwin, Piaget, Freud, and Skinner) addressed old facts from the perspective of new questions.

Seventh, formal operations places an overemphasis on the understanding of single systems and underemphasizes the relationship between multiple systems of reference. Several theorists (Commons, Richards, & Kuhn, 1982; Labouvie-Vief, 1982b, 1984; Sinnott, 1981, 1984) have suggested that formal operations does not allow a thinker to understand the relativistic nature of knowledge and reality. Relativistic thinking has been regarded as either intersystemic or metasystematic in nature. Labouvie-Vief (1982b) argued that intersystemic thinking

> reveals the basic duality of logical truth. This realization initiates a movement from logical absolutism to logical relativism. . . . Much as truth now is relativistic, one's actions must be singular and particularized. The erosion of logical certainty throws the self explicitly back on its own resources. (p. 182)

Commons et al. (1982) described metasystematic reasoning as

> . . . cognitions about systems . . . (which) are required in the formation of a framework (or "metasystem") for comparing and contrasting systems with one another. The relationship between one system to another such system is expressed as a metatheory and is found by comparing axioms, theorems, or other limiting conditions of systems within the framework of a "super-system" that contains all of the variant systems. (p. 1059)

As an example of metasystematic reasoning, Commons et al. (1982) showed how Einstein's general theory of relativity could be viewed as a higher-order integration of what physicists assumed to be two different and completely independent systems: the inertial system and the gravitational system.

Eighth is the inability of formal operations to "know itself" as a system of thought. Because the individual is constrained by the system (i.e., formal operations) from which he or she reasons, the individual does not know of the existence of that system. Piaget suggested, for example, that the formal thinker does not understand the structure of logical–mathematical thought in any conscious or self-reflective manner (see Ginsburg & Opper, 1969). Formal thought structures, from Piaget's viewpoint, seem to be below the individual's level of awareness.

How, then, could have Piaget identified the structure of formal operational intelligence? It seems as if Piaget would have had to extract himself from the system of formal thought in order to theorize about the structure of formal thought. Such an "extraction" exhibits an intersystemic or metasystematic quality. Thus, it would seem as if Piaget had to use a mode of reasoning beyond formal operations in order to conceptualize the nature of formal operations.

The World View Generated by Formal Operations

At this juncture, it is useful to summarize our presentation of the basic characteristics and limitations of formal operational thought by a brief description of the world view of the formal thinker. At the most general level, a world view is a metaphorical statement intended to represent the ultimate nature of reality. Kramer (1983) noted that formal operational thinking gives rise to a *mechanistic* world view. The metaphor that underlies the mechanistic world view is that of the "machine" (Pepper, 1942; Reese & Overton, 1970). Viewing reality as if it were a machine leads the formal thinker to conceptualize reality as a collection of stable, permanent, complex, and knowable entities. The terms *stable* and *permanent* imply that the "machines" that comprise reality are "closed systems" that do not exchange energy with surrounding systems and are therefore not capable of influencing or being influenced by other closed systems. Despite the affirmation that these closed systems may be very complex and intricate, it is nevertheless assumed that they consist of elements or subunits that may interact with one another and may be separated from one another. Finally, the notion of *knowability* suggests that it is possible to understand the closed, interactive systems that make up reality through experimentation and hypothetico-deductive thinking (i.e., through the type of scientific thinking that is the hallmark of formal operations). Scientific research will uncover, it is assumed, a set of universal, abstract, invariant and absolute rules, laws, and principles that govern the behavior of reality's elements and entities.

After having examined the basic assumptions of the mechanistic world view and the mode of thought upon which it is based (i.e., formal operations) vis-à-vis the manner by which Piaget conceptualized the nature and growth of knowledge, we were struck by a glaring inconsistency. Formal operations generated a view of reality characterized by reductionism, stability, and absolute knowability, but Piaget viewed reality as holistic, open, self-transforming, and relativistically knowable. Piaget could not have possibly viewed reality from a mechanistic perspective, because he argued that knowledge is an active construction.

What then is the world view espoused by Piaget? Several theorists have suggested that Piagetian theory has its basis in an *organismic* world view.

The root metaphor in this world view (see Pepper, 1942; Reese & Overton, 1970) is that of a living, biological organism, in general, and a developing embryo, in particular. All forms of biological life are integrated forms that defy reduction. Furthermore, biological organisms are essentially active rather than passive. The transformations that characterize embryonic development, for example, have their basis in the internal blueprint contained in the genome, not in the external environment. According to the organismic world view, the external environment is viewed as a theatre stage upon which embryonic development is played out. Several writers (Broughton, 1978, 1984; Edelstein & Noam, 1982) have observed that the essence of Piagetian theory is not accurately represented by the organismic world view. To be sure, Piaget has conceptualized humans as active organisms who are producers of their own development; he also viewed the human mind as an integrated whole that defies an atomistic, piecemeal analysis. But, as we have emphasized earlier in this chapter, Piaget did not assign a passive role to the environment. Instead, he posited a relationship of mutual influence between mind and environment.

The last writings of Piaget (1980) reflected a *contextual* or *dialectical* conceptualization of knowledge and cognitive growth. The metaphor, which underlies a contextual world view, is that of a historic, dynamic event. Viewing reality from this perspective, emphasizes the following:

1. The fabric of reality (as well as the nature of the knowledge we may attain about reality) is continuously changing over time, because reality (as well as our knowledge of reality) is open and self-transforming.
2. To know anything in a changing world means to know it from a particular perspective or context; therefore, knowledge must be relative (not absolute), because knowledge is always constructed from a particular perspective.
3. Knowledge of reality has its basis in the changing relationship between the subject and object of knowledge. Both the organism and its environment are viewed as active forces that cannot be separated from one another.
4. Because all knowledge is changeable, contextual, and relative, attempts at knowing reality give rise to knowledge that is characterized by its paradoxical and contradictory quality. The knower–known relationship is paradoxical, in that the knower is viewed as structuring the external world to the same extent that the external world structures the knower.
5. Because the human knower constructs contradictory forms of knowledge, the hallmark of mature cognition must be the dialectical synthesis of contradiction (i.e., mutually exclusive systems of knowledge) into a more all-encompassing whole.

The reader is directed to Baltes, Cornelius, and Nesselroade (1979), Overton (1976), Reese and Overton (1970), Riegel (1975), and Pepper (1942) for further discussions of the characteristics of the organismic, mechanistic, and contextual world views.

SUMMARY

Ironically, Piaget's theory of cognitive development has been regarded by many as espousing a purely organismic world view. But, Piaget's conceptualization of mature cognition (i.e., formal operations) would, at best, allow adult thinkers to construct a mechanistic understanding of knowledge and reality. On close examination, Piaget's conceptualization of knowledge and reality seems to have its roots in a contextual/dialectic world view.

The problems and shortcomings of formal thinking have set the stage for major conceptual revisions in Piagetian theory. Thus, proponents of genetic-epistemological theory need to identify and examine adult styles of thinking that are qualitatively different from those that are characteristic of formal operations. These styles of thinking unique to adulthood have been termed *postformal* in nature. In the next chapter, we review current theory and research bearing on the growth of postformal thinking during the adult years.

3

Postformal Styles of Adult Thinking

If Piaget's assertion that formal thought constitutes the crowning achievement of human ontogeny is accepted . . . a pessimistic view of adulthood becomes a logical necessity.

G. Labouvie-Vief
Logic and Self Regulation from Youth to Maturity

In this chapter we describe the basic features of postformal thought. Of the various conceptualizations of postformal thought, the dialectical framework of Basseches (1980, 1984a, 1984b) seems to be the most representative of features associated with mature thinking. We review the evidence bearing on the various conceptions of postformal thinking and point to the need for integrations of postformal theories with empirical findings on age differences in cognitive function.

GENERAL CHARACTERISTICS

Recently, Kramer (1983) identified three basic characteristics of postformal reasoning. First, postformal thinkers possess an understanding of the relative, nonabsolute nature of knowledge. Knowledge and reality are viewed as temporarily true (or real) rather than universally fixed. Second, postformal thinkers accept contradiction as a basic aspect of reality. With regard to physical reality, for example, a physicist might come to understand light as being both a wave and a particle. In the personal domain, an individual might realize that a relationship with another person cannot be described in terms of love or hate alone, but by the simultaneous existence of these apparently contrasting emotions. Third, postformal thinkers possess an ability to synthesize contradictory thoughts, emotions, and experiences into more coherent, all-encompassing wholes. Instead of viewing a contradictory situation as one that forces a choice between alternatives, the postformal reasoner views it as one that calls for an integration of alternatives.

Two additional characteristics can be added to Kramer's description of postformal thought. First, if the postformal reasoner views reality (and knowledge of reality) as relative and contradictory, then reality (and knowledge of reality) must necessarily be conceptualized within an "open systems" framework. Thus, postformal thinking may predispose adults to view reality as an integration of open interdependent systems that change and evolve over time. Second, postformal thinking is grounded in contextualism. That is, postformal reasoners create new principles based on the changing circumstances of life, rather than search for absolute, universal principles that apply across all contexts and circumstances.

The characteristics of postformal thought are also represented in other conceptions of mature thinking. For example, Dittmann-Kohli and Baltes's (1986) neo-functionalist description of adult intelligence suggests that adults develop the capacity for wise decision-making. Furthermore, Dittmann-Kohli and Baltes (1986) have proposed that wisdom entails the following characteristics:

1. Skill or expertise within the domain of personal knowledge.
2. Emphasis on the pragmatic or practical aspects of intelligence and knowledge.
3. Emphasis on the context of the problem.
4. Uncertainty as a characteristic of problems and solutions.
5. Reflection and relativism in judgments and actions.

This characterization of wisdom is nearly identical to the descriptive characteristics of postformal thinking.

ASPECTS OF POSTFORMAL THOUGHT

Several authors have described various aspects of postformal thinking. As previously mentioned, Arlin (1975, 1977, 1984) has conceptualized postformal thought as a mode of problem finding that she contrasted with the problem-solving quality of formal thought. Koplowitz (1984) has argued that postformal thinking embraces the principles of: nonlinear causality, the complete interdependence (and nonseparability) of variables, the open nature of boundaries and systems, and the existence of self-constructed entities and objects within a self-constructed and contextual world. In contrast, formal thinking embraces the principles of: linear causality, independence and separation of variables, the closed nature of systems and boundaries, and the existence of permanent and stable entities and objects within a permanent and stable external world.

Basseches (1980, 1984a, 1984b) has viewed postformal thinking as *dialectic thinking*. The term *dialectic* has a long history of use (and misuse) within philosophy, and in the 1970s was embraced by the developmental psychologist, Klaus Riegel. Riegel (1976) published a "Dialectic Manifesto" (1976) in which he called for the abandonment of Piagetian theory. He maintained that Piagetian theory emphasized equilibrium and stability at the expense of disequilibrium and change. Rather than arguing for the supremacy of one theoretical position over the other, Basseches has employed the notion of "dialectic" in a manner that allows an integration of the major ideas of both Piaget and Riegel.

Basseches focused his conception of postformal thought on the means by which the adult thinker envisions reality as a multitude of structured wholes, forms, and systems that continuously change and evolve over time. Basseches proposed that the adult thinker understands and integrates the continuously changing systems in a changing world via the principle of the dialectic. The term *dialectic* refers to developmental transformations through forms, which occur via constitutive and interactive relationships (Basseches, 1984a).

The dialectic principle emphasizes that because systems are open rather than closed, they evidence movement, transformation, and change. But changes in a system occur via the constitutive and interactive relationships between the "whole" of the system and the "parts" of the system. The parts of a system have a constitutive relationship with the whole of the system, in that the parts of the whole are created by the whole and do not have an existence independent of the whole. Likewise, the whole of a system does not exist without the parts, which combine themselves nonadditively to create the whole. Therefore, the notion of constitutiveness implies that it is the relationship between the parts and the whole that creates the parts and the whole.

Relationships are also interactive. Interactive relationships are characterized by mutual (i.e., reciprocal) influence. The elements of a relationship are changed by one another and change one another; they have a paradoxical/contradictory relationship with one another. The changing nature of these interactive relationships creates the changes that move the system over time.

Basseches (1984a) summarized the major differences between formal operational thought and dialectic modes of thinking as follows:

> Formal operational thinking can be understood as efforts at comprehension relying on applications of an implicit model of an unchanging structured whole, a closed system of lawful relationships among possibilities, to their phenomenal world. Dialectic thinking can be understood as efforts at comprehension relying on the application of an implicit model of dialectic, developmental transformation via constitutive and interactive relationships, to the phenomenal world. (p. 218)

Basseches, unlike Riegel, has connected equilibrium, constancy, and stability with dialectic thinking. But, unlike Piaget, he noted that this type of dialectic equilibrium cannot compensate for all of the perturbations that could impinge upon a system. Thus, Basseches makes a suggestion, which seems paradoxical; namely, he argued that what is *constant* over time is *change* over time. This viewpoint is expressed in the following passage:

> From the perspective of dialectical thinking, what remains recognizable across a range of changes is the historical process as a evolving whole. Any change at all, no matter how radical, can be equilibrated if it can be conceptualized as a moment in a dialectical process of evolution. New events are integrated within a conception of a process as later steps in the evolution of that process. (Basseches, 1984a, p. 230)

At this point, we present an example that contrasts formal thought with dialectic (i.e., postformal) thought. This example, which is drawn, in part, from Basseches (1984b, pp. 26–27) deals with the topic of marriage and the problems that could arise between a husband and a wife. A formal thinker would be predisposed to view the partners of a marriage as two individuals who always have a unique constellation of fixed and stable traits. The traits that characterize the husband's personality exist independently of those that characterize the wife's personality. Therefore, the marriage of these individuals represents a connection between two elements (husband and wife) that have an existence outside of the relationship they are about to enter. Also, the marriage of these two individuals may be viewed as a connection or relationship that represents the *simple* and *static* interaction of the traits that characterize the husband and the wife. This interaction would be viewed as simple in the sense that the husband's and wife's contributions to the relationship can be assessed independently of each other. The interaction would be viewed as static in the sense that these two sets of fixed traits give rise to a specific relationship that remains fixed and stable over time. Finally, the formal thinker would regard marital problems as the result of a permanent flaw or shortcoming in either the husband's or the wife's personality (i.e., one of the marriage partners made a bad choice, he or she picked a partner who possessed a constellation of traits that were essentially incompatible with his or her mates'). Or it would be assumed that marital problems develop because, in some cases, the interaction of the personalities of two "good people" proves to be problematic (i.e., they were two nice people who weren't meant for each other).

The dialectic thinker views a marriage and the problems that may arise within it in a different manner. The dialectic thinker would be predisposed to view the traits of the man and the woman who enter into marriage as constantly evolving over time. More importantly, it would be assumed that the personalities of both the husband and wife could not exist independently of one another because what (or who) a man is as a husband is influenced by his relationship with what (or who) a woman is as his wife and vice versa. This means that a marriage would be viewed as a constitutive relationship between two parties in which it is the relationship that makes the parties of the relationship (i.e., husband and wife) what (or who) they *are*. Furthermore, marriage would be viewed as an interactive relationship in a dynamic rather than a static sense. A dynamic interactive relationship is one in which the parties of the relationship mutually change each other and are changed by each other over time. A marriage, therefore, is viewed as a "whole" relationship that displays movement and change over time because of the constitutive and interactive relationship between the "parts" (i.e., the husband and wife) of the marriage, which could not exist independently of the "whole" (i.e., the marriage, itself). Finally, the dialectical thinker conceptualizes marital problems as a relationship between two individuals that has evolved in an increasingly maladaptive manner, with the maladaptivity affecting the "whole" of the relationship (i.e., the marriage) to the same extent that it interferes with the growth of the parties of the relationship (i.e., the husband and wife who "create" and are "created by" the relationship). Viewing a problematic relationship from this perspective allows the husband and the wife not to blame each other as the cause of the problem and to value their relationship as something that was meaningful at one point in its growth and evolution. For the dialectic thinker, the crucial issue in understanding marital problems becomes: "How does the relationship need to change in response to the changes it has brought about in us in order for it to continue?" (Basseches, 1984b, p. 27).

We conclude this section with two tables that compare and contrast the characteristics of formal and postformal thought. We present a revised version of Table 2.1 in Table 3.1, which describes the differences between formal and postformal thinking on the dimensions that characterize the various Piagetian stages. In Table 3.2, we present a description of the contrasting world views of the formal and postformal thinker.

POSTFORMAL THOUGHT: THE RESEARCH EVIDENCE

We have described the general characteristics of formal and postformal modes of thought, and we now present a summary of the empirical research bearing on the formal/postformal distinction. This summary is not meant to be an all-inclusive, critical review of the research investigating postformal development. Rather, it is intended to acquaint the reader with the form and content of the research that has been conducted in this area. We review studies that have focused on four aspects of postformal thinking: (a) the relativistic nature of knowledge and the limits of pure logic; (b) the development of metasystematic thinking; (c) a change in emphasis from problem solving to problem finding; and (d) the development of dialectic thinking.

TABLE 3.1. A Revised Version of Table 2.1 Indicating the Relationship Between Formal Operations and Postformal Operations

STAGE	NATURE OF OPERATIONS	OBJECTS OF OPERATIONS	TYPE OF EGOCENTRISM	TYPE OF CONSERVATION	TYPE OF EQUILIBRIUM
Formal Operations	Operations are second-order mental activities (i.e., they are thoughts that thoroughly coordinate the reciprocal relationships between all thoughts within a particular thought system).	Operations are directed to the propositions that characterize the "possible" relationships that exist between the variables within a closed system (i.e., operations are intrasystematic).	The constructive qualities of human cognition cannot be seen as responsible for the construction of the seemingly nonsubjective and nonrelative, absolute laws and principles they construct; the abstract and hypothetical take precedence over the real.	Conservation of abstract laws, rules, and principles which are viewed as universal, absolute, and nonrelative.	The INRC Group coordinates the twin forms of reversibility: negation and reciprocity into a coherent whole for those possible propositions that characterize a given closed system.
Postformal Operations	Operations are at least third-order mental activities (i.e., they are thoughts that attempt to coordinate the thoughts that emerge from different systems of thought).	Operations are directed to an analysis of the relationships that characterize interdependent systems that evolve over time (i.e., operations are inter-systematic).	The constructive properties of the mind as well as the relativistic properties of all knowledge are realized; the danger at this stage is not so much an egocentrism as it is an unwillingness to make firm commitments in the context of a knowledge base that is characterized by relativism.	Conservation of the changing, self-transforming nature of open systems; a commitment to uncertainty and relativism.	A form of equilibrium develops that has at its basis an understanding of the inherent disequilibrium of open systems.

TABLE 3.2. A Comparison of Formal and Postformal World Views

WORLD VIEW OF THE FORMAL THINKER	WORLD VIEW OF THE POSTFORMAL THINKER
Logical analysis will reveal the permanent and absolute laws and principles that regulate the behavior of the elements and entities that comprise reality. Knowledge, because it can be logically deduced, is viewed as absolute and noncontextual.	There are limits to logical analysis because logic is a construction of the mind rather than a given of reality. Knowledge, because it is a construction of the mind, must be nonabsolute and contextually relative.
Reality is best described as a collection of closed, static, unchanging systems at rest.	Reality is best described as a whole that consists of multiple, integrated, self-transforming systems in movement.
Reality consists of systems as well as variables within systems that are independent of one another and can be separated from one another "one at a time."	Reality consists of systems and variables within systems that are totally interdependent of one another and thus cannot be separated from one another "one at a time."
Unidirectionality of variables (linear causality).	Reciprocal influence of variables (nonlinear causality, interactiveness).
Parts of a whole exist independent of the whole.	Parts of a whole are constituted by their relationship to the whole.
Avoidance and separation of contradiction.	Acceptance of contradiction and synthesis into more inclusive wholes.
Emphasis on the hypothetical and abstract.	Emphasis on real events that characterize real life.

Relativistic Thinking

The first researcher who examined the growth of postformal thought (without ever using the term *postformal*) was William Perry (1968). He conducted a longitudinal study in which he interviewed students at Harvard University about their educational and personal experiences. Perry found that freshman students approached various intellectual and ethical problems from a dualistic perspective. These students assumed that there was only one correct answer to a particular problem and that it was the task of authority figures (e.g., professors) to teach them to distinguish the one correct answer from wrong alternatives. With time, this dualistic perspective was replaced by the realization of the inherent subjectivity of experience. This led the students to conceptualize all knowledge and value systems (even those espoused by authorities) as relative and contextual. At this level, students felt as if they were adrift in a sea of uncertainty, because there were several viewpoints that seemed to be of equal merit and validity. Finally, the students reached a developmental level at which they still understood the relativity of knowledge, but were no longer overwhelmed by it. In addition to their acceptance of the contextual and subjective nature of knowledge and values, they had become committed to a particular intellectual and/or ethical point of view. These students, in other words, were capable of transcending subjectivity via personal commitment.

Perry's (1968) ideas about cognitive development during the college years were drawn from a nonrepresentative sample, and he did not replicate or extend his findings to older groups. However, his ideas about the growth of contextual relativism have served as a basis for subsequent studies. Murphy and Gilligan (1980), for example, used Perry's theory to chart a new conception of adult moral development. Murphy and Gilligan noted that a disparity existed between Kohlberg's (1976) description of adult morality and the view of adult morality fostered by Perry's notion of contextual relativism. Kohlberg claimed that adult morality is characterized by the generation of logically derived absolute principles. In contrast, Perry argued that adult morality is characterized by a commitment to principles that are viewed as relative and changeable over time. These researchers examined the responses of adolescents and young adults to Kohlberg's moral judgment interview. Results showed that when longitudinal data were scored from the perspective of Kohlberg's scoring system, a significant number of subjects evidenced a *regression* in their dominant stage of moral development. However, when the same data were scored using Perry's system it was discovered that young adults evinced a *progression* in their level of moral reasoning. In another study, Gilligan and Murphy (1979) found that patterns of moral reasoning for real-life problems and concerns manifest the same shift from absolutism to contextualism during the adult years.

Sinnott (1980, 1981, 1984) has also discussed the relativistic nature of postformal thought. Although she believes that relativistic thinking can be directed to several different content areas (e.g., physical sciences, mathematics), she contends that it is easiest to study relativistic reasoning within the domain of interpersonal reality. Sinnott (1984) used the term *necessary subjectivity* to describe relativistic thinking within the area of interpersonal relations. Necessary subjectivity means that interpersonal reality is characterized by mutually contradictory frames of reference. It also suggests that contradictory frames of reference serve as the basis for personal growth and development. This contrasts with the view of physical reality in which subjectivity should be avoided because it is considered to be the product of faulty thinking. In order to examine the growth of relativistic thinking, Sinnott (1984) presented a group of adults ranging from 26 to 89 years of age with a variety of problems that were tested for the presence of formal operations and relativistic (i.e., postformal) operations. These problems demanded combinatorial and/or proportional forms of reasoning that were directed to highly abstract and artificial problems (e.g., putting letters of the alphabet into various combinations) or problems that involved real-life issues and circumstances. Results showed that adult subjects were most likely to use relativistic, postformal thinking styles to deal with real-life rather than abstract problems.

King, Kitchner, Davison, Parker, and Wood (1983) conducted a study that tested Kitchner's and King's (1981) Reflective Judgment Model. This model, which is similar to Perry's (1968) analysis of the growth of contextual relativism, postulates the existence of a series of seven structural stages, each of which describes the assumptions upon which individuals justify their beliefs about reality and knowledge. More specifically, King et al. (1983) have characterized each of these stages in the following way:

Stage 1. There is the belief in the absolute correspondence between what is real and what is perceived. Therefore, beliefs require no justification, because to observe reality means to know reality.

Stage 2. There is the belief in the existence of an objective reality and absolute knowledge of this reality. It is the role of authority figures (e.g., professors) to know and transmit objective knowledge. Therefore, personal beliefs are justified by their correspondence to the beliefs of authorities.

Stage 3. There is the belief that authorities may be temporarily unaware of particular types of absolute knowledge. It is also assumed that although such missing knowledge will ultimately be obtained, it is permissible to believe in what "feels right" to the self.

Stage 4. There is the belief that there is an objective reality that can never be known with certainty. Therefore, all knowledge, even that knowledge possessed by authorities, must be conceptualized as "relative" to the individual's point of view.

Stage 5. There is the belief that not only is knowledge subjective/relative, but all of reality is subjective/relative as well. Because reality and knowledge of reality can only be understood through subjective interpretation, it is believed that understanding is contextual and nongeneralizable.

Stage 6. There is the belief that even though all knowledge is subjective, some forms of knowledge may be judged as more valid than others. This claim is based on the premise that there are principles of inquiry which generalize across contexts.

Stage 7. There is the belief that knowledge is the end result of the process of critical inquiry. Valid knowledge claims may be made by evaluating the work of many individuals over a long period of time. The process of critical inquiry, however, may give rise to fallible knowledge. Therefore, all knowledge claims must remain open to reevaluation vis-à-vis the formulation of new theoretical paradigms and the accumulation of new data.

The subjects in the King et al. (1983) study were 59 individuals from three different educational levels who were tested twice over a 2-year period. The mean ages of the subjects at each educational level at the onset of the study were as follows: high school juniors = 16.2 years; college juniors = 19.6 years; doctoral students = 28.2 years. The high school and college students were matched to the doctoral students on high school SAT (Scholastic Aptitude Test) scores, size of home town, and sex. At both times of testing, all subjects were administered the Reflective Judgment Interview (Kitchner & King, 1981) and the Concept Mastery Test (Terman, 1973). The former measure, which consists of a set of four dilemmas within the areas of current events, science, religion, and history, assesses subjects' understanding of the nature of knowledge and the justification of beliefs. The latter measure, which consists of a number of word identification and analogy problems, assesses subjects' verbal ability.

At the time of first testing, significant differences were observed in the subjects' stage levels of epistemic understanding. More specifically, subjects in the high school, college, and graduate school groups received mean stage scores of 2.8, 3.6, and 6.0 on the Reflective Judgment Interview. At the time of seconding testing, all groups displayed a significant gain in their stage level of epistemic understanding. The mean stage scores for subjects in the high school, college, and graduate school groups were 3.6, 4.2, and 6.3, respectively, on this second occasion. These gains held true even when gains in subjects' verbal abilities were statistically controlled.

Perry's (1968) description of the growth of postformal thinking skills also served as the basis for an empirical investigation conducted by Benack (1984). She hypothesized that relativistic thought, more so than dualistic thought, enables an individual to empathically understand another person's experience. Benack's (1984) position was grounded in the speculation that:

> The dualist sees peoples' experience as generally reflecting the nature of the external world. He or she typically perceives the experience to be identical with reality; not as "how I see things" but as "the way things are." . . . He or she typically does not differentiate "my experience," "others' experience," and "reality," but assimilates all of these to a general category of "the way we know things to be."
>
> With the rise of relativism comes the ability to recognize multiple subjective perspectives on common situations. The relativist is able to differentiate not only "my experience," from "your experience," but "my perspective" from "your perspective." . . . the relativist *expects* that people will have somewhat different interpretations of the same event. He or she sees no contradiction in multiple views of a situation, each having "validity" or "truth." (p. 345)

The subjects in Benack's study were 20 graduate students enrolled in a counseling course who ranged from 21 to 42 years of age. All subjects were administered a semistructured interview that assessed their level of relativistic thought in two different ways. First, the subjects were asked to make a number of concrete moral judgments, and the dualistic versus relativistic nature of their thought was inferred from their responses. Second, the subjects were asked to make explicit statements about their understanding of the nature of knowledge, truth, and reality. The subjects' levels of empathic understanding were measured by observing their behavior over an average of five role-played counseling sessions. In all, eight different measures of empathy were recorded during these sessions. These measures of empathy included: breadth, accuracy, specificity, and tentativeness of the empathic response, as well as overall empathy and nondirectiveness.

Benack (1984) found that most subjects ($n = 15$) displayed either completely dualistic or relativistic thought when confronted with tasks that assessed their implicit and explicit epistemological orientations. Subjects who evidenced purely relativistic thought scored significantly higher on all empathy measures than did those who evinced purely dualistic thought. These results held true when both the average scores and the peak scores of these groups were compared.

A smaller number of subjects displayed "mixed" epistemological orientations. Some of these subjects ($n = 3$) displayed relativistic thought when asked to state their explicit epistemological orientation, but dualistic thought when their epistemological orientation was implicitly inferred from their responses to concrete problems. The remaining subjects ($n = 2$) displayed the opposite orientation. Results showed that these subjects' explicit epistemological orientations were more predictive of their empathic responses than were their implicit epistemological orientations.

We end this section on relativistic thinking by briefly describing the contents of a paper authored by Sinnott (1981). In this paper, she pointed out that not only do individuals tend to replace dualistic modes of thought with relativistic modes of thought, but that the shift from absolutism to relativism can be observed in the development of various scientific disciplines. For example, Sinnott (1981) contrasted the prerelativistic (i.e., mechanistic) concepts of Newtonian physics with the relativistic concepts of Einsteinian physics. Sinnott also argued that the manner in which contemporary psychologists view *development* seems to be shifting from an absolutistic orientation to a relativistic orientation. An inspection of Table 3.3 will reveal a brief list of the prerelativistic and relativistic concepts that Sinnott (1981) has identified within both physics and psychology.

Metasystematic Reasoning

Commons, Richards, and Kuhn (1982) postulated that formal operations involves operations on the elements of a system, whereas postformal operations involves operations that are applied to different systems. Cognitions about diverse systems and their interrelationships were termed *metasystematic* operations by these researchers. To test their hypothesis, Commons et al. presented undergraduate and graduate students with some traditional measures of concrete and formal thinking. Also, subjects were required to

TABLE 3.3. Prerelativistic and Relativistic Concepts
in Physics and Developmental Psychology

	TYPE OF CONCEPT	
DISCIPLINE	PRERELATIVISTIC	RELATIVISTIC
Physics	1. No event or principle exists that cannot be known and understood.	1. Unknowable events and principles exist.
	2. Events are stable.	2. Observed events are in motion. Motion must be taken into account in the observation.
	3. Natural laws and principles conform to verbal conventions.	3. Natural laws and principles may appear contradictory in terms of verbal conventions.
Developmental Psychology	1. The characteristics of self and other are viewed in Aristotelian terms.	1. The characteristics of self and other represent the interplay between the constantly changing organisms in a constantly changing world.
	2. Humans attain a stable stage of cognitive development and manifest stable personality traits.	2. Humans are evolving systems. Stages, and traits are artificial abstractions.
	3. Present models give rise to empirical studies that produce contradictory results; therefore, these models cannot be true.	3. Contradictory models that describe behavior in the limiting case may be related by transforms to derive truly general laws.

Source: Adapted from Sinnott, J.D. (1981). The theory of relativity: A metatheory for development? *Human Development, 24*, 293–311.

analyze the similarities and differences between four stories that were written in such a way that they could be interpreted in a concrete, formal, or postformal manner. Results indicated that success on the formal operational reasoning problem seemed to be a necessary cause for the emergence of postformal (metasystematic) thought.

In a recent study of the differences between undergraduates and graduate students' appraisals of stories, Richards and Commons (1984) found that few undergraduate students displayed metasystematic thinking, whereas most graduate students did. Of the 31 students who exhibited postformal thought, only one failed to display formal thought. And, as predicted, not all the students displaying formal thought were capable of metasystematic reasoning.

Armon (1984) has also provided support for the concept of metasystematic thinking in adulthood. In her research she investigated the ability of adults to reason about the *Good* (a general system of evaluative reasoning) and the *Good Life* (the evaluative reasoning system applied to concrete domains such as work, marriage, and education). The development of these valuing systems is indicative, she argued, of structural change that differentiates formal from postformal reasoners. She suggested that postformal reasoners evince a coherent and holistic personal value system that allows them to understand the legitimacy of other value systems. Formal reasoners, however, were hypothesized as *not* able to accept the legitimacy of value systems different from their own. The evidence for a *structural* distinction between formal and postformal (i.e., metasystematic forms of thinking) comes from Armon's combined cross-sectional and longitudinal research conducted over a 4-year period. Initially, 43 subjects were interviewed using both Kohlberg's Standard Form Moral Judgment Interview and Armon's Good Life Interview. A subsequent repeat testing with these same measures was conducted 4 years later with only four subjects discontinuing their participation. The age range of the subjects was 5–13, 23–30, 31–47, and 48–72, with nearly equal numbers of subjects in each of the respective categories. The results were generally supportive of the concept of postformal reasoning in adulthood. No subject below the age of 26 displayed postformal reasoning, using either the Kohlberg or Armon interview. In addition, subjects' scores on both measures were found to be highly related. Stage sequentiality and progressive, ordered movement without the skipping of stages was supported in the longitudinal assessments of both Moral Judgment and the Good. Stage change analyses revealed that 11 of 22 adults over the age of 30 progressed at least one-half a stage in reasoning about the Good, whereas no subjects evidenced regression. A parallel set of data was reported for Moral Judgment, with 7 out of 22 adults over the age of 30 showing positive stage progression across the same 4-year period and only one subject displaying a regression of one-half stage.

Armon (1984) also reported correspondence between stages in reasoning about the Good and the Good Life with the General Stage Model developed by Commons and Richards (1984). The lowest levels of Armon's subjects' reasoning corresponded to the stage of formal operations as described by Commons and Richards; the highest levels of Armon's subjects' reasoning corresponded to Common's and Richard's description of metasystematic operations. These results support the notion that qualitative changes in thinking extend into adulthood and are related to meta-ethical change at this juncture of the life span. This view has also been echoed in Kohlberg's recent recasting of his scoring methodology and his continued longitudinal analysis of moral reasoning from adolescence through adulthood (Colby, Kohlberg, Gibbs, & Lieberman, 1983).

Problem Finding

Arlin (1975) conducted the first empirical study to suggest the need for a fifth (i.e., postformal) stage in Piagetian theory. She regarded formal thinking as primarily involved in the task of problem solving (i.e., solving a problem within a known system) and postformal thinking as primarily geared to the task of problem finding (i.e., transcending known systems in search of new systems that create new problems). She presented college freshmen and seniors with a variety of formal thinking tasks: chemical combinations, pendulum, and projection of shadows, and a measure of problem finding. The problem-finding task involved having subjects raise questions about a collection of 12 common objects. The level of generality expressed in the subjects' questions was taken as an index of problem finding. Very generalized and abstract questions, for example, were assumed to reflect a problem-finding orientation, whereas very specific and concrete questions were assumed to reflect a preoccupation with problem solving. Results indicated that success on the Piagetian measures of formal operations was a necessary precondition for generalized problem finding.

Recently, Arlin (1984) studied problem solving and problem finding in a group of young adult artists. Subjects were given several traditional measures of formal thinking as well as a problem-finding task. All subjects performed equally well on the measures of formal thought. Those subjects who were judged as producers of highly creative and original works of art, however, scored higher on the measure of problem finding than the artists whose work was rated lower in creativity. Differences between artists who were classified as either formal or postformal were also found in responses to the question, "Could any of the elements in your drawing be eliminated or altered without destroying its characteristics?" Similar to the findings of Getzels and Csikszentmihalyi (1976), less creative artists viewed their work as fixed, unalterable, and finished. Highly creative artists, in contrast, viewed their works as changeable and unfinished.

Arlin (1984) suggested that the highly creative artists use relativistic thinking skills in order to (a) accept the idea that their work evolves and changes over time, and (b) actively produce new perspectives from which to view their work. Perkins (1981) suggested that people who want to be creative and who value creativity are likely to become creative. Thus, the motivation to be creative may, in part, fuel the recognition of the relativity of one's productions and facilitate the development of certain aspects of postformal thought.

Arlin's analysis of the relationship between problem solving, problem finding, and creativity vis-à-vis the tendency to conceptualize artistic efforts in either an absolute or relative manner has widespread utility. Consider, for example, playwright Peter Shaffer's description of Mozart's musical compositions from the perspective of Arlin's dichotomy

> Mozart's incomparability lies in the absolute nature of his achievements: The best of them cannot be even slightly rewritten without diminishment. Of course, great art always attests to the existence of absolutes: That is why the

greatest offers the largest comfort — even as, temporarily, it can also induce the greatest despair. At certain moments in art galleries, for example, we get the uneasy feeling we are not judging perfect paintings but that they are judging us. (*The New York Times*, September 2, 1984)

Dialectic Thinking

Sinnott and Guttman (1978) were the first researchers to study the growth of dialectic thinking during the adult years. They sought to determine if older adults employ dialectic principles in the resolution of real-life problems and conflicts. For example, they examined whether or not older adults cast decision-making processes within a thesis→ antithesis→ synthesis framework, and if older adults connect their own personal histories with the relevant contextual dimensions surrounding a problem. Furthermore, these researchers examined the relationship between the growth of dialectic modes of thought and the presence of Piagetian operational abilities.

The subjects in the Sinnott and Guttman (1978) study were 447 older adults who were approximately 70 years of age. Subjects were asked if they had made an important decision during the past year and to describe the way they went about making the decision. Subjects were also given a battery of Piagetian tasks that measured their logical thinking abilities. These tasks assessed concrete operational skills, such as multiple classification, and formal operational skills, such as the isolation of variables.

Of the 447 subjects, 109 described a critical decision they had to make that was tied to a particular life event. It was found that 32 of these 109 subjects experienced conflict-free decisions. A total of 77 of the 109 subjects reported making decisions that were characterized by conflicts between the biological, psychological, social, financial, and/or environmental dimensions within which individual and social life evolves (cf. Riegel, 1976). A total of 11 of these subjects reported that they could *not* resolve their conflicts, 41 subjects resolved their conflicts *without* the aid of a dialectic synthesis, and 25 subjects resolved their conflicts via the implementation of a *dialectic synthesis* of the conflicting dimensions that constituted the problem. Next, Sinnott and Guttman (1978) performed a series of analyses to determine the degree to which Piagetian logical abilities were related to whether or not subjects: (a) made decisions that they experienced as conflict-free; (b) resolved their conflicts; and (c) resolved their conflicts through dialectical synthesis. Surprisingly, these analyses revealed that logical thinking skills were *not* significantly related to any of the above-mentioned research questions. An important implication of these findings is that postformal thinking about personal conflicts and formal thinking about standard Piagetian laboratory tasks are relatively independent from one another.

Basseches (1980, 1984a, 1984b) operationalized his notion of postformal development by constructing a scoring system that describes 24 "moves-in-thought," each of which calls attention to a unique type of dialectic thinking. These 24 moves-of-thought can be grouped into four different schemata, each of which captures a generalized aspect of dialectic thinking. Motion-oriented Schemata, for example, focus on the processes of change and recognize the dialectic roots of change (e.g., thesis → antithesis → synthesis). Form-oriented Schemata call attention to the primacy of wholes and conceptualize wholes as forms or systems. Relationship-oriented Schemata direct the thinker's attention to the interactive and constitutive nature of relationships. Meta-formal Schemata integrate the notions of movement, systems, and relationships in a meaningful way.

Using this scoring system, Basseches (1980) interviewed freshmen, seniors, and faculty members at a small liberal arts college about their understanding of the function of education and the process of education. He found that faculty members displayed a higher incidence of dialectic thinking than did seniors, whereas seniors displayed a higher incidence of dialectic thinking than did freshmen.

Basseches (1984a), in a related study, presented freshmen, seniors, and graduate students with pairs of arguments on a variety of issues in which one element of each pair expressed a dialectic point of view and the other expressed a nondialectic perspective. Results indicated increased comprehension of and preference for the dialectical points of view with advancing grade level. Comprehension of the nondialectical arguments was not related to grade level.

Basseches (1984a) also investigated the development of the four different types of dialectical schemata. He reported that a relatively large number of college freshmen but a small number of faculty members evidenced just one mode of dialectic thought. These subjects only displayed some of the form-oriented schemata that call attention to the existence of wholes and systems. They focused on the holistic nature of one particular system, and did not display the ability to integrate diverse systems in a holistic manner. Also, they viewed contradictions as flaws within a system rather than as facilitators of growth and transformation within that system. Thus, Basseches theorized that the dialectical schemata that recognize the existence of single, isolated systems emerge along with formal operational thought.

Next, Basseches identified three groups of transitional subjects. These groups consisted of approximately equal numbers of students and faculty, who were conspicuous because they displayed all but one specific cluster of dialectic schemata. Some of these transitional subjects, for example, were labeled Formalists. These subjects were termed formalists because they did not manifest the cluster of dialectic schemata that argues against the efficacy of viewing reality as a number of stable, closed systems. They seemed to have a great deal of difficulty understanding that development entails change and movement because they failed to grasp the interactive nature of relationships. Another group of subjects was termed Nonformalists. In comparison to the formalists, they understood the changeable nature of systems, but they did not understand the form of the change. They lacked an appreciation of how a single system can become more differentiated (with regard to itself) yet more integrated (with regard to other systems) over the course of time. The third transitional group was labeled Value-relativists. They displayed an unwillingness to make any sort of value judgment and were unable to transcend the subjective nature of reality. Value-relativists, in other words, lacked the ability to commit themselves to a set of values because they felt overwhelmed by the changing, evolving nature of those values.

A third group of subjects, primarily faculty members, evinced all four of the dialectical schemata. These individuals seemed to have reached a form of dialectic equilibrium in that they understood: (a) the open, self-transforming nature of systems; (b) the constitutive and interactive relationships that exist both within and between systems; and (c) the need to make firm commitments to principles that they expected to change over time.

Kramer and Woodruff (in press) conducted a study that investigated the hypothesis that formal operational thinking is a necessary precondition for the development of two distinct forms of postformal reasoning: dialectic thinking (i.e., the acceptance and integration of contradiction into a more all-inclusive whole) and relativistic thinking (i.e., the acceptance of contextual relativism). The subjects were young, middle-aged, and older adults, who were matched on educational level. They were administered several measures of formal operational thought (e.g., separation of variables, coordination of internal and external frames of reference), along with two dilemmas designed to measure postformal reasoning (i.e., a career dilemma and a hostage problem). The results indicated that with increasing age adults displayed an increased awareness of relativity, an acceptance of contradiction as a basic aspect of reality, and an ability to synthesize contradictions into higher-order wholes. Contrary to expectation, however, was the finding that an awareness of relativity was a necessary precondition for the development of formal operations. But formal operations was found to be a necessary precondition for the development of dialectic thinking. Kramer and Woodruff interpreted these results by suggesting that dialectic synthesis is a skill that is more closely allied with a contextual world view than is the acceptance of relativity.

As can be seen, there are many different conceptual and methodological approaches to the study of dialectic thinking. Common to these divergent approaches is a commitment to some form of constructivism. Constructivism implies that knowledge structures are created by individuals and are not simply direct copies of external reality. The notion of constructivism pervades most current views of human cognition. Moshman (1982), for example, has suggested that all theories of human cognition have a foundation in constructivism. The most sophisticated form of constructivist thinking, however, is seen in the work of Piaget. Moshman (1982) suggests that Piaget's theory, and by necessity Piaget's own thinking, falls within the dialectical constructivist paradigm. Moshman's (1982) viewpoint on this issue is consistent with our position already expressed in chapter 2. In that chapter, we suggested that Piaget's theory does not fit precisely into an organismic world view but has a strong basis in dialectical constructivism.

CRITIQUE OF POSTFORMAL THEORIES OF ADULT COGNITIVE DEVELOPMENT

We have outlined what we believe to be the main features of postformal thought and have presented a brief overview of the research that has investigated the formal/postformal distinction. The postformal research is limited, because the quality of studies has *not* kept pace with the level of theorizing that has surrounded the topic of postformal development. This may be because of the inherent difficulty in constructing and scoring sound measures of postformal thinking. The abundance of theory may be a signal of a "paradigm shift" in the study of adult cognitive development (cf. Kuhn, 1970). When theorists realized the inadequacies of existing paradigms (e.g., when developmentalists realized the problems with applying Piagetian theory to adult development), they responded with a rash of new adjustments before they could adequately operationalize and empirically test those adjustments. Despite this problem, there is tentative empirical support for the existence of postformal modes of thought. Some psychologists support the existence of cognitive structural stages extending well beyond formal operations (Commons & Richards, 1984; Labouvie-Vief, 1984; Richards & Commons, 1984). Other developmentalists, however, suggest that changes in thought beyond formal operations do not meet the criteria that define true structural stages (Basseches, 1984a, 1984b; Gibbs, 1979). For example, Basseches (1984b) has commented:

> Thus, if the notion of "stage" of cognitive development is meant as a technical term, presupposing the attributes of Piagetian structures, the conception of dialectical schemata presented here is consistent with Kohlberg's articulated assumption that there are no postformal cognitive stages. (p. 267)

It is not necessary to adhere to only one of the several conceptions of postformal thought. But these stylistic aspects of adult thinking that have been identified in postformal research must be taken into account in order to advance both theory and research on cognitive development in adulthood. Furthermore, we agree with Basseches' (1984b) point that postformal reasoning may not be representative of a genuine thought "structure" in the traditional Piagetian-structural sense. Therefore, our position is that postformal cognitive development should be regarded as a set of *styles* of thinking that emerge during adulthood (i.e., relativistic thinking, metasystematic reasoning, problem finding, and dialectic thinking), not as a true structural stage of thought.

Not only do we have doubts about the true "stage-like" nature of postformal operations, we also have reservations about the structural stage-like qualities of all of the other Piagetian stages (i.e., sensori-motor, preoperations, concrete operations, and formal operations). Several developmentalists (Brainerd, 1978; Donaldson, 1978; Gardner, 1983; Gelman, 1979) have commented, for example, that the cognitive performance of children and adolescents is so inconsistent and variable that it is difficult to embrace the existence of a set of truly "structural" stages that comprise cognitive development.

Finally, it must be noted that formal and postformal theories of cognitive development portray adults as competent reasoners who are capable of constructing an increasingly sophisticated understanding of physical and social reality. This outlook on adult cognition seems to be overly optimistic in light of well-documented trends showing age-related declines in reasoning (Horn, 1982). Furthermore, the postformal view does not seem to represent how adults actually make complex judgments under uncertain conditions. For example, several researchers (Johnson-Laird, 1983; Kahneman & Tversky, 1984; Nisbitt, Krantz, Jepson, & Kunda, 1983; Tversky & Kahneman, 1971, 1973, 1974, 1981, 1983) have shown that adults employ a set of "intuitive heuristics" to help them solve problems under conditions of uncertainty that are essentially irrational and illogical in nature. Thus, proponents of the postformal approach to the study of adult cognition have yet to integrate their assumptions about the positive qualities of adult thinking with the more negativistic characteristics of adult thought that have been reported by the previously mentioned researchers.

SUMMARY

In this chapter we discussed Basseches' (1980, 1984a, 1984b) conceptualization of postformal cognitive development, a conceptualization that highlights the features of dialectic thinking. Next we presented and discussed several research studies that have shown that adulthood is characterized by the growth of several components of postformal reasoning: relativistic thinking, metasystematic reasoning, problem finding, and dialectic thinking. We concluded that adults think in a manner that is largely consistent with postformal accounts of cognitive development. However, we have come to regard postformal cognitive development as characterized by the emergence of a set of *styles* of thinking, not as a genuine structural stage of thought.

4

The Domain Specificity
of Adult Thinking

The questions which belong to different domains of thought, differ very often not only in the kinds of subject matter that they are about, but in the kinds of thinking that they require.

G. Ryle
Dilemmas

In the previous chapter, we presented theoretical and empirical evidence that suggested that adulthood is characterized by the transition from formal to postformal styles of thinking. In this chapter, we examine: (a) the nature of the developmental relationship between formal and postformal styles of thought, and (b) the manner by which adults develop advanced thinking skills within particular domains of knowledge. Specifically, we discuss and compare three models. First, we consider a Standard Model, in which postformal cognitive development is conceptualized as an all-encompassing and unitary structured whole. This model suggests that the attainment of formal operations is necessary for the attainment of postformal thought. Second, we describe a Differentiation Model, which suggests that adults develop postformal styles of thinking in some domains and content areas to the exclusion of other domains and content areas. According to this model, individuals begin to display advanced thinking skills within specific domains upon entry into formal operations. This model conceptualizes postformal development during adulthood as the end point of a differentiation process that has its beginnings in adolescence. Like the Standard Model, the Differentiation Model assumes that the first three stages of cognitive development (i.e., sensori-motor, preoperational thought, and concrete operations) are best conceptualized as unitary and all-encompassing structured wholes. Third, we present a Modularity Model, which has its origins in part in Piagetian theory, but which also takes into account non-Piagetian theory and research in philosophy, developmental psychology, cognitive psychology, and neuropsychology. This Modularity Model suggests that humans possess a number of genetically hard-wired, autonomous cognitive subsystems through which they come to understand different aspects of reality. Within the parameters of each of these cognitive modules or subsystems, individuals may display qualitatively different styles of thinking. Further, this model suggests that the style of thinking (e.g., formal versus postformal) that an adult manifests within the context of any cognitive module is relatively independent of the style of thinking that he/she displays within the context of another cognitive module. We begin with a description of these models.

THE STANDARD MODEL

The Standard Model is prototypical of Piaget's early (i.e., pre-1972) conceptualizations regarding the stage-wise characteristics of cognitive development. This model captures the general underpinnings of structural stage theory, in that cognitive development is presumed to involve qualitative cognitive change through a progression of stages satisfying the following criteria:

1. Invariant Movement
2. Qualitative Restructuring
3. Hierarchical Integration
4. Structured Wholeness
5. Universal Progression

With regard to the first of these criteria, the Standard Model implies that individuals progress through a cognitive–developmental sequence in a manner that will not allow for either stage skipping or for backwards stage movement (i.e., regression). Consequently, postformal thinking skills should be observed only in those individuals who already possess consolidated formal operational thinking skills. Thus, formal operations is viewed as a necessary precondition for the growth of postformal operations.

The Standard Model also suggests that there is a qualitative difference (i.e., a difference in form rather than a difference in degree) between the structure of the thought systems that describe each of the stages of cognitive development. The qualitative differences between formal and postformal styles of thought were discussed in the previous chapter.

Hierarchical integration implies that each stage of cognitive development should be viewed as both an incorporation and an extension of the stage that preceded it within the developmental sequence. This means that postformal thought structures have their basis in formal thought structures. The notion of hierarchical integration assumes invariant movement, because each stage has its basis in each preceding stage.

The criteria of invariant movement, qualitative restructuring, and hierarchical integration are shared and presumed valid by all of the three models we discuss in this chapter. The last two criteria, structured wholeness and universal progression, are not shared and require closer examination.

The concept of structured wholeness maintains that each of the stages within the cognitive developmental sequence is characterized by the existence of a number of highly generalizable and interrelated thought structures, which all reflect a qualitatively identical level of cognitive organization. Thus, each Piagetian stage is reflective of a mode of thought that is both unitary and all-encompassing. This means that: (a) the structural characteristics of one's thought is not affected by the content area or domain to which one's thought is directed; (b) an individual may evince a form of cognitive sophistication that is consistent with one (and only one) of the Piagetian stages; and (c) instances of decalage and/or unevenness in development are either unexpected, unimportant, or treated as a nuisance if they occur. When the structured-wholeness criterion is applied to a postformal developmental stage, it yields the proposition that if an adult is capable of postformal thinking, this level of thought will be displayed regardless of content. For example, if a person displayed postformal thinking skills in the area of mathematics, then it would be also expected that he/she would display postformal reasoning skills within other areas, such as literary or poetic analysis.

The position that cognitive structures are all-pervasive and unitary raises several problems. First, Piagetian theory addresses mainly the study of logical–mathematical thought structures. Thus, the standard version of Piagetian theory seems to have erred when it equated a very specific and narrow mode of thought (i.e., logical–mathematical understanding) with the most general and all-encompassing mode of thought structures (i.e., not unlike Spearman's, 1927, "g" factor of intelligence). Thus, the Standard Model concerns itself with a specific form of thought, but it also suggests that this specific mode of thought forms the substrate of all modes of thought.

Second, the Standard Model suggests that the demonstration of competence in such diverse areas as interpersonal awareness, visual art, poetry, music, physics, or philosophy is dependent on the application of logical–mathematical thought structures to these various content areas or domains. Given this assumption, the Standard Model maintains that both the musical composer and the electronics engineer apply the same type of logical–mathematical reasoning to the problem-solving and problem-finding demands that surround these professions. This position is difficult to accept on commonsense grounds and in light of current research findings suggesting the multidimensionality of adult intelligence (Dixon, Kramer, & Baltes, 1984; Horn, 1970; Horn & Donaldson, 1980; Reinert, 1970; Schaie, 1983). Further, Gardner (1983) has suggested that individuals possess a number of different types of neurologically based intelligences that are brought to bear on problems in different intellectual domains. From Gardner's perspective, logical–mathematical reasoning is only one type of intelligence.

Third, we disagree with the standard version of structured wholeness, which suggests that everything that one could possibly know about has to be known at the same qualitative level (i.e., stage level) of logical–mathematical organization. This assertion does not take into account the obvious fact that different adults display qualitatively different levels of sophistication within different cognitive domains. For example, a skilled musical composer displays postformal thinking skills with regard to musical composition, but probably uses formal (or even concrete) thought when dealing with problems and concepts in other domains. This argument regarding the lack of structured wholeness seems just as meaningful when one considers the cognitive skills of young children. It has already been mentioned in chapter three, for example, that it is becoming increasingly difficult to accept the notion of structured wholeness as descriptive of the first three Piagetian stages (see Brainerd, 1978; Donaldson, 1978; Gelman, 1979). Consistent with this position, Kagan (1984) has argued that:

> The five-year-old who knows that a mosquito remains small in size, even though it appears large under a magnifying glass, does not know that the amount of water in a large flat dish remains unchanged after all of it has been poured into a tall, thin cylinder. On the one hand, the psychologist can attribute to the five-year-old the general competence Piaget calls *conservation of quantity*, and rationalize the child's failure with the containers of water as being due to his inability to extend the principle to this specific problem. On the other hand, the psychologist can deny the general competence and treat the conservation of size or quantity as a set of highly specific competencies tied to highly specific situations. (p. 237)

Also, consider the notion of structured wholeness in light of the following problems developed by Peter Wason and Philip Johnson-Laird (Johnson-Laird & Wason, 1970; Wason, 1966; Wason & Johnson-Laird, 1972) and commented upon by Gardner (1985):

Problem A. Four cards are laid in front of you displaying, respectively, an E, K, 4, and 7. You are informed that each card has a letter on one side and a number on the other. And, you are then given a rule, "If a card has a vowel on one side, then it has a vowel on the other side," whose truth-value you are expected to evaluate. Finally you are given the opportunity to turn over two, but only two, cards in order to determine if the rule is correct.

Problem B. Four cards are laid in front of you, each card has the name of a city on one side and a mode of transportation on the other side. The four cards display, respectively, the following words: "Manchester," "Sheffield," "Train" and "Car." You are then told to evaluate the truth-value of the following rule, "Everytime I go to Manchester I travel by train." Finally, you are given the opportunity to turn over two, but only two, cards in order to determine if the rule is correct.

Problems A and B contain to-be-evaluated rules that are formally *identical* to one another. In responding to problem A, the majority of subjects realize the necessity of turning over the card with the vowel (E) printed on it and the irrelevancy of turning over the card that bears the consonant (K). However, only about 10% of the adults tested give the correct response when required to choose the second card. These subjects realize that of the two numbered cards (4 and 7), it is essential to turn over the card with the 7 printed on it, *not* the card with the 4 printed on it. With regard to problem B, the vast majority of adults tested (approximately 80%) select the appropriate pair of cards. They select the cards with the words Manchester and Car printed on them, rather than the cards that bear the words Manchester and Train. Choosing this latter pair of cards (Manchester and Train), however, would have been analogous to the incorrect response offered by 90% of the subjects to problem A (i.e., choosing the card marked with the E and the 4). Gardner (1985) has argued that differential success rates on problems A and B are inconsistent with the notion of structured wholeness. He has suggested that the key to understanding these results is to be found in the familiarity and personal meaning that adults attach to the contents of problems A and B, *not* to the existence/nonexistence of a set of highly generalizable and abstract logical rules. More specifically, Gardner (1985) commented that:

> The results clearly challenge any notion that individuals are "logic machines," capable of applying the same modes of reasoning, independent of the specific information in a problem. Thus humans are notably different from an ideal computer: the actual contents of a problem (vowels versus vehicles) cannot make any difference for such a syntactically governed apparatus. Yet . . . the content of specific problems determines how all of us (except highly trained logicians) will proceed on an apparently simple reasoning task. (p. 363)

Fourth, the assertions made by the Standard Model concerning structured wholeness create problems vis-à-vis the criterion of universal progression. The concept of universal progression implies that not only will all individuals pass through a stage sequence in an invariant manner, but they will also pass through *all* of the stages that comprise the stage sequence. In terms of Piaget's traditional stage theory, this means that all individuals should reach the stage of formal operations; in terms of the postformal theories, it suggests that all individuals should display postformal thought. However, several reviewers (Brainerd, 1978, 1979; Day, 1978; Keating, 1980; Neimark, 1975, 1979) have observed that a significant minority (or perhaps even a majority) of adults never attain consolidated formal operational thinking skills. Thus, the manifestation of integrated formal thinking seems to be the exception rather than the rule. If formal operational thinking is a prerequisite to postformal thinking, the attainment of the postformal stage must be a rarity. In this sense, postformal theory serves as a description applied only to individuals who are exceptionally gifted in most or all domains of thought.

In light of these issues, the Standard Model has abandoned the criterion of universal progression. That is, most individuals do not evince the apex of cognitive development, but all individuals do progress through the stages in an invariant and theoretically anticipated manner. Also, it has suggested that individual differences in the manifestation of the terminal stage of cognitive development may be accounted for in part by individual differences in personality (e.g., levels of motivation, curiosity, cognitive style), genetic potential, and/or the differential experiences and opportunities afforded by various psycho-social environments.

The Standard Model is presented in Figure 4.1. Each of the three adults represented in this figure has achieved a different terminal stage of cognitive development: postformal operations for adult *A*, formal operations for adult *B*, and concrete operations for adult *C*.

THE DIFFERENTIATION MODEL

In 1972 Piaget published an important article in *Human Development* that was a reconceptualization of his earlier views of adult cognitive development, and we refer to this work as an example of a Differentiation Model. Piaget's Differentiation Model makes the same assumptions as the Standard Model concerning the stage criteria of invariant progression, qualitative restructuring, and hierarchical integration, but the reconceptualized model makes different assumptions regarding structured wholeness and universal progression.

Piaget (1972) suggested that formal operations may not be a unitary and all-encompassing stage of cognitive development as originally suggested (Inhelder & Piaget, 1958). The accumulating evidence encouraged Piaget to propose that individuals develop formal-thinking skills in *some* domains or content areas (not all domains and content areas) as a function of their unique interests, aptitudes, motivations, and life experiences. Piaget articulated this revised position in the following manner:

> All normal subjects attain the stage of formal operations or structuring if not between 11–12 to 14–15 years, in any case between 15 and 20 years. However, they reach this stage in different areas according to their aptitudes and their professional specializations (advanced studies or different types of apprenticeship for the various trades). . . . (1972, pp. 9–10)

Piaget suggested that during formal operations, the *content* of one's thought determines the *structure* of one's thought. But at all of the earlier stage levels, the structure of thought is not affected by the content of thought. In

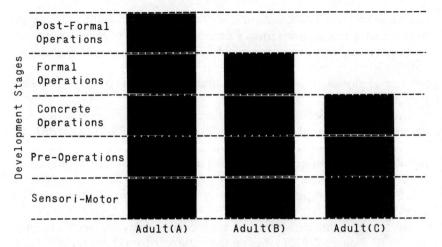

FIGURE 4.1. An illustration of the Standard Piagetian Model.

other words, the first three stages (i.e., sensori-motor, preoperations and concrete operations) were still seen as unitary structured wholes within the framework of the Differentiation Model. To again quote Piaget:

> It is one thing to dissociate the form from the content in a field which is of interest to the subject and within which he can apply his curiosity and initiative, and it is another to be able to generalize this same spontaneity of research and comprehension to a field foreign to the subject's career and interests. To ask a future lawyer to reason on the theory of relativity or to ask a student in physics to reason on the code of civil rights is quite different from asking a child to generalize what he has discovered in the conservation of matter to a problem on the conservation of weight. In the latter instance it is the passage from one content to a different but comparable content, whereas in the former it is to go out of the subject's field of vital activities and enter a totally new field, completely foreign to his interests and projects. Briefly, we can retain the idea that formal operations are free from their concrete content, but we must add that this is true only on the condition that for the subjects the situations involve equal aptitudes or comparable vital interests. (1972, p. 11)

Although Piaget did not suggest the need for a more advanced stage of cognitive development, his revised theory has several implications for the conceptualization of postformal thought. First, postformal thinking develops within a particular domain only if formal-thinking skills have developed within that domain. Second, postformal thinking skills represent the end product of a branching/differentiation process that begins at the onset of formal operations. Third, individual differences among adults are expected to be found with regard to terminal developmental level within different cognitive domains. Thus, someone might have a postformal understanding of judicial/legalistic concepts and a formal understanding of concepts within the area of physics, whereas another adult may have the opposite cognitive profile.

Several writers (Berzonsky, 1978; Dulit, 1972) have arrived at a view similar to the one expressed in Piaget's (1972) paper. Dulit (1972) contended that the first three of Piaget's stages are invariant, hierarchical, and universal, but that there is a branching into parallel tracks in adolescence or early adulthood. Although formal operations is a logical and optimal outgrowth of the prior stages, it is just one of several tracks representing cognitive development.

Berzonsky's branching model of adult cognitive development is an integration of Piaget's (1972) ideas on the nature of formal operations, Guilford's (1959) "Structure of Intellect Theory," and Phenix's (1964) discussion of the different realms of meaning. Berzonsky's model can be represented as a tree with one trunk and various branches (see Fig. 4.2). The trunk of

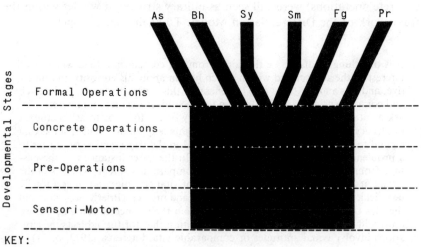

KEY:
As- Aesthetic Knowledge
Bh- Behavioral Content
Sy- Symbolic Content
Sm- Semantic Content
Fg- Figural Content
Pr- Personal Knowledge

FIGURE 4.2. Berzonsky's Branching Model of formal operations: An illustration of the Differentiation Model.

the tree consists of the first three of Piaget's stages. Berzonsky argued that these stages meet the criteria of structured wholeness (i.e., they are relatively unitary and all-encompassing modes of thought) and universal progression (i.e., normal individuals will ultimately progress through these stages and attain consolidated concrete operational thought). As illustrated in Figure 4.2, normal development involves advancing to the top of the tree trunk.

Branches of the tree represent the various content areas within which an adult might develop formal thinking skills. Guilford's (1965, 1967) Structure of Intellect Model includes four general content areas of intelligence: figural, behavioral, semantic, and symbolic. *Figural content*, for example, refers to the ability to observe, manipulate, and represent concrete objects in a sophisticated manner. Successful problem solving on traditional Piagetian measures of formal thought (e.g., pendulum task, rods task) may reflect advanced development within this content area. *Semantic content* consists of a domain of knowledge that involves the articulation of ideas and meanings that are expressed within a verbal medium. Reasoning about issues in literary works may be representative of this domain of knowledge. *Behavioral content* is a form of knowledge in which an individual displays an expertise in understanding psychological dynamics and processes. Coping successfully with real-life interpersonal problems and developing a personal identity are aspects of behavioral content. *Symbolic content* refers to a domain within which representational knowledge is gained through the manipulation of arithematic and algebraic symbols as well as letters. Individuals who manifest a flair for mathematics and/or logic may be viewed as having a great deal of cognitive sophistication within this content area.

Berzonsky described two additional forms of knowledge, which have their basis in the work of Phenix (1964). The first, *aesthetic knowledge*, refers to the type of knowing that exists within music, literature, and the visual arts. Knowledge of this type is immediate, personal, attained by direct perception, and is nongeneralizable. The second, *personal knowledge*, involves an understanding of human relationships from an "I-Thou" rather than an "I-It" framework.

With regard to the tree metaphor, the adolescent or young adult who has arrived at the top of the tree trunk makes a decision about which of the various branches of knowledge will be developed and which will be ignored. It is likely that this decision is neither deliberate nor conscious. See Figure 4.3 for an illustration of the cognitive profiles of three different adults. This figure combines Berzonsky's (1978) branching model with a conception of a postformal stage of cognitive development. Adult A, who might very well be an accomplished musician and composer, has developed postformal thinking skills within the aesthetic and symbolic branches, formal skills within the personal and behavioral branches (he or she may possess reasonably good interpersonal skills and abilities that would account for success

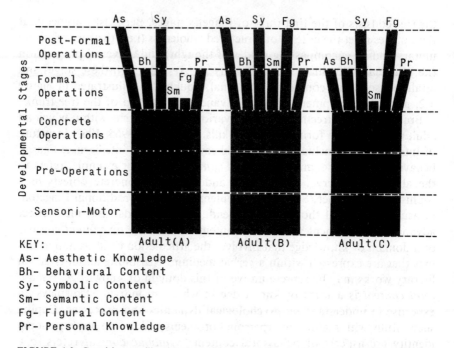

FIGURE 4.3. Cognitive profiles for three different adults: An illustration based on the Differentiation Model.

in dealing with other musicians on a one-to-one basis and easing various rivalries and tensions between other musicians), and due to a lack of interest and aptitude, he or she may possess a very limited understanding of issues and problems that pertain to the semantic and figural branches (e.g., poetry, tinkering with automobile engines). Examination of the cognitive profiles of adults B and C will show their respective strengths, weaknesses, and occupations.

The Differentiation Model seems to be a more accurate representation of adult cognitive development than the Standard Model. However, the limitation of the Standard Model still applies, in that there is mainly one type of knowing (i.e., logical–mathematical), which may eventually become directed to different cognitive domains. The Differentiation Model suggests that some adults may apply formal or postformal modes of logical–mathematical thinking to the solution of interpersonal problems, while other adults use the same type of logical–mathematical thinking in order to understand concepts within mathematics and/or the physical sciences. That logical–mathematical reasoning is presumed necessary for advanced reasoning in the other branches can be seen in the research on identity formation and postconventional moral development in late adolescence and young adulthood (Berzonsky & Barclay, 1982; Berzonsky, Weiner, & Raphael, 1975; Kuhn, Langer, Kohlberg, & Haan, 1977; Tomlinson-Keasey & Keasey, 1972). The vast majority of these studies have been conducted under the guiding hypothesis that advanced understanding about self and interpersonal relationships depends on advanced understanding of logical-mathematical concepts. Alternatively, Gardner (1983) and others have argued that individual differences in cognitive profiles represent the development of qualitatively different and neurologically independent frames (i.e., modules) of cognition. We discuss this alternative view (i.e., the Modularity Model) in the next section of this chapter.

THE MODULARITY MODEL

The stage criterion of structured wholeness and the primacy of logical-mathematical reasoning lead to rejection of the Standard and Differentiation Models. Both of these models regard cognition as a *horizontal mental faculty* (Fodor, 1983). This term suggests that the mind consists of a number of psychological processes and mechanisms (i.e., faculties), such as perception, memory, and judgment, which are brought to bear on various content areas. For example, a physician may use the same mental faculty—the faculty of judgment—in resolving a personal or bioethical dilemma and in diagnosing a patient's illness. This position seems consistent with the criterion of structured wholeness, in that an identical level and type of reasoning is used when one reasons within different content areas because one employs the same generalizable mental faculty. Similarly, aesthetic judgment is simply the application of the horizontal faculty of judgment to the process of drawing aesthetic distinctions. According to this view of knowledge, then, there is no such thing as an aesthetic faculty (see Fodor, 1983).

Both the Standard and Differentiation Models viewed logical-mathematical reasoning as a type of horizontal mental faculty—perhaps the only mental faculty. The Standard Model, through its version of structured wholeness, took the view that adults could only know the world "one stage at a time" via the application of the same level of logical-mathematical organization to problems within various content areas. The Differentiation Model, through its modified version of structured wholeness, implied that there is one primary mental faculty, logical-mathematical understanding, which is applied with differential success (i.e., different levels of logical-mathematical organization) to problems within different content areas (e.g., the aesthetic domain, the moral/ethical domain, the medical/scientific domain, etc.).

Recently, many philosophers, cognitive psychologists, and neuropsychologists have argued against the existence of horizontal mental faculties in favor of *vertical mental faculties*. Vertical mental faculties refer to distinct and independent types of knowledge systems (i.e., multiple modules or intelligences) that are: (a) content- or domain-specific, (b) genetically based, hard-wired, and associated with relatively distinct neural structures, (c) computationally autonomous, in that they do not share or compete for such horizontal cognitive resources as memory and attention, and (d) cognitively impenetrable (Fodor, 1983).

The Modularity Model is based on Fodor's (1983) ideas about the nature of vertical mental faculties. Fodor, who is a philosopher, has proposed that the mind consists of a number of cognitive subsystems or modules that are just as "cognitive" as logical–mathematical thought and that are separate and distinct from logical–mathematical thought and independent of each other in terms of course of development and level. That is, each vertical faculty or module is computationally autonomous and develops independently from other faculties in an orderly sequence.

The perceptive reader may notice a strong connection between Fodor's concept of vertical mental faculties and Franz Gall's theory of Phrenology. Fodor, in fact, has suggested that a great deal of his philosophical heritage has its basis in Gall's version of faculty psychology. Gall is looked upon skeptically by most cognitive psychologists, according to Fodor (1983), because

> Gall made two big mistakes, and they finished him: he believed that the degree of development of the mental organ can be measured by the relative size of corresponding brain area, and he believed that the skull fits the brain "as a glove fits the hand." Phrenology followed as the night the day . . . and with all sorts of fraud and quackery, for none of which Gall was responsible but for much of which he appears to have been retrospectively blamed. (p. 23)

As was previously mentioned, Fodor, by inclination and training, is a philosopher. However, this does not imply that the modularity position is solely philosophical (rather than scientific) in nature. Several contemporary neuropsychologists have also argued for the validity of the modularity perspective. For example, Gazzaniga (1985) has stated:

> I argue that the human brain has a modular-type organization. By modularity I mean that the brain is organized into relatively independent functioning units that work in parallel. The mind is not an indivisible whole, operating in a single way to solve all problems. Rather there are many specific and identifiably different units of the mind dealing with all of the information they are exposed to. The vast and rich information impinging upon our brains is broken up into parts, and many systems work on it. These modular activities frequently operate apart from our conscious verbal selves. (p. 4)

Neither Fodor nor Gazzaniga provide a list or the names of the types or "modules" of vertical mental faculties. In order to gain an understanding of what these various modules "might be," it is necessary to turn to the work

of Gardner (1983) on the one hand, or to the work of multivariate intelligence theorists (Baltes, Cattell, Horn, Reinert, Schaie, and Thurstone) on
the other.

Gardner (1983) has postulated the existence of seven different cognitive
modules or "frames" of human intelligence. Gardner's criteria for identifying each specific module of intelligence were as follows: (a) it can be independently destroyed or spared relative to other intellectual functions as a
result of brain damage; (b) it allows for the existence of exceptional individuals such as idiot savants and prodigies within particular domains; (c) it performs a specific and unique type of operation and/or computation that may
be triggered by certain types of internally or externally presented information; (d) it displays an identifiable developmental history characterized by
qualitatively distinct levels of competence; (e) it possesses an evolutionary
history that can be discerned via analysis of the capabilities of other species;
(f) its existence can be supported by the results of experimental psychological research; (g) its existence can be supported by the results of psychometric
research; and (h) it performs its operations and computations on data that
are encoded within a specific *symbol system*. Using these criteria, which are
based in part on Fodor's description of vertical mental faculties, Gardner
has identified seven modules or frames of intelligence as follows:

   I. Linguistic Intelligence
  II. Musical Intelligence
 III. Logical–Mathematical Intelligence
 IV. Spatial Intelligence
  V. Bodily–Kinesthetic Intelligence
 VI. Intrapersonal Intelligence
VII. Interpersonal Intelligence

As can readily be seen from an examination of this list of intelligences, Gardner treated logical–mathematical intelligence as one module of intelligence,
but not the only module. Speaking directly to this point, Gardner has
emphasized that "Piaget has painted a brilliant portrait of development in
one domain — that of logical–mathematical thought — but has erroneously
assumed that it pertains to the other areas, ranging from musical intelligence
to the interpersonal domain" (1983, p. 134).

Although Gardner did not offer his theory as an explanation of cognitive
development and change during the adult years, it clearly has implications
for these concerns. In combining Gardner's modularity position with recent
advances in Piagetian theory, the following picture of adult cognitive development emerges:

   1. Humans possess several knowledge structuring systems (i.e., modules
or intelligences), each of which is structurally and functionally independent
of the others.

2. Each knowledge structuring system has a developmental sequence connected with it such that each system has the potential to progress from a sensori-motor level to a postformal mode of knowing.

3. Over the course of cognitive development, it may become easier to distinguish one knowledge structuring system from another knowledge structuring system.

4. The majority of individuals will probably move through the first three Piagetian stages (sensori-motor, preoperations and concrete operations) within the context of each knowledge structuring system without difficulty. The manifestation of formal and postformal styles of thinking within each of these knowledge structuring systems, however, is unlikely.

5. Because an individual may arrive at different end states within each of the different knowledge structuring systems, decalage or unevenness in development is the rule rather than the exception. Thus, decalage (not structured wholeness) is expected throughout the entire course of cognitive development.

6. Different knowledge structuring systems may display different rates of acceleration across the life span. For example, logical–mathematical intelligence may develop most quickly in childhood and adolescence, linguistic intelligence may develop most quickly in early childhood, and personal intelligence may develop at a relatively fast rate in middle adulthood.

7. There may be individual differences in the rate at which the individual knowledge structuring systems develop. Individual differences, unevenness, and/or decalage with regard to terminal development may be accounted for by a variety of genetic, biological, psychological, and/or socio-historical events and processes. That is, independent development of the various modules can be attributed to hard-wired neuro-behavioral circuitry, environmental influences, or interactions of such factors.

One possible metaphor for the Modularity Model is a bush. A bush consists of various branches that emanate from the base of the plant rather than from a central trunk. Consider each of the branches of the bush to be a different type of human intelligence or knowledge structuring system. Consider the idea that the growth and differentiation of the various branches of human intelligences are analogous to the growth and differentiation of a bush. During infancy and childhood the different intelligences may be very difficult to separate from one another. As development proceeds through adolescence and adulthood, however, the differential growth of the intelligences may become more and more apparent.

Figure 4.4 illustrates a developmental progression for the seven types of intelligence described by Gardner (1983). (In this figure Intrapersonal Intelligence and Interpersonal Intelligence have been combined under the general heading of Personal Intelligence.) Note that this person has developed postformal cognitive skills within all of the frames of intelligence. Because people

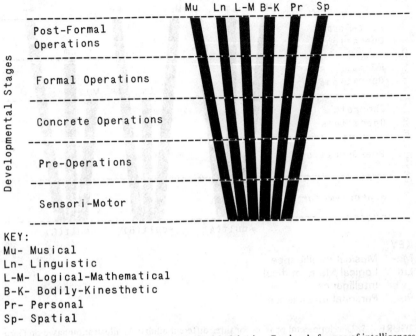

FIGURE 4.4 An illustration of the Modularity Model using Gardner's frames of intelligences.

are generally not evenly or fully developed across all frames, we have presented (in Fig. 4.5) the cognitive profiles for three different adults, all of whom show an unevenness in three branches of intelligence: musical, logical–mathematical, and personal.

Inspection of Figure 4.5 reveals that Adult A has developed postformal thinking skills within the frames of musical and logical–mathematical intelligence and formal thinking skills within the frame of personal intelligence. Perhaps this individual possesses the skill to compose and perform a flute concerto along with the ability to cast a musical composition within a framework of mathematical progressions and relationships (see Hofstadter's *Goedel, Escher, and Bach*), and he or she may be reasonably adept at his or her understanding of "self" and "others." Adult B is just as musically gifted as adult A. However, Adult B does not deal with mathematical concepts and relationships at a postformal level, but he/she has postformal skills within the area of personal intelligence. Adult C, in contrast, possesses concrete thinking skills with regard to musical endeavors, formal skills with regard to logical–mathematical problems, and postformal skills within the area of personal intelligence. Note that both adults B and C display formal thought structures with regard to logical–mathematical intelligence and post-

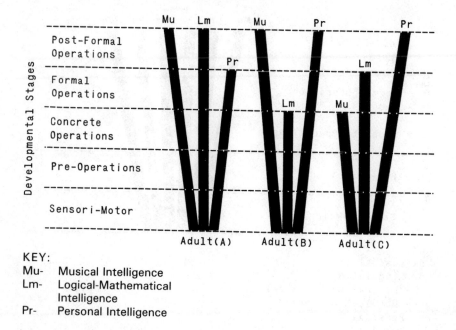

KEY:
Mu-   Musical Intelligence
Lm-   Logical-Mathematical
        Intelligence
Pr-   Personal Intelligence

FIGURE 4.5. Developmental profiles for three different adults: An illustration based on Gardner's Modularity Model.

formal thought structures with regard to personal intelligence. However, Adult B may have developed postformal thought within the realm of personal intelligence *before* he/she developed formal thought within the realm of logical–mathematical intelligence; or Adult C may have developed postformal thought within the realm of personal intelligence *after* he/she developed formal thought within the realm of logical–mathematical intelligence.

There are several sources of support for the contention that personal intelligence is not dependent on logical–mathematical intelligence and that logical–mathematical and personal types of intelligence may develop at different rates. First, different brain structures may be associated with emotional and cognitive function. Gardner (1983) argued that personal intelligence has its neurological basis in the frontal lobes, whereas logical–mathematical intelligence has its locus in the left parietal lobe as well as the temporal and occipital associative areas contiguous to the left parietal lobe. Second, these types of intelligence may have different developmental antecedents. Piaget (1969) noted that logical–mathematical operations are constructed from the actions that individuals perform on *objects*. Gardner (1983) noted that personal intelligence may be constructed from reciprocal transactions that take place interindividually between different *selves*. Third, logical–mathematical intelligence may develop earlier than personal intelligence, in part because of cultural–educational influences and bio-maturational changes. Personal intelligence might proceed more quickly in adulthood because of various interpersonal, social, and societal responsibilities associated with this developmental period (e.g., parenting, work). Also, using the framework of Baltes, Reese, and Lipsitt (1980), it can be suggested that the normative age-graded influences that predominate in early life are more likely to affect logical–mathematical growth than personal growth, and the nonnormative life events that predominate in mid-life are more likely to affect moral and personal growth than logical–mathematical intelligence.

CRITIQUE OF MODULARITY

One of the attractions of modularity theory is the attempt to link cognitive organization to brain organization, but this attempt seems either premature or unfounded. For example, Gardner (1983) suggests that the different modules of intelligence have different loci in the brain. One of the main criticisms of Gardner's theory is that there is little if any real basis for suggesting the organization of intelligence that Gardner proposes from neurobehavioral research. Generally, links between brain function and structure and cognitive function remain undetermined.

Probably the best evidence for modularity comes from work showing that language is a relatively hard-wired autonomous domain (Chomsky, 1975). But it does not follow that there are also hard-wired structures for music, math, or personal intelligence. Modularity models derived from multivariate analytic studies of age changes and age differences in adult intelligence suggest differential growth of multiple intelligences, without reference to a structural/functional correspondence of brain organization with cognitive function (Baltes & Nesselroade, 1972; Cunningham, 1980; Garrett, 1946; Reinert, 1970; Schaie, 1983). There are two justifications for ignoring brain function in the conceptualization of adult intelligence. First, brain organization may simply not be related to cognitive function in a direct or measurable fashion. Second, curiously, although there is continuous change in brain function during the adult years in terms of neuronal loss, buildup of neurofibrillary tangles and plaque, and so on (see Bondareff, 1985), these changes do not seem to affect cognitive function until relatively late in life. Even computerized axial tomography (CAT scans) has not yielded a direct correspondence between degree or locus of brain damage and reduced or differential cognitive function. For example, Obler and Albert (1985) have noted that CAT scans, as well as other measures of brain status such as evoked potentials and blood flow, may be too gross to provide a reliable index of language functions in the left hemisphere.

Another criticism of the modularity view has to do with the nature of modules or intelligences and how they are constructed. It is a mistake to view the descriptive systems of knowledge and the processes of cognition as isomorphic. Statements about adult knowledge are not simply linguistic expressions of mental content. There is much recent evidence to suggest that knowledge and thinking develop by being organized within areas or domains (cf. Kiel, 1981; 1986). Thus, the development of a modular organization of knowledge may be primarily functional, rather than structural. Also, the wide individual differences in type and degree of cognitive differentiation suggest that individuals actively construct and organize knowledge systems (Carroll, 1984). Gardner's theory bypasses the role of the individual in creating unique domains of knowledge. In contrast we take the view that the neurophysiological correlates of domain-ordered knowledge do *not* exist on a purely *a priori* basis. The neurophysiological correlates of domain-ordered knowledge grow, to a large extent, out of the effects of experience upon an undifferentiated nervous system. (Note that the evidence supportive of the modularity position – Gardner's data collected from adult stroke patients – may be called into question because it examines the effects of physical damage on a nervous system that has already been "framed" or "modulated" through experience.)

A final criticism of the modularity view concerns the failure of modularity theorists to distinguish between *modules* and *domains*. Modules may be regarded as hard-wired, autonomous, and cognitively impenetrable information analyzers (cf. Fodor, 1983). Modules, for example, may provide the individual with the ability to detect angles and edges, experience depth, and discriminate various rhythms and pitches. Also, modules may have, more or less, the same location within the nervous system in most, if not all, individuals. The purpose of these built-in modules seems to be to get information into the cognitive system. Domains, in our view, may be regarded as organized knowledge representations that are self-constructed, interdependent, and cognitively penetrable. Knowledge about the physical and social world that the developing person deems important is represented, organized and stored in a domain-specific manner. Given this distinction between modules and domains, it seems as if modularity theorists have failed to: (a) recognize the active role played by the individual in the construction of knowledge domains, (b) identify the processes responsible for the development of knowledge domains, (c) examine the manner by which domains are altered due to age and experience, and (d) call attention to the manner by which the nature of domain-specific knowledge constrains its generalizability.

LIMITATIONS OF THE GENETIC–EPISTEMOLOGICAL APPROACH TO THE STUDY OF ADULT COGNITION

Research conducted within the context of genetic–epistemological theory has provided valuable information about the nature of adult cognitive change. Specifically, researchers have discovered that adulthood is the developmental period that is marked by the emergence of postformal styles of thinking. But postformal accounts of adult cognition, even when they are viewed within the context of all the models discussed in this chapter, cannot adequately explain the development of advanced styles of domain-specific thinking. Furthermore, research conducted within the genetic–epistemological tradition seems to portray adult cognitive development in an overly optimistic and restricted manner. For example, postformal theorists take great effort to point out the positive features of adult cognitive growth (e.g., how adults begin to conceptualize knowledge in a relativistic and dialectic manner and become capable of problem finding as well as problem solving). Postformal theorists have failed to acknowledge, however, a large number of empirical studies that have shown that adults usually think in a rather irrational and illogical manner (Kahneman & Tversky, 1984; Tversky & Kahneman, 1981, 1983). And they have not recognized a large body of research within the information-processing and psychometric traditions that has identified significant age-related decline in various basic mental processes (e.g., attention, memory) and fluid mental abilities. Furthermore, genetic-epistemological theorists, in general, and postformal theorists, in particular, seem to regard such basic cognitive processes as memory and attention as mere "performance variables" that have little significance or importance. Thus, genetic–epistemological accounts of adult cognition run the risks associated with any competence theory of cognitive development (see chapter 1). More specifically, postformal theories create an unnecessary and artificial separation between the different components of cognition (i.e., thought structures, knowledge systems, and basic mental processes are not viewed as equally important components of an intentional, unified, and goal-directed cognitive system). In order to develop a truly comprehensive perspective on adult cognition, it will be necessary to go beyond the confines of genetic-epistemological theory and research. Thus, there is a need to review the current research within the information-processing and psychometric approaches and to integrate the results of these studies with genetic–epistemological theory and research. These goals will be addressed in subsequent chapters.

SUMMARY

In this chapter we presented and evaluated three models: a Standard Model, a Differentiation Model, and a Modularity Model. Each model was evaluated by its ability to explicate the domain-specific nature of postformal styles of thinking. Although there are strengths associated with each of these models, all are incapable of explaining the interrelationship between the complexity and specificity of adult thought.

We suggested that postformal thinking styles are likely to manifest themselves in some, but not necessarily all, of the knowledge domains that have been actively constructed by the individual over time. Furthermore, we proposed that the transfer of postformal thinking from one domain to another is constrained by the nature of the knowledge within the domains.

Genetic–epistemological theory and research, even though it provides valuable insight into the nature of adult cognition, is overly limited. Consistent with competence theories of cognition, it artificially separates the components of cognitive activity and views basic cognitive processes (e.g., attention, memory) as mere performance variables.

5

Developmental Changes in Cognitive Processes

In 1980, Simon declared . . . "Everything of interest in cognition happens above the 100 millisecond level—the time it takes you to recognize your mother." . . . I take exactly the opposite viewpoint: "Everything interesting in cognition happens BELOW the 100 millisecond level—the time it takes you to recognize your mother." To me the major question . . . is this: "What in the world is going on to enable you to convert 100,000,000 retinal dots into one single word "mother" in one-tenth of a second?" Perception is where it's at!

D. Hofstadter
Artificial Intelligence: Subcognition as Computation

In previous chapters we presented evidence that suggests that adulthood is characterized by the emergence of postformal styles of thinking within specific knowledge domains. Researchers and theoreticians working within the context of genetic–epistemological theory, however, have failed to integrate their view of adult cognitive development with that espoused by psychologists working within the confines of other theoretical approaches. Due to the lack of such an integrative effort, we have maintained that postformal models of adult cognition provide an overly optimistic picture of age-related cognitive change. Therefore, the major goal of this chapter is to address the issue of age-related cognitive change from the psychometric and information-processing points of view. An empirical account of adult age differences in intelligence and information-processing skills is a necessary ingredient in any comprehensive treatment of adult cognition. In this chapter, we review many of the research findings bearing on age differences in various aspects of intelligence, memory, attention, problem solving, and information processing. We begin by considering the psychometric studies of age-related changes in adult intelligence.

THE PSYCHOMETRIC APPROACH

Contrasting Views of Intelligence

Everyone agrees that intelligence changes during the adult years, but there is less agreement as to how it changes. The debate between Horn and Donaldson (1976) and Baltes and Schaie (1976) over the plasticity of adult intelligence allows us to conclude that, sooner or later, some degree of intellectual decline occurs on some measures for all people. Part of the tenuousness of this conclusion can be attributed to the wide range of individual differences, both qualitative and quantitative, that can be observed among middle-aged and older adults in the expression of intelligence. A second factor contributing to the tenuousness of this statement has to do with measurement issues. Cohort and generational influences, ability-extraneous factors such as fatigue and motivation, and individual differences in the validity and reliability of measures make it difficult to draw precise conclusions about the nature of age-related changes in intelligence. A third factor contributing to the problem is that intelligence can be conceptualized in several contrasting ways. In different cultures, and at different points in historical time, there is variation in the value that is placed on particular abilities. For example, in a culture and time in which knowledge is changing rapidly, a relatively high value may be placed on the skill of rapid information acquisition, and, correspondingly, individuals who possess such skills may be awarded a greater status.

In an article that appeared in the *Journal of Educational Psychology* in 1921, prominent psychometricians were asked the following question: What do you conceive intelligence to be and by what means can it best be measured (Intelligence, 1921)? Some of the responses were as follows:

1. The ability to carry on abstract thinking. (Louis M. Terman)
2. The ability to give true or factual responses. (E. L. Thorndike)
3. The ability to learn to adjust oneself to the environment. (S. S. Colvin)
4. The ability to adapt to new situations, which reflects the general modifiability of the nervous system. (Rudolf Pintner)
5. The capacity to acquire abilities. (Herbert Woodrow)
6. A group of complex mental processes traditionally defined as sensation, perception, association, memory, imagination, discrimination, judgment, and reasoning. (M. E. Haggerty)

Is it a problem that there are so many different conceptualizations of intelligence? In trying to make sense out of the enormous literature bearing on adult intelligence, it is useful that a wide variety of approaches and frameworks for organizing the data on age-related changes in adult intelligence exist.

The definitions given above do not address the question of whether or not intelligence is different at different ages and whether different criteria should be used for defining intelligence at different ages. In adulthood, as well as childhood, there are many ways for individuals to develop and express unique styles of thinking and unique cognitive abilities. For example, Professor X is considered intelligent because he makes important but not necessarily creative or highly visible contributions to one's field. Yet Professor Y within the same discipline shows distinction by having many creative and stimulating ideas and is well-known in the public media, even though she is considerably less active than Professor X in the actual conduct of research.

There are many different ways of being intelligent in all fields and vocations, suggesting the usefulness of multiple criteria for evaluating adult abilities. Schaie (1978) emphasized the importance of taking into account the situations in which older adults exercise their abilities. For example, Scheidt and Schaie (1978) asked older people about their everyday activities as the first step in developing situationally based measures of competence.

The importance of contextual issues in the conceptualization and assessment of intelligence is also recognized in Robert Sternberg's (1984) triarchic model of intelligence. One of the components of Sternberg's model is a *contextual* subtheory, which relates intelligence to the external world of the individual. From this perspective, intelligence can be viewed as the manifestation of competent behavior in everyday contexts. Intelligence involves matching one's abilities to the tasks one is faced with in the everyday world. According to Sternberg, the three most common ways of matching abilities to contexts involve changing the environment, selecting a new environment, or changing oneself (i.e., developing one's abilities). For example, it may be that as we grow older, we develop an understanding of what is required to be successful in particular environments and situations, and we then select environments, situations, or tasks that match our particular strengths, interests, and abilities. However, at any age, we sometimes choose particular tasks because of the challenge, the novelty, and the opportunity for diversification and cognitive growth that they offer. Dittmann-Kohli and Baltes (1986) and others (Labouvie-Vief & Chandler, 1978) have also emphasized such pragmatics in their formulations of adult intellectual development.

A second aspect of Sternberg's theory is represented by the *componential information processes* or subabilities that determine what information is encoded by the system and how efficiently the individual learns, thinks, and perceives. According to Sternberg (1984), there are three functionally distinct types of components. The first type, metacomponents, refers to the higher-order processes used in monitoring and regulating performance, planning, strategy selection, and decision making. The second type, performance components, refers to the processes that are used in the execution of performance such as speed of stimulus encoding and rate of comparison of one stimulus with another. The third type, referred to as knowledge acquisition components, is used in gaining new knowledge. Sternberg proposed several general knowledge acquisition components that are involved in the acquisition of practically all kinds of knowledge. Several lines of research lead to the conclusion the componential subprocesses may decline with age.

A third aspect of Sternberg's theory addressed the question: At what point in task performance do the component abilities most reflect "intelligent" performance? Some tasks most adequately reflect one's intelligence when they are novel or unfamiliar and assess how quickly one can master a new kind of problem. Alternatively, other tasks will most adequately tap one's intelligence only when they are performed after many hours or even many years of learning. Older adults seem to be "less intelligent" than younger adults in the acquisition of new information.

Sternberg (1984, 1985a) and many other contemporary intelligence theorists frequently find themselves struggling with some of the same complexities and controversies that faced the early theorists such as Spearman (1927), Thorndike (1926), and Thurstone (1938). For example, because of the conceptual and methodological problems involved in the measurement of intelligence, Thorndike (1926) proposed a distinction between *altitude* (degree of difficulty of the tasks that the individual can do successfully), *width* (referring to the number of tasks of a given difficulty that the individual can accomplish), and *speed* (referring to the amount of time required to produce the correct response to a task). This threefold distinction continues to have important implications for the measurement and conceptualization of adult intellectual development.

Another long-standing problem in the conceptualization of adult intelligence has to do with representing the factors that cause intelligence to change with time. It is generally accepted that there are multiple antecedents, some of which are based on heredity or natural ability, and some of which are based on environmental influence or acculturation. Although all cognitive behavior can be considered as a product of the interaction of genetic and environmental influences, the relative contribution of heredity or environment may be greater at different points in the life span, at different points in learning, and for different abilities.

Spearman (1927) emphasized the contribution of a general ability factor, or g, in accounting for the consistency of individual performance across cognitive tasks, but he also recognized that there are task-specific abilities (s's) that account in part for intraindividual differences in performance across tasks. The g factor is assumed to be central to accounting for the lack of variability (i.e., consistency) across various subtests of intelligence. Reinert (1970) took the view that general ability is a useful concept in early cognitive development, but g becomes differentiated with development and acculturation during the early and middle years of life. Another interesting approach to this issue was suggested by Cattell (1971). His triadic theory postulated three types of mental abilities or powers. Some abilities were conceptualized as *general capacities* or (*g*'s), which exert influence on all types of cognitive performance. Second, some abilities were *provincials* or (*p*'s), which have to do with the functioning of particular sensory and motor systems. Third, there are *agencies* or (*a*'s), which are aids or acquired cognitive skills based on education, training, and proficiencies based on particular interests.

Abilities, Contents, and Processes of Intelligence

Many psychometric theories of adult intelligence are based on factor analytic or multivariate analyses of multiple measures of intellectual performance. Those who have applied this approach to the study of intellectual aging have recognized that there are multiple abilities and multiple antecedents associated with the development of abilities in adulthood (Cunningham, 1980; Horn, 1970; Reinert, 1970; Schaie, 1979). In addition, it is important to distinguish between multiple intellectual abilities, the multiple content areas within which these multiple abilities may be manifest, and the multiple processes that comprise all skilled problem solving in real-life contexts. In this section we examine the multiple abilities, content areas, and processes of intelligence as they relate to adult cognitive development.

Multiple Abilities

How many unique or independent abilities are there? How many abilities must be measured in order to provide a complete description of adult intelligence? Thurstone (1938) was one of the pioneers in the search for the number of unique or primary intellectual abilities. Thurstone's Primary Mental Abilities (PMA) test consists of the factors of verbal meaning, reasoning, space, number, and word fluency. The PMA test has been used extensively by Schaie and his colleagues in their sequential investigations of adult intelligence (Schaie, 1983; Schaie & Labouvie-Vief, 1974; Schaie & Strother, 1968). Figure 5.1 provides a summary of Schaie and Labouvie-Vief's (1974) cross-sectional and longitudinal data showing how the five abilities changed with age from the 1963 to the 1970 data collection. Note that the cross-sectional comparisons yield greater losses than the longitudinal comparisons. This difference is evident by looking at the lines that connect the 1963 and 1970 data. It can be seen that each birth cohort displays a stable trajectory, with the younger cohorts showing systematically higher positions than the older ones. Schaie had obtained a similar pattern when he compared 1956 with 1963 data (Schaie & Strother, 1968), and he reported similar findings at the 21-year follow-up in 1977 (see Schaie, 1983).

There is evidence to suggest that the number of primary mental abilities

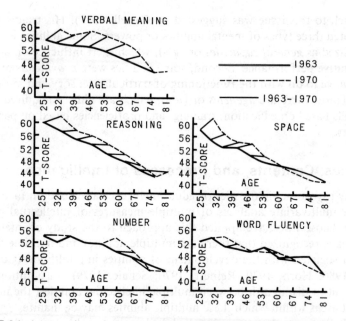

FIGURE 5.1. A comparison of two cross-sectional data collections (1963 and 1970) and the longitudinal change from 1963 to 1970 on the five subtests of Thurstone's Primary Mental Abilities test. Data are from Schaie's cohort sequential research on adult intelligence. [Source: Adapted from Schaie, K.W., and Labouvie-Vief, G. (1974). Generational versus ontogenetic components of change in adult cognitive behavior. A fourteen-year cross-sequential study. *Developmental Psychology, 10,* 305-320.]

is greater than five. Ekstrom, French, and Harman (1979) have described 25 basic mental abilities that meet a satisfactory level of factorial independence. See Table 5.1 for a list of these abilities and the tests by which they are measured.

These 25 mental abilities show different patterns of change with advancing age, although it is generally reported that age-related change can be roughly described by two age-performance curves. That is, some abilities remain relatively stable across the adult years or improve slightly, and others on this list show a reliable and substantial decline with advancing age. Age-related declines are found on measures of immediate memory, spatial relations, and abstract thinking (Horn, 1970; Labouvie-Vief, 1985). No decline or only a minor age-related decline is obtained on measures of word fluency, vocabulary, and recall of learned or overlearned information.

Horn (1982) pointed out that a developmental model based on 25 mental abilities is much too unwieldy. He suggested that it is difficult, if not impossible, to represent all of the 25 mental abilities in a model that is inter-

TABLE 5.1. Twenty-five Primary Mental Abilities

THE ABILITY	EXAMPLES OF TESTS REPRESENTING THE ABILITY
Verbal Comprehension	Vocabulary, reading comprehension, understanding grammar and syntax
Verbal Closure	Anagrams, hidden words, incomplete words
Word Fluency	Word endings, word beginnings, word naming
Expressive Fluency	Making sentences, simile interpretations
Associative Fluency	Selecting associations and opposites
Object Flexibility	Uses tests, combining objects
Logical Reasoning	Nonsense syllogisms, diagramming relationships, decoding and deciphering
Concept Formation	Word grouping, verbal relations
Induction	Letter sets and series, classifications
General Reasoning	Word problems, using rule systems
Estimation	Width determination, spatial judgment, quantitative estimation
Number Facility	Addition, subtraction, mixed numerical operations
Spatial Orientation	Card rotation, cube comparisons
Visualization	Paper folding, shape recognition
Speed of Closure	Gestalt completion, incomplete figures, concealed objects
Flexibility of Closure	Hidden figures, embedded figures, copying figures
Perceptual Speed	Finding letters, number comparisons, identical pictures
Figural Flexibility	Toothpicks, planning patterns
Figural Fluency	Decorations, alternate signs, make a figure
Integration	Following directions, internalizing rules, manipulating numbers
Visual Memory	Orientation memory, system-shape recognition
Span Memory	Digit span-visual, letter span-auditory, tone reproduction
Associative Memory	Picture-number pairs, serial recall
Meaningful Memory	Sentence completion, sentence recall
Sensitivity to Problems	Listing problems, finding deficiencies

Adapted from Ekstrom, R.B., French, J.W., & Harman, M.H. (1979). Cognitive factors: Their identification and replication. *Multivariate Behavior Research Monographs*, No. 79.2.

nally consistent, parsimonious, coherent, and empirically sound. For this reason, Horn (1970) moved up the ladder of abstraction to the description of two second-order factors referred to as *crystallized* and *fluid* intelligence. Crystallized intelligence is considered to be a rough representation of the extent to which individuals have incorporated the valued knowledge of their culture. It is indicated by a large inventory of behaviors that reflect the breadth of culturally valued knowledge and experience, the comprehension of communications, and the development of judgment, understanding, and reasonable thinking in everyday affairs. The primary mental abilities that are associated with the crystallized intelligence factor are verbal comprehension, concept formation, logical reasoning, and general reasoning. Tests used to measure the crystallized factor include vocabulary, simple analogies, remote associations, and social judgment. Crystallized abilities generally have been found *not* to decline with advancing age. In fact, crystallized forms of intelligence may even show slight increases with age up to the sixth decade (Horn, 1970, 1982). Horn and Donaldson (1976) suggested that crystallized intelligence may increase with age because of the cumulative effects of experience (see Fig. 5.2).

The fluid intelligence factor is a second-order representation of those mental abilities that are *not* imparted by the culture, such as those abilities and processes associated with extracting complex visual–spatial information under time pressure. Abilities represented by the fluid intelligence factor include seeing relationships among patterns, drawing inferences from rela-

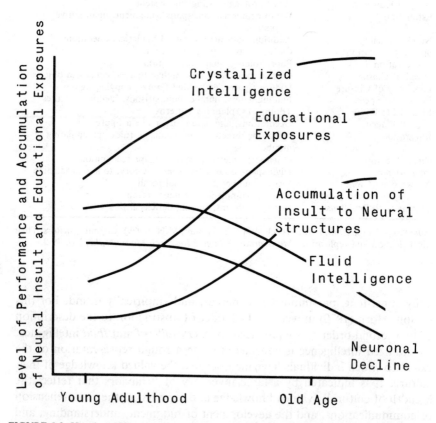

FIGURE 5.2. Horn's (1970) conception of the development of crystallized and fluid intelligence in relation to the accumulation of educational exposures, age-related decline in the physiological base, and the accumulation of insult to neural structures [Source: Adapted from Horn, J.L. (1970). Organization of data on life-span development of human abilities. In L.R. Goulet & P.B. Baltes (Eds.), *Life-span developmental psychology: Research and theory* (pp. 423–466). New York: Academic Press.]

tionships, and comprehending implications. The primary mental abilities that best reflect this factor are induction, figural flexibility, and integration. Tasks measuring this factor include letter series, matrices, and topology. A large body of empirical research has unequivocally indicated that fluid abilities show a *decline* with aging (Horn, 1970, 1982). Horn and Donaldson (1976) have suggested that fluid abilities decrease as a function of age-related physiological and neurological change and the cumulative effects of injury and/or disease such as a stroke.

As shown in Figure 5.2, fluid intelligence declines with aging, and crystallized intelligence improves gradually during the adult years. These changes are presumed to be related to the accumulation of educational exposures, the accumulation of insult to neural structures, and declines in the physiological basis of performance. It is important to note that practically all performance that is referred to as "cognitive" represents some combination of the factors of crystallized intelligence (i.e., transferable experience) and fluid intelligence (i.e., slowing of the control processes). Three hypothetical curves showing age-related changes in level of performance on tasks involving different proportional combinations of experience and control processes are depicted in Figure 5.3. It is reasonable to hypothesize that the greater the involvement of the individual's highly practiced or specialized skills, the more likely it is that level of performance will not decline with advancing age (see Denney, 1984). Conversely, age-performance decline is presumably a function of the extent to which capacity-limited, fluid-like control processes are required in task performance. These issues are discussed further in chapter 6.

Multiple Content Areas

Humans exhibit different degrees of strength and facility in different content areas, such as in particular quantitative domains, in the sciences, in the arts, in social interactions, and/or in particular sports and games. Given the wide range of content areas within which one can display a high level of cognitive performance, it seems reasonable to conceptualize intelligence as dependent on the specific knowledge as well as the general procedures and control operations that are involved in carrying out a particular skill within a particular content area. Examples of some of the content areas in which skilled behavior and reasoning have been studied include mathematics (Kintsch & Greeno, 1985), physics (Larkin, 1981), computer programming (McKeithen, Reitman, Rueter, & Hirtle, 1981), music (Wolf, 1976), medical expertise (Lesgold, 1983), and game domains such as chess and bridge (Charness, 1985; Chase & Simon, 1973). Intellectual performance is substantively domain specific in that specialized skills are frequently unrelated to general ability measures (Coates & Kirby, 1982) and unrelated to general information-processing skills (Chase & Simon, 1973). Results from a study

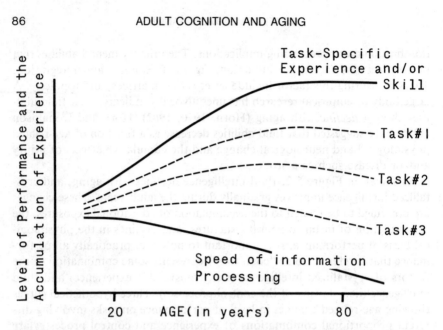

FIGURE 5.3. Level of performance in relation to the accumulation of skill and the slowing in processing speed. Hypothetical or stereotypical performance is shown as a function of age for three tasks, each involving different proportions of task-related experience and speed-dependent control processes. Individually specialized and highly practiced skills depend largely on the accumulation of experience, and slowing of cognitive processes has little effect on level of performance (Task 1). The level of performance of many skills depends on a relatively balanced mix of task-specific experience and task-general control processes (Task 2). Level of performance on unfamiliar, speeded, nonverbal tasks declines with aging (Task 3).

by Salthouse (1984) of younger and older skilled typists showed that skilled older adults maintained a high rate of typing in spite of age-related declines in general perceptual motor performance. Salthouse found that the older adults were more sensitive to characters farther in advance of the currently typed character than younger adults (i.e., older people needed to pre-view more letters in advance in order to maintain a fast rate of transcription typing). One implication of Salthouse's data is supported in the literature on job performance; that is, task-specific components are frequently better predictors of specific job performance than are measures of general aptitude (Welford, 1977). In the next chapter, we discuss the evidence showing that performance becomes increasingly specific to task requirements as skill level increases.

Multiple Processes

Individual differences in intelligence have also been attributed to the various processes or mechanisms presumed to comprise cognitive functioning (Hunt, 1978). One person might be exceptional with regard to memorizing briefly presented information, another person might show an extraordinary speed of mental calculation, and yet another person might stand out because of an ability to quickly retrieve factual-type information from memory. A high level of performance on a particular test of intelligence or in a particular everyday cognitive task might depend on one's ability to process information quickly, or it might depend on a different process, or on some combination of processes. Processing domains refer to such operations as encoding, selective attention, working memory, and integrating new and old information. From this perspective, Neisser (1967) defined cognition as "all the processes by which the sensory input is transformed, reduced, elaborated, stored, recovered, and used" (p. 4). What these processes are and how they change with age is at the heart of an information processing approach to intelligence as discussed in the next section.

AGING AND INFORMATION PROCESSING

The information-processing paradigm has served as a useful model for guiding the investigation of developmental differences in the rate and efficiency of encoding, storing, and retrieving information. An information-processing model of cognitive aging suggests that the speed of processing may be reduced, or the volume or size of mental capacity may be reduced, so as to represent slower processing rates or to restrict cognitive efficiency with aging. Special attention has been paid to age differences in the speed and efficiency of the *control processes* (e.g., effortful mental processes), which construct and transform information within the human cognitive system. According to this model, computational processes or control processes *operate* in roughly the same way for everyone, young and old, but individuals differ from each other in the efficiency and speed of these mental processes. For example, Birren (1974) noted that as a consequence of age-related slowing of information transmission, older adults can be considered to be living in a functionally different environment from that of younger people.

One of the most pervasive findings in the research on cognitive aging is the slowing of the rate of processing information (Birren, 1965, 1974; Birren, Woods, & Williams, 1985; Cerella, 1985b; Salthouse, 1982, 1985, 1986). It appears that decrements in the rate of information processing can account for many of the age-related differences in cognition. Older adults are differentially slowed as the complexity of information to be processed increases (Cerella, Poon, & Williams, 1980; Salthouse, 1985). Similarly, older adults generally exhibit a greater disadvantage relative to younger adults as conditions of processing load (i.e., arranging task demands to exceed the individual's established level of performance) are increased (Plude & Hoyer, 1981; Plude, Kaye, Hoyer, Post, Saynisch, & Hahn, 1983).

Age-related declines have been found with regard to the processes of encoding, retrieval, and working memory dynamics (Craik, 1977; Fullerton, 1983; Light & Anderson, 1983; Poon, 1985; Salthouse, 1985). Older adults have more difficulty than younger adults in moving information from short-term memory or consciousness into long-term memory (Craik, 1977) and in accessing or retrieving information from long-term memory (Burke & Light, 1981). Such findings have been obtained in many studies of age differences in information processing that have used a wide variety of materials ranging from nonsense syllables to sentences and prose (see Burke & Light, 1981).

Research conducted from the information-processing tradition has addressed a wide array of cognitive performance, ranging from the most basic processes involved in the transmission of sensory input to such higher order skills as problem solving and decision making. We begin our review of the information-processing literature by considering those studies that have examined *attention*.

ATTENTION

The study of attention is concerned with the nature of the limitations in processing information and with information selection processes. Attentional processes and mechanisms determine in part which of the many bits of information received by the senses reaches conscious awareness. The concept of attention has been used to refer to a variety of functions, including alertness, span of consciousness, perceptual span, selectivity in the processing of particular signals relative to other stimuli (i.e., distractors), localization of targets in search and filtering tasks, visual orienting of attention, and attentional preparedness or expectancy. Although these are overlapping and somewhat imprecisely defined functions, we think it is useful to view attention as a construct that involves at least these aspects. In this section, we review the studies bearing on adult age differences in attention.

Selectivity

The general two-process model of selective attention (Neisser, 1967; Solso, 1979) posits a preliminary set of preattentive processes that provides the data for the subsequent filtering and search processes. Such preattentive processes as iconic visual storage and the early neural transmission of visual information are reported to be slower with advancing age (DiLollo, Arnett, & Kruk, 1982; Walsh & Thompson, 1978). Recent studies of aging and preattentive processing have interpreted age-related slowing in terms of differential aging of the transient and sustained channels of processing (Kline, Schieber, Abusamra, & Coyne, 1983; Owsley, Sekuler, & Siemsen, 1983; Sturr, Kelly, Kobus, & Taub, 1982). These visual channels can be distinguished at a neuroanatomical level, and functionally, the transient and sustained channels can be distinguished by their temporal response properties and their differential sensitivity to information varying in size and spatial frequency. The transient channels are associated with the transmission of fast-moving information, and the sustained channels are associated with the processing of relatively detailed, stationary information. Kline and Schieber (1981) suggested that there may be a transient to sustained shift in channel functioning with increasing age, and this shift may account for a variety of observed age-related changes in visual information processing.

The *search* processes of selective attention have been assessed in tasks wherein the subject is required to locate one target or several target characters within a display consisting of varying numbers of distractors and/or target(s). Slopes that relate target-detection time (or error rate) to the number of characters in the display typically show an age-related deficit in search performance (Plude & Hoyer, 1981, 1986; Salthouse & Somberg, 1982). The *filtering* processes of selective attention have been assessed in nonsearch tasks, wherein a particular position in a visual display is specified as relevant and all other display positions are specified as irrelevant. Wright and Elias (1979) found no age differences in the amount of interference associated with nontarget stimuli using such a task. Farkas and Hoyer (1980), Madden (1983), and Plude and Hoyer (1986) have also reported that focused attention does not decline with aging. However, Cerella (1985a) repeated the Wright and Elias (1979) study using a corrective adjustment for the age-reduction parafoveal discriminability and obtained an age-related focused-attention deficit. Cerella (1985a) also demonstrated an age deficit in identification speed and accuracy as a letter was moved away from the fovea toward the parafovea. Identification thresholds were reduced by about one-third for older adults (mean age = 72.2 years) compared to younger adults (mean age = 20.7 years), suggesting a constricted "perceptual window" with aging. By extending Cerella's results to the interpretation of aging differences on visual search tasks, it is reasonable to suggest that limitations associated with the identification of parafoveal characters rather than (or in addition to) capacity-limited search processes may account for age deficits in visual search performance.

Plude and Hoyer (1986) examined age-related nontarget interference under two conditions — search and filtering. In the search condition, if the target appeared, it could be in any of five spatial locations within the array. In the filtering or nonsearch condition, if the target appeared, it was always in the center position of the array. In both experiments, one involving a between-groups comparison of search and filtering conditions and the other using a within-subjects comparison, an age-related divided-attention deficit was obtained under search but not under filtering conditions. Similarly, a comparison across conditions based on response times to targets only when they appeared in the center (foveal) position revealed a divided-attention effect in the search, but not in the filtering condition. Clearly, both data-limiting and capacity-limiting factors are involved in describing aging differences in visual selectivity.

Expectancy and Preparation

The development and use of preparation and selectivity can be inferred from improvements in performance as the opportunity to select stimulus information and to prepare for particular imperative events is increased. The optimal preparatory interval between a warning or precue stimulus and fast/accurate performance is age-related (Gottsdanker, 1980; Madden, 1984; Plude, Cerella, & Poon, 1982; Rabbitt & Vyas, 1980; Talland & Cairnie, 1964).

In a recent series of experiments on age differences in the use of two types of expectancy information, Hoyer and Familant (1983) found no age reduction in the ability to use *a priori* probabilistic information to aid the spatial localization of an imperative stimulus in a visual search task. The investigators also examined age differences in the use of briefly presented pre-cue information by varying the length of the interval between the presentation of an informative pre-cue and the onset of the imperative stimulus. Under these conditions, older adults required more time to process pre-cue information compared to younger adults (i.e., 500 msec compared to 250 msec). When expectancy is based on *a priori* probabilistic information, no age differences in the use of expectancy information were obtained. However, when expectancy is based on a pre-cue presented just prior to the onset of the imperative stimulus, then age-related slowing in the rate of processing information affects the efficiency of use of expectancy information.

Madden (1983) reported that older adults (63–77 years) benefited more than younger adults (19–27 years) when uncertainty about the spatial location of target information was reduced in a visual search task. In the last session of Madden's experiment, subjects viewed two different kinds of displays: cued and noncued. In the cued displays, targets appeared in any of four positions, whereas in the cued condition, targets were confined to two positions of a specified diagonal pair. Reaction time was reduced in the cued compared to the noncued trials for both age groups, but the magnitude of the cueing benefit was larger for the older adults (16%) than for the younger adults (11%).

Attention and Automaticity

Underwood (1974) showed the effect of extended practice on auditory information processing by comparing the performance of naive subjects with that of Neville Moray, an experimental psychologist who has spent many hours performing in auditory detection experiments. Naive subjects were instructed to not pay attention to (i.e., shadow) one list of letters or numbers while a second list of items was being presented. The task was to detect a single item appearing in either list. There was no difference in detection rates between Moray and the unpracticed subjects when the item appeared on the shadowed list. However, there was a huge difference between Moray and the other subjects when detecting items in the nonshadowed list, especially when the items were spoken in the same voice. In this condition, the naive subjects detected 8% of such items, whereas Moray detected 67%. Moray's extremely high level of performance presumably occurred because his extensive practice enabled him to select auditory information with minimal use of attentional capacity. Although there is no age comparison, it is reasonable to infer that there would not be group differences between young and middle-aged adults under highly practiced conditions, even though unpracticed older adults typically show a deficit in shadowing performance relative to unpracticed younger adults (Olsho, Harkins, & Lenhardt, 1985).

There is a growing body of evidence to suggest that there are two general modes of information processing, which are described as automatic and controlled or effortful (Hasher & Zacks, 1979; Kahneman & Treisman, 1984; Schneider & Shiffrin, 1977). Automatic processing is fast, accurate, and effortless, in that it is not affected by capacity-limiting factors such as simultaneous tasks or increases in display size, memory set size, or task complexity. In contrast, effortful or controlled processing requires active, conscious control on the part of the perceiver and is capacity-limited, in that it is affected by complexity and information load factors. Shiffrin and Schneider (1977) found that subjects who developed an automatic target detection strategy were unaffected by increases in the number of targets and distractors, whereas subjects who had to rely on controlled processing showed typical decrements as a function of these load factors. Adult age differences in automatic and controlled processing have been investigated in several studies (Madden & Nebes, 1980, Plude & Hoyer, 1981; Plude et al., 1983; Salthouse & Somberg, 1982). The main finding in these studies is that a traditional pattern of age-associated decrement in information processing is obtained under conditions requiring effortful processing, and no minimal age differences in performance are obtained under conditions of automatic processing. This result is consistent with the "real world" observation that older adults frequently show no noticeable deficits in performing well-practiced skills, even though there may be a decline in performing novel tasks or in acquiring and processing new information (Hoyer, 1985, 1986; Salthouse, 1984). Recall from our earlier discussion of Salthouse's (1984) study of age and skill in typing that older adults relied on a strategy of looking further ahead while typing. Apparently, this strategy enabled the older typists to maintain a high rate of typing performance in spite of basic slow downs in psychomotor reaction time. That traditional measures of processing speed showed a typical pattern of age-related decline for these subjects suggests that skilled performance cannot be described or predicted by general age-performance functions.

Age differences in cognitive performance are frequently attributed to a deficit in processing capacity (Craik & Byrd, 1982; Guttentag, 1985; Hasher & Zacks, 1979; Hoyer & Plude, 1982). The most direct evidence in support of this interpretation is that age differences are greater when two or more tasks must be performed simultaneously than when the tasks are performed individually (Broadbent & Heron, 1962; Madden, 1985; Somberg & Salthouse, 1982; Talland, 1962; Wright, 1981). Although it is well-established that older adults are at a disadvantage when mental resources or capacities need to be shared while performing two or more tasks, older adults may not be at a disadvantage when they are highly practiced with regard to the tasks involved in the dual-task situation.

The effects of experience or practice also apply to the analysis of perceptual identification and pattern recognition with age. Suppose as you were driving home, you were passed by the automobile that you owned 4 years ago. Probably you would still recognize this particular car, and you would do so on the basis of relatively subtle features. The act of recognition would be relatively immediate, even though you might not be any better than most other people under standard conditions designed to test your general ability to discriminate types of cars or other categories of objects.

It is paradoxical that despite our facility in object recognition, we can be so terrible at rendition (e.g., drawing faces or typefaces). Fodor (1983) noted in this regard that humans cannot describe or mimic what their own language sounds like, but we can easily discriminate it from other dialects and languages. Fodor uses this sort of evidence in part as support for his modularity position. This kind of discrimination can be attributed to the specialization of input analyzers, which develops in part as a function of experience.

Attentional Performance and Age: A Summary

In summary, age-related deficits in attentional performance are most evident under capacity-limited conditions. It also has been shown that practice-related factors can produce benefits in the attentional performance of older adults. Practice or experience may bring about a criterion adjustment at the encoding or identification stages of information processing, or the effect may involve a change in the accessibility of particular knowledge or information in memory. The problem of explicating the role of cumulative, age-acquired experience in cognitive function is complicated in several ways. First, some of the factors associated with improved preparation and selectivity (i.e., practice, stimulus familiarity) may produce decrements in other aspects of performance (i.e., alertness decrement). Second, the relation between performance benefits and costs and the readiness to select particular targets may be relatively domain specific because the processes of attentional selectivity and preparation have become dedicated to expected information.

MEMORY

A distinction is usually made between short-term (or primary) memory and long-term (or secondary) memory. Primary memory is conceptualized as a limited-capacity store. It has been likened to consciousness, in that we are aware of the information in primary memory as it is being used. If information is stored more permanently "out of mind" and for durations longer than the span of consciousness, the information is presumed to be stored in secondary memory, which is conceptualized as an unlimited, relatively permanent store. In this section we review age differences in primary and secondary memory processes.

Mechanics of Memory

Memory should be regarded as a set of active processes that control the manner by which information is encoded, stored, transformed, and retrieved. Clearly many of the active or dynamic aspects of memory, such as encoding and retrieval processes, overlap in function with the effortful or control processes already discussed under the topic of attention. The effortful or control processes of memory are those that are responsible for actively manipulating information in primary memory; such processes include effortful computation, integration, transformation, and synthesis. Although there are no age-related differences or only small differences in span measures of primary memory (Botwinick & Storandt, 1974; Craik, 1977; Fozard, 1980; Gilbert & Levee, 1971), working memory and other effortful memory processes show a reliable decline with aging (Hasher & Zacks, 1979; Talland, 1966). Working memory refers to "a limited capacity work space that can be divided between storage and control processing" (Baddeley & Hitch, 1974, p. 76). Craik (1977) and others (Botwinick & Storandt, 1974; Gilbert & Levee, 1971) have observed that relative to younger adults, older people have little trouble with a digit span forward task (i.e., repeating a list of numbers in the order in which they were presented), but elderly adults show a deficit on a digit span backward task (i.e., repeating a list of numbers in the reverse order).

Age differences in the rate of memory search have been assessed using a procedure developed by Saul Sternberg (1969). Memory search involves finding information in memory (i.e., was there a 4 in the presented memory set, 1, 2, 3, 6?). Older adults are not as fast as younger adults in searching the contents of short-term memory (Anders & Fozard, 1973; Anders, Fozard, & Lillyquist, 1972; Erikson, Hamlin, & Daye, 1973; Madden & Nebes, 1980; Plude & Hoyer, 1981; Salthouse & Somberg, 1982). Salthouse (1982) has estimated that there is a 60% slowing in the rate of memory search between the ages of 20 and 50 years.

Older adults are also slower at gaining access to information stored in long-term or secondary memory (Poon & Fozard, 1978, 1980). Although the speed of retrieval is slower with aging, several studies have shown that the processes of semantic activation are relatively unaffected by age (Bowles, Obler, & Poon, 1985; Chiarello, Church, & Hoyer, 1985; Howard, McAndrews, & Lasaga, 1981; Howard, Shaw, & Heisey, 1986). Information in long-term memory is retained within some sort of a knowledge representational system, and particular information can lead to the activation or priming of other information in the semantic network. These semantic networks appear to remain intact with aging and may actually become more elaborate and refined with use (and age).

The topic of how long-term memories are organized is of current concern to cognitive researchers. Tulving (1972, 1983), for example, proposed that there were two different memory storage systems: one for handling personal events and one for handling semantic materials. The episodic–semantic dichotomy refers not only to the types of information that are stored, but also to differences in the conditions of memory retrieval and to the degree of vulnerability to interference. Brown (1975) observed that the episodic-semantic distinction is like Piaget and Inhelder's distinction between "memory in the strict sense" and "memory in the wider sense." Remembering a specific telephone number is an example of an episodic memory, whereas remembering that telephones are communication devices is an example of a semantic memory. In general, there are age-related declines in accessing information stored in both the episodic and semantic systems.

Knowledge Actualization

Lachman and Lachman (1980) described knowledge actualization as a type of memory or knowing that is relatively permanent, nonepisodic, and nonlinguistic, and that has been acquired during a lifetime of formal and informal education. Knowledge actualization refers to the accumulation, access, and use of information in the natural environment and *not* to memory performance assessments derived from experimental tasks designed to test "pure" memory processes. According to Lachman and Lachman (1980), the types of cognitive processes involved in knowledge actualization are locative processes, inferential processes, and metamemory processes. Locative processes refer to relatively automatic, unconscious, and strategy-free information retrieval processes. Inferential processes refer to effortful, conscious, and deliberate control processes for constructing information. Metamemorial processes refer to a constellation of cognitive capacities concerned with the individual's self-assessment of and knowledge about his/her own memory processes and abilities.

Does having knowledge about the strengths and weaknesses of one's own cognitive system lead to improved cognitive performance? If so, older adults could either minimize or compensate for age-related losses in the mechanics of memory and other information-processing functions, as has been suggested by some investigators (Perlmutter, 1980, 1986). Perlmutter (1980) emphasized the role of knowledge actualization in her discussion of the discrepancy between the pessimistic findings typically obtained in laboratory studies of memory aging and the numerous observations of continued high levels of competence in everyday functioning on the part of older adults. Although there are only a few studies on this topic, preliminary findings suggest that there are no age-related losses in knowledge actualization and that there may even be gains in such skills with aging (Camp, 1985).

In a recent review of memory from a life-span perspective, Perlmutter (1986) emphasized that it is useful to examine the development of memory in terms of age-related changes in memory capacities (e.g., encoding and retrieval processes) and age-related changes in the contents of memory (e.g., world knowledge, metacognitive knowledge). It is clear from the research that many aspects of the mechanics or capacities of memory show a decline with advancing age. However, the studies of memory contents suggest that much information about the past is available to adults of all ages (Bahrick, 1984; Botwinick & Storandt, 1974; Perlmutter, Metzger, Miller, & Nezworski, 1980; Storandt, Grant, & Gordon, 1978). Older adults possess a great deal of knowledge about the status of their memory system (e.g., Perlmutter, 1978), and they may use this information to compensate for (or mask) declines in the mechanics of memory. Current investigators of knowledge actualization, metamemory, and metacognition readily acknowledge that further work is needed in order to develop adequate measures of the contents of memory (Cavanaugh & Perlmutter, 1982; Dixon & Hultsch, 1983; Perlmutter, 1986; Zelinski, Gilewski, & Thompson, 1980).

Personal Memory

Personal memories, which may be regarded as stored in the episodic system, figure prominently in everyday life, but developmental differences in the characteristics of personal memory have been rarely investigated. Most nondevelopmental studies of personal memory have focused on forgetting. There are many examples and experimental findings that suggest that forgetting is frequently quite deliberate and selective. For example, Neisser (1981) showed that John Dean's recollections of the Watergate events were unintentionally distorted in a direction consistent with Dean's personal view of himself. This distortion of the "facts" was more evident than the predicted bias for constructing the "gist" of past events. Other studies have shown that people selectively distort information about accidents that they have witnessed (Loftus, 1979), about how they have raised their children (Robbins, 1963), and about what they used to believe (Goethals & Frost, 1978; Goethals & Reckman, 1973). Perhaps every time we recall a personal memory, we change it. Blackburne-Stover, Belenky, and Gilligan (1982), for example, discovered that changes in moral reasoning were related to the ability to accurately recall past events and experience. Specifically, these researchers found that women who displayed an increase in their stage level of moral reasoning tended to significantly distort their memories of the conditions and events that surrounded their previous decision about whether they should terminate an unwanted pregnancy via an abortion. But they also found that women who displayed no change in their level of moral reasoning did not display any significant alteration in their memories of the events and experiences that surrounded their previous abortion decision. More recently, Nigro and Neisser (1983) have examined the importance of the perspective from which the past event is reexperienced in personal memory. They found that the remememberer's perspective is related to characteristics of the original event, to the individual's purpose in recalling that event, and to the length of the recall interval. Greenwald (1980) has suggested that adults actively review their past in such a way as to create a favorable image of themselves as having been "good" and "efficacious."

The revision of autobiographical memories is presumed to be a continuous process throughout the life course, with recall of previous events subject to reinterpretation as new events are experienced (Cohler, 1982; Whitbourne, 1985). One of the procedures currently used to assess autobiographical memory is based on a method first reported by Galton (1879) to study his own episodic memory. Galton's method consisted of inspecting a word until he was able to describe a personal experience associated with the word. A modified version of Galton's method has been used with older adults in recent studies by Fitzgerald and Lawrence (1984), Franklin and Holding (1977), Rubin (1985), and Sperbeck, Whitbourne, and Hoyer (in press). These investigators presented prompt words to different aged adults, instructed them to think of an associated experience from their lives, and to date the remembered experience. Older adults generally report older memories, but of course there is a confound between age of the individual and age of memory. Sperbeck, Whitbourne, and Hoyer (in press) found no relationship between age and number of memories retrieved or between age and the speed with which memories were retrieved. These results are in agreement with other findings on autobiographical memory, which show no clear pattern of adult age differences in the accessibility of personal memories (Franklin & Holding, 1977; Fitzgerald & Lawrence, 1984; see Rubin, 1985).

Memory Training

Can anything be done to remediate age-associated declines in memory performance (Poon, 1985)? An important question for both practitioners and basic researchers in the field of aging and memory is the extent to which older adults can be taught to use mnemonics and other cognitive strategies to improve memory performance. A related question is the extent to which observed declines in memory performance can be attributed to the use of relatively less efficient learning and memory strategies on the part of older persons, rather than attributing such declines in memory and cognitive performance to irreversible changes brought about by aging of the functions of the brain and central nervous system.

Mnemonic techniques are learning strategies that can be used to enhance the acquisition and retention of information. One of the oldest mnemonic strategies is the method of loci. Ancient Roman orators were taught to use this method in a series of stages. First, a large number of places in a public building were memorized in a strict serial order, so that each location could be clearly visualized. Next, after a speech was prepared, its content was divided into a series of visual images, which represented key words or ideas in the speech. Each of these images was then associated with one of the places in the public building. To recall the main ideas of the speech, one simply imagined traveling through each of the places in the building.

A similar mnemonic strategy is the peg-word method. Images of concrete objects rather than locations are used as the pegs to which the images to be remembered are attached. In the rhyming peg-word method, each peg word rhymes with the number indicating its position in a list: "One is a bun, two is a shoe, three is a tree," and so on. Bower and Reitman (1972) showed that the peg-word method and the method of loci yielded essentially identical recall performance under a variety of test conditions with young adults. Also, Yeasavage, Rose, and Bower (1982) showed that practice with a mnemonics-plus-elaboration technique improved name/face recall in a manner similar to the method of loci for elderly adults.

In a review of the studies examining adult age differences in the use of mnemonic strategies, Poon, Walsh-Sweeney, and Fozard (1980) concluded that older adults can learn to improve their memory; 14 of 17 studies suggested that the use of mnemonics immediately improved the paired-associate and list-learning performances of trained elderly adults compared to no-training control subjects.

The memory training program developed by Baltes and his colleagues at the Max Planck Institute in West Berlin, Federal Republic of Germany (Baltes & Kliegl, 1986; Kliegl, Smith, & Baltes, 1986) is probably one of the most systematic demonstrations of the beneficial effects of training on the elderly. Following Chase and Ericsson's (1982) approach, these investigators have shown that older people can increase their digit memory span to over 40 items using a modified method of loci mnemonic. Note that without training, typical subjects are able to repeat four to eight items in the correct order. The best elderly person (a 70-year-old) in the West Berlin study was able to repeat a string of 120 digits at a presentation rate of 8 seconds per item. The training programs used by Baltes and Kliegl (1986) extend over 30–50 sessions. The programs consist of three components: training of working memory, acquisition of a knowledge system about digits, and learning a mnemonic system (method of loci) for encoding and retrieving information.

Although elderly adults can clearly benefit from the use of mnemonic systems, Baltes and his colleagues have found that younger adults frequently benefit more from the training. Further, some investigators have shown that the gain in retention on the part of the elderly is not as durable as it is for younger adults. Hellenbusch (1976) found that both young adults and the elderly benefited from the peg-word mnemonic system, but the gain for the older participants was evident immediately after learning, but not after a 2-week retention interval. Another age difference is that older adults may be less able to apply a general mnemonic strategy to a wide variety of cognitive tasks. Hellenbusch (1976) also reported that almost twice as many young adults (83%) as elderly (44%) were able to transfer a learned mnemonic strategy to a new learning task.

The work on adult age differences in the use of mnemonics suggests that there is a failure or a difficulty on the part of older adults to spontaneously use imagery and other effective mnemonic strategies when learning and remembering. Hulicka and Grossman (1967) found that the paired-associate learning performance of older adults can be improved by instructing and encouraging participants to use self-generated images in relating paired items to one another. Similarly, Robertson-Tchabo, Hausman, and Arenberg (1976) showed that older adults do not spontaneously use the method of loci mnemonic, although older adults can use this mnemonic effectively when instructed to do so.

CONCLUSIONS AND IMPLICATIONS

In this chapter, we examined the component processes and abilities of cognition identified as important by the adherents of the information-processing and psychometric paradigms. Research conducted within these traditions has shown that fluid mental abilities and information-control processes decline with age. However, it has also been shown that deficits do not occur in performance under highly practiced conditions. Nevertheless, it can be concluded from our review of the literature that with increases in age, adults process less information in a progressively less efficient manner and become less adept at acquiring new information and applying general reasoning strategies to the solution of novel problems.

In the earlier chapters, we observed that the formal and postformal models of adult cognitive development ignored the effects of age-related declines in the basic components and processes of cognition. Recall that postformal conceptions of adult cognition emphasized the dialectical, relativistic, and open-ended aspects of thinking — aspects that were overlooked by formal operations models of adult cognition. Obviously, the information-processing and psychometric models that were discussed in this chapter are also constrained in that they do not consider the postformal aspects of adult thinking.

There is little direct correspondence between the empirical work concerning age differences in intelligence and information processing and extant developmental theory and research on stylistic changes in adult thinking. Ecologically irrelevant tasks designed by psychologists for laboratory purposes are representative of the work of the former approach; whereas real-life, everyday functional assessments of cognitive performance are indicative of work in the latter tradition. As Perlmutter (1980) has noted, the lack of correspondence between these two different models and methods of assessing cognitive development should not be surprising. This gap arises because until recently much of the research on cognitive aging has been conducted as an extension of general cognitive research. In the aggregate, the research enterprise has generated huge inventories of findings that, taken together, do not yield a theory of cognitive development in adulthood. A similar gap has characterized the child development literature as Klahr and Wallace (1976) have remarked:

> On the one hand, we have Inhelder and Piaget's theoretical account, and, on the other, the complex set of results obtained from the experimental studies. A gap exists between the hypothetical structures and processes which form the basis of the theory and the level of performance as represented by the experimental data. (p. x.)

The information-processing and psychometric approaches emphasize the subprocesses and component abilities that constitute intelligence or cognition. Although it is useful to study a singular process or ability, there are limitations to ignoring the overall organization of abilities. Older adults frequently exhibit a reduced speed and efficiency in information *processing* and in the mechanics of cognition, but such age-related losses may not interfere with cognitive effectiveness in real-world contexts. Many of the contexts and tasks of adulthood require decisions, choices, and actions that reflect relatively complex styles of *thinking*, which do not appear to be captured by laboratory-based studies of intelligence and information processing. Furthermore, the cognitive processes and mental abilities studied in the information-processing and psychometric traditions are considered in isolation from the knowledge structures that they are used to create. The *knowledge* that adults construct (*not* just the processes that aid in the creation of that knowledge) should be viewed as a part of the development of adult cognition. Thus, new and expanded views of mature cognition are needed that take account of age-related changes in processing, thinking, and knowing. In the next chapter, we propose this type of an integrative model of adult cognition.

SUMMARY

In this chapter we described the nature of adult cognitive change from the information-processing and psychometric perspectives. In general, it was shown that with increasing age, adults process less information in a progressively less efficient manner and become less adept in general problem solving. However, older adults can display relatively high levels of cognitive performance within specialized skill areas.

We noted that the psychometric and information-processing perspectives provide an overly restrictive view of adult cognition. We called for the development of a new perspective on adult cognition that recognizes the importance of knowledge systems and thinking styles, as well as the processes and mechanics of cognition (i.e., information control processes and fluid mental abilities).

6

Knowledge Encapsulation:
Processes and Products

Recent work emphasizes a new dimension of difference between individuals who display more or less ability in thinking and problem solving. This dimension is the possession and utilization of an organized body of conceptual and procedural knowledge . . .

R. Glaser
Education and Thinking: The Role of Knowledge

This chapter is divided into three sections. In the first section, we present theory and research bearing on the cognitive science perspective of adult cognition. Consistent with a cognitive science point of view, we suggest that adult cognitive development is marked by the emergence of and increased differentiation of domain-ordered knowledge specializations. We also argue that the development of a knowledge-based organization of cognition in adulthood is unidirectional (i.e., toward increased differentiation and complexity) and increasingly resistant to modification and/or reversibility. Furthermore, we propose that a mature or final form of knowledge is *a priori* unspecifiable, because it is dependent on the particular characteristics or constraints of the domains within which knowledge is represented and the developing individual's unique level of mastery within those domains. A major component of cognitive development through life, therefore, involves the continuous process of integrating new information and skills within knowledge domains. Support for our position comes from: (a) nondevelopmental research on the acquisition and use of cognitive skills, (b) cognitive performance differences between novices and experts within and across domains, and (c) the general observation that most older adults continue to function competently on everyday tasks and in skilled domains, even though standardized assessments of cognitive ability are likely to yield age-related declines.

Second, we briefly summarize and critique the genetic–epistemological, psychometric, information-processing, and cognitive science approaches to the study of adult cognitive change. Each of these theoretical perspectives offers an important but incomplete conceptualization of adult cognition. Thus, the development of a new perspective that paints a more comprehensive picture of adult cognition is needed.

Third, we present our Encapsulation Model of adult cognition. The Encapsulation Model: (a) integrates and extends the best features of the genetic–epistemological, cognitive science, information-processing, and psychometric perspectives, (b) unifies the three most prominent strands of adult cognition: *processing, knowing,* and *thinking,* (c) stresses the functional/ adaptive quality of adult cognitive activity, and (d) describes how basic psychological processes become encapsulated within the forms of domain-specific knowledge and thought.

THE COGNITIVE SCIENCE APPROACH:
POINTS OF DEPARTURE

Consider the following professional roles: musician, physicist, historian, surgeon, and entrepreneur. Because of the kinds of abilities that are necessarily involved in these and most fields of endeavor and the tremendous amount of knowledge that is required to be proficient in any one domain, individuals are rarely expert at more than one or two of these fields during the life course. Yet the bulk of theory and research on adult cognitive development gives emphasis to the study of abilities that are presumed to cut across particular cognitive specializations. In the information-processing literature, for example, much attention is given to the study of age deficits in central processes that are presumed to be independent of particular knowledge domains. Similarly, in the psychometric literature, age differences in general ability or general capacity as represented by notions like Spearman's (1927) g, and Cattell's (1971) and Horn's (1970) conceptions of fluid intelligence are the predominant concern. Even in the early applications of Piagetian theory to the analysis of adult cognition, logical–mathematical reasoning was conceptualized as an all-encompassing, general form of reasoning.

It has been reported that there are significant losses in fluid abilities, general reasoning processes, and speed of mental processes with advancing age (Horn, 1970; Kausler, 1982; Salthouse, 1982). However, if we look at the effects of aging within particular areas or domains of cognitive specialization (i.e., expertise), recent evidence as well as general observation indicate that adults continue to function competently in their vocations and in their everyday avocational roles (Charness, 1985, 1986; Cole, 1979; Perlmutter, 1980). Psychologists interested in studying cognitive development during adulthood, therefore, are faced with an interesting paradox. Empirical research indicates a deterioration of generalized cognitive ability with age, whereas everyday observation indicates that with increasing age there is stability (and sometimes even enhancement) of cognitive performance within areas of specialization and expertise. Glucksberg (1985) has commented on this matter in the following way:

> The paradox of expertise . . . suggests limitations of the componential approach to skilled functioning. And it poses an important puzzle: How does expertise work, in each of the many domains that require expertise? This may well be one of the more important areas of research in cognitive psychology in the next few decades: the analysis of complex, expert performances are . . . more than the sum of their parts. (pp. 8–9)

In recent years, several relatively distinct research directions have emerged that bear on the resolution of the above-mentioned paradox. One line of investigation has shown the beneficial effects of training on those generalized measures of intelligence that typically manifest age-related deficits (Blieszner, Willis, & Baltes, 1981; Denney, 1979; Fozard & Popkin, 1978; Hoyer, Labouvie, & Baltes, 1973; Schultz & Hoyer, 1976; Willis, Blieszner, & Baltes, 1981). The results of these training studies demonstrate that there is a considerable degree of plasticity in adult intelligence.

A second research direction is represented by those studies aimed at explicating the differential and multidimensional nature of adult intelligence. These studies, which offer a more optimistic picture of adult intellectual development, suggest that intelligence is best construed as a complex system of changing abilities (Horn, 1982), each of which displays different patterns of age-related change. Research based on the Cattell–Horn model of fluid and crystallized intelligence, for example, has revealed that fluid mental abilities exhibit significant age-related decline, whereas crystallized forms of intelligence exhibit stability and/or positive growth over time.

Caution is in order in interpreting the meaning of age differences found on domain-general measures of fluid intelligence. On the one hand, such measures are intended to provide a pure assessment of cognitive ability, relatively independent of cultural and experiential influences (Horn & Donaldson, 1976). On the other hand, it is difficult, if not impossible, to view tasks of fluid intelligence as being unaffected by cultural/experiential influences when one considers the enormous role played by cohort effects (i.e., sociohistorical change) on adults' performance on these measures (cf. Labouvie-Vief, 1985). More importantly, it seems as if many assessments of fluid intelligence are artificial, because they do not take into account the actual contexts in which adults think. Thus, the significance of the robust finding that fluid mental abilities decline may *not* be that intelligence declines, but that with age much of everyday cognitive performance depends less on fluid abilities and increasingly more on contextual and domain-related factors.

Other writers (Dittmann-Kohli & Baltes, 1986; Dittmann-Kohli & Kramer,

1985; Willis & Schaie, 1986) have suggested that the fluid components of intelligence and the fundamental information-processing abilities that appear to cut across substantive domains may be of far greater importance in accounting for aspects of intelligence in early adulthood or adolescence than in later adulthood. If cognitive processes and fluid abilities become increasingly organized and integrated within domains of knowledge with aging (as we propose in our Encapsulation Model), then the practical and theoretical importance of age-related decline in domain-general measures of intelligence is attenuated.

Similarly, caution is in order when interpreting the finding that crystallized intelligence remains stable or increases with age (Horn, 1970, 1982). Typically, measures of crystallized intelligence take the form of vocabulary tests (e.g., "What is the difference between laziness and idleness?") or questions that assess the presence of factual information (e.g., "Who wrote Hamlet?" or "How far is it from New York to Paris?"). It is difficult to view the above-mentioned items as ecologically relevant and meaningful. Despite the fact that crystallized intelligence is regarded as accumulated knowledge, it is difficult to envision how such knowledge is necessary for the solution of everyday tasks. Furthermore, there seems to be no acknowledgement by psychometricians concerning the organization (i.e., domain-specific nature) of crystallized forms of intelligence.

A third line of research that bears on the resolution of the previously mentioned paradox is represented by the cognitive science approach to the study of cognition. This approach suggests that intelligent problem solving has its basis in the possession and utilization of a great deal of specific knowledge about the world. The fundamental claim of this approach differs dramatically from the more commonsensical notion about skilled performance that pervades the information-processing and psychometric points of view. Adherents of these approaches have suggested that sophisticated problem-solving ability has its basis in the implementation of very powerful and very *general* control processes and fluid mental abilities (e.g., general reasoning skills, general memory abilities) that comprise the human cognitive system. Alternatively, proponents of the cognitive science approach have suggested that general mental processes and abilities play a minor role in the problem-solving process. Consistent with this cognitive science orientation, Goldstein and Papert (1977) have argued that

> there has been a change in paradigm. The fundamental problem of understanding intelligence is not the identification of a few powerful techniques, but rather the question of how to represent large amounts of knowledge in a fashion that permits their effective use and interaction . . . the problem-solver (whether man or machine) must know specifically how to use its knowledge — with general techniques supplemented by domain-specific pragmatic know-how. (p. 84)

Waldrop (1984), in tracing the influence of the cognitive science orientation on the study of artificial intelligence *(AI)*, has similarly commented that

> By the mid-1970s the conventional wisdom in *AI* had undergone a fundamental change. The essence of intelligence was no longer seen to be reasoning ability alone. More important was having lots of highly specific knowledge about lots of things—a notion inevitably stated as, "Knowledge is power". (p. 1280)

Similarly, Hillman (1985) has noted that

> by the mid-1970s researchers had turned their attention to more restricted domains of application. The prevailing philosophy was, and still is, that the expert's knowledge is the reason for expert performance, whereas knowledge representation and inference schemes provide the mechanisms for its use. The search for comprehensive knowledge representation theories and general-purpose reasoning systems has been, for all practical purposes, abandoned. (p. 22)

Thus, in contrast to the early efforts to represent human problem solving as a general process (Newell & Simon, 1972), contemporary cognitive scientists suggest that human problem solving proceeds through the use of domain-specific knowledge or task-specific heuristics (Duda & Shortliffe, 1983).

Given the important role ascribed to knowledge within the framework of the cognitive science approach, we present various descriptions of knowledge and knowledge heuristics.

Knowledge Heuristics

To paraphrase Waldrop (1984), it seems as if 100 years of psychology have not necessarily improved upon 3,000 years of philosophy—no one can yet say exactly what knowledge *is*. Despite the inherent elusiveness of the nature of knowledge, several cognitive scientists have proposed different ways to conceptualize knowledge. Kolers and Roediger (1984), for example, have suggested that knowledge should be conceptualized as a set of procedures rather than as a singular, concrete propositional entity. Anderson (1982), on the other hand, has made a distinction between *declarative* knowledge and *procedural* knowledge. Declarative knowledge consists of factual information that can be used to solve a problem, whereas procedural knowledge consists of a set of rules that determine how and when declarative knowledge is to be applied. Declarative and procedural forms of knowledge are sometimes referred to as *heuristics*, intuitive rules of thumb, which govern the problem-solving process. One way to think about cognitive growth, therefore, is that it consists of the successive replacement or integration of old heuristics with new and more powerful heuristics. Rather than becoming faster at mental computations or developing more memory capacity, it appears that the human cognitive system becomes more powerful by actively constructing more sophisticated heuristics for handling information.

According to Newell and Simon (1972), humans use heuristics to determine which of an extremely large number of potential paths toward a solution may be followed. For example, exhaustive trial-and-error searches of possible moves in the middle of a typical chess game branch a thousandfold for every set of move possibilities and their replies. Simon and Chase (1973) pointed out that a complete analysis of only three moves deep requires charting approximately one million branches. However, computer-generated simulations of chess games or solutions to anagrams may not reflect how adults approach such problems. In both cases, the task of carrying out blind, random generations of all combinations and then comparing these generations to a recognizable solution exceeds the capacity of human memory. In other cases, blind exhaustive search is simply not representative of how adults approach and solve problems.

A distinction can be made between heuristics and algorithms. A heuristic may lead to a solution, but it also might not. An algorithm is a sure solution strategy. As a way of illustrating the differences between algorithms and heuristics, consider the anagram CLOMPY, in which the letters can be rearranged to form an English word. One algorithm or sure solution for this problem is to list all 720 combinations of these six letters, compare each of these combinations to all other six-letter words stored in the mental lexicon, and then select the correct match. Computers can use this sort of algorithm efficiently. However, most humans use a heuristic procedure to solve anagram problems that involves the generating and testing of educated guesses (i.e., trying PLY as a suffix and COM as a prefix, thus producing the solution).

Humans do not use algorithms, even though they always lead to solution, for two reasons. First, they may not have the mental capacity (i.e., working memory space) to carry out the solution in a deductive–logical fashion. Second, there may not be an algorithm available, either for the task or in the person's repertoire. For example, there is no algorithm that we know of for writing a book on adult cognition!

The strategies involved in solving anagrams also help to illustrate other aspects of knowledge and its representation. Try the anagram DYOMLE. The speed of reaching the solution depends on the use of syntax or what one knows about English words and how they are formed, how quickly one can manipulate these letters in working memory, and the availability and rate of access to one's mental lexicon. If the correct solution, MELODY, is not in the individual's lexicon, solution to the anagram DYOMLE may not be possible. Similarly, if the capacity of working memory is exceeded (e.g., a 10-letter word presented orally and to be parsed without visual aid), a solution may not be possible. Third, not knowing the structure or syntax of

English words disables solution. Thus, this kind of problem suggests that knowledge may necessarily be both declarative (i.e., lexical, syntactic) and procedural (i.e., the mental rules involved in the rearranging of letters).

Hofstadter (1979) has commented that a specific piece of knowledge can be represented in either a declarative or a procedural manner. To quote his musical example:

> Consider the recall of a melody. Is the melody stored in the brain note by note?. . . . If so, then melodies are stored declaratively. Or is the recall of a melody mediated by the interaction of a large number of symbols, some of which represent tonal relationships, others of which represent emotional qualities, others of which represent rhythmic devices, and so on? If so, then melodies are stored procedurally. In reality, there is probably a mixture of these extremes in the way a melody is stored and recalled. (1979, p. 363)

Categories, Prototypes, and Schemas

Declarative and procedural forms of knowledge may be viewed as categories, prototypes, or schemas. Rosch and Mervis (1975) have clearly shown that adults use categories and prototypes as organizers of information about people, places, and things. Knowledge schemas are also presumed to assist in the organization and acquisition of knowledge. Fodor (1985), for example, suggested that knowledge schemas fill in incomplete perceptual information. He also pointed out that modern cognitive psychologists use this evidence to argue that perception is "smart"—that there is more information in the individual's perception of a physical stimulus than there is in the stimulus that prompts the perception.

Research on the selectivity of information processing also suggests the importance of the individual's particular knowledge of cognitive function. In perceiving, we recognize, actively select, and subjectively interpret only part of the vast array of information to which we are exposed. Numerous investigators have emphasized the role of "top-down" factors in perception (Hoyer & Plude, 1982; Rock, 1983), memory (Bransford, Barclay, & Franks, 1972; Tyler & Voss, 1982), and schematic processing (Abelson, 1981; Fiske & Kinder, 1981; Mischel, 1981).

The beneficial effects of having "schemas" and knowledge categories for the integration and/or storage of new information are particularly clear in the area of memory. It has been shown that isolated pieces of information are vulnerable to forgetting unless they are integrated within schemas or domains of some type (Bower, Black, & Turner, 1979; Bransford & Franks, 1971; Mandler & Johnson, 1977; Neisser, 1981; Nelson & Gruendel, 1981). As Neisser (1984) has pointed out, we quickly forget loosely ordered bits of information, but we seldom forget information that is part of some well-established knowledge system, such as our personal history or our first language system. In studies of age-related changes in memory retrieval (Hultsch, 1971), it has been shown that isolated bits of information are more difficult to retrieve with advancing age but that adult age differences in recall of organized information are relatively small or nonexistent. Thus, functionally, individuals impose an organization on incoming information by combining it with information already in memory.

Expert Knowledge

Knowledge, we have argued, manifests itself in certain forms (e.g., declarative knowledge, procedural knowledge, schemas, etc.). Furthermore, knowledge has a developmental history (i.e., knowledge evolves sequentially through various forms or stages). Neves and Anderson (1981), for example, have described the stages involved in the acquisition of cognitive skills as follows. The first stage is *encoding*, where a set of facts required by the skill are committed to memory. Second, facts become procedures in the *proceduralization* stage. The third stage is called *composition*, by which the previously established procedures are made faster with practice. A fourth stage, labeled *automization*, occurs when processing becomes asymptotic, independent of load factors, and resistant to interference (Logan, 1980). Thus, given sufficient exposure (e.g., trials, practice), there is considerable evidence to suggest that some types of information can be accessed either automatically or in a highly constituted form (Schneider & Shiffrin, 1977). William James' (1890) description of the changes in performance that accompany experience and training are consistent with the above-mentioned portrayal:

> When we are learning to walk, to ride, to swim, skate, fence, write, play, or sing, we interrupt ourselves at every step by unnecessary movements and false notes. When we are proficient, on the contrary, the results not only follow with the very minimum of muscular action requisite to bring them forth, they also follow from a single instantaneous "cue." The marksman sees the bird, and, before he knows it, he has aimed and shot. A gleam in his adversary's eye, a momentary pressure from his rapier, and the fencer finds he has instantly made the right parry and return. A glance at the musical hieroglyphics, and the pianist's fingers have rippled through a cataract of notes. (p. 114)

Another way to chart the developmental course of knowledge is to maintain that knowledge becomes increasingly expert during the adult years. The shift from novice to expert is one that is characterized by highly skilled problem solving within a particular domain and most typically occurs in adult life. Although no common taxonomy exists for distinguishing experts from novices, there are fundamental differences in the ways in which experts and novices represent, apply, and become introspectively aware of knowledge systems. In highly structured domains (e.g., physics), expertise seems to be rule-based and procedural, whereas in less-structured domains (e.g., certain kinds of writing, painting, and music), expertise is most likely based on a blend of different skills: rapid and efficient integration coupled with inductive processes.

Despite the fact that there exists no consensus concerning the definition and/or characteristics of expertise, it is widely acknowledged that the development of expertise is more highly dependent on the growth of acquired knowledge than on the luck of genetic inheritance. Charness (1985, 1986), for example, has offered an analogy between the components of the human cognitive system and the computer — "acquired knowledge representations," he suggested, are analogous to computer "software," while the neural substrate, he argued, is analogous to computer "hardware." Furthermore, he proposed that software components are more important than hardware components for the development of cognitive expertise. More specifically, Charness reviewed evidence that suggests that expertise within the domains of chess, music, and physics is primarily dependent on at least 10 years of extensive work, study, and practice within these domains. See Table 6.1 for a summary of Charness' analysis of the software and hardware components that account for differences in expert versus novice performance.

Generally, experts are not conscious of the knowledge, processes, and rules that enable them to perform competently. Despite the presence of knowledge structures that permit the solution of highly complex problems in a domain, experts may not necessarily be able to describe how they arrive at a decision. This suggests that an intuitive approach to problem solving is characteristic of expertise. In fact, experts have great difficulty understanding how novices, who are accessing the same information as themselves, arrive at a different decision or outcome. It seems that expertise within any domain gives rise to a set of intuitions that are derived from the selective processing of relevant information. Lesgold (1983), for example, has reported that expert radiologists often have difficulty informing novices of diagnostic errors (see also Lesgold, Feltovich, Glaser, & Wang, 1981). An expert would accurately identify a large white blotch on an x-ray photograph as a collapsed lung, whereas novices (medical residents) would diagnose the same stimulus as a large tumor. Further, the expert does not consciously entertain the idea that the blotch ever was a tumor in making the diagnosis. However, if questioned the expert can point out in rule form the visual differences between a tumor and a collapsed lung on an x-ray. The expert radiologist also reports not having an understanding of what led the novice radiologist to suspect that the blotch was a tumor, suggesting that the radiologist's visual diagnostic skills might be a type of automatized perception.

Much more needs to be known about how physicians arrive at solutions in diagnostic problem-solving tasks. For example, Elstein, Shulman, & Sprafka (1978) discovered that expert and novice physicians differed from

TABLE 6.1. Factors That Underlie "Novice" Versus "Expert" Performance

TYPES OF FACTORS

HARDWARE	SOFTWARE*
Asymptotic speed of elementary processes such as attention and recognition	*Size* of the knowledge-base in long-term memory
Size and storage capacity of working memory	Whether information in the knowledge base is represented in a declarative or a procedural manner
Time necessary to create a new chunk of information in long-term memory (i.e., consolidation rate of long-term memory processes)	Whether information in the knowledge base is organized in a linear or hierarchical manner
Predisposition to code incoming information within the context of different symbol systems (e.g., linguistic vs. visual/ spatial vs. kinesthetic symbol systems)	The manner by which information in the knowledge base is symbolized (e.g., whether the information in the knowledge base is symbolized in a bodily/ kinesthetic vs. a visual/spatial manner)

Source: Adapted from Charness, N. (1985). *Age and expertise: Responding to Talland's challenge.* Paper presented at the third George A. Talland Memorial Conference on Aging and Memory, Cape Cod, MA; and from Charness, N. (1986). Expertise in chess, music, and physics: A cognitive perspective. In L.K. Obler & D.A. Fein (Eds.), *The neuropsychology of talent and special abilities.* New York: Guilford Press.
*With increasing levels of expertise, the following software changes are likely to occur: (a) increase in the size of the knowledge base, (b) the tendency for knowledge to be represented in a procedural rather than a declarative manner, (c) the tendency for knowledge to be organized in a hierarchical rather than a linear manner, and (d) the tendency for knowledge to be symbolized in different ways (e.g., knowledge originally symbolized in a bodily/kinesthetic manner may become symbolized in a visual/spatial manner). Furthermore, these changes in software are likely to produce changes in: (a) the nonasymptotic speed of elementary processes, (b) the size of the chunks of information capable of being manipulated in working memory, and (c) the rate at which information is consolidated in long-term memory. Thus, the changes in software (i.e., changes in knowledge representation and organization) which accompany expertise are likely to produce changes in the information-processing abilities of experts. Previous researchers, however, tended to view these *outcomes* of expertise (i.e., domain-specific information-processing abilities) as the *causes* of expertise.

each other with regard to the size of their underlying knowledge base. These researchers also found that experts and novices displayed the same style of reasoning (i.e., they both generated a limited number of tentative hypotheses relatively early in the diagnostic process) when confronted by a medical problem. In contrast, Patel and Groen (1986) reported that the accuracy of physicians' diagnoses is related to the type of reasoning processes they employ. These investigators showed that the explanations of those cardiologists who made an accurate diagnosis of acute bacterial endocarditis were accounted for by a model consisting of pure forward reasoning through a network of causal rules. Cardiologists making inaccurate diagnoses employed a mixture of forward and backward reasoning, beginning with a high level hypothesis and proceeding in a top–down fashion to the generation of irrelevant rules.

Kuipers and Kassirer (1984) have commented on the difficulty of obtaining information from expert physicians.

The expert physician, with many years of experience, has so "compiled" his knowledge that a long chain of inference is likely to be reduced to a single association. This feature can make it difficult for an expert to verbalize information that he actually uses in solving a problem. Faced with a difficult problem, the apprentice fails to solve it at all, the journeyman solves it after long effort, and the master sees the answer immediately. Clearly, although the master has the knowledge we want to study, the journeyman will be much easier to study. . . . (p. 367)

Likewise, Rose (1985), in his review of the research on the novice/expert shift, has proposed that

only novices proceed according to formal rules; as they become more proficient, people rely increasingly on context and experience. Expert pilots, for example, don't think of themselves as flying an airplane but as simply flying. Chess masters don't analyze hundreds of board positions; they sense the right move popping into their heads. What guides them is not analytic thought, apparently, but intuitive response. (p. 51)

Automatically applying an intuitive, highly compiled knowledge system may be sufficient for expert cognitive performance *only* when there is no benefit to construct or integrate new information. New information requires the reorganization of prior knowledge and current experience. For example, much of medical expert knowledge can be represented as a set of highly structured rules of the form, "If the symptoms are _____, then the diagnosis is _____," or "If the diagnosis is _____, then the prescription is _____." In fact, medical expert computer programs such as INTERNIST (Pople, 1977), an internal medicine diagnostic program, and MYCIN (Shortliffe, 1976), which diagnoses bacterial diseases, contain several hundred production rules. However, there are many exceptions to specific rules in the real-life practice of medicine, in part because each patient is different and because not all of the extant rules in medicine have been ideally formulated. For example, if a patient is not responding satisfactorily to a prescribed drug dosage, the physician draws inferences from a reservoir of acquired experience that is patient specific and generalizable from similarly unique cases. This new knowledge or discovery (Pople, 1977; Shortliffe, 1976) can then be formulated as a revision of the original rule. Thus, an expert's ideal response to the exceptional case is integrative and constructive. It is not purely dependent on the implementation of an automatized preexisting rule system.

Not only is expert knowledge automatized and intuitive, expert knowledge is also domain-specific. In recent studies comparing novices and experts, for example, it has been reported that rapid and efficient information processing is specific to the kind of information represented within the knowledge domain. More specifically, observed differences between experts and novices in particular domains such as chess or physics have been shown to depend on the extent and organization of specific knowledge bases in long-term memory (Simon & Simon, 1978). Experts differ from nonexperts in chess mainly in terms of component perceptual and memorial abilities, not in terms of measures of logical thinking and general problem solving (Chase & Simon, 1973; DeGroot, 1965). A chess master, for example, could reconstruct the positions of approximately 25 pieces from a game after having seen the display for 5 seconds, whereas a novice player could remember the locations of only about one-quarter as many pieces after the same exposure. However, even though the expert was able to process large masses of domain-specific information without loss of detail compared to the nonexpert, experts and novices were not found to differ from each other with regard to general (i.e., nonspecific) measures of span memory and working memory. Further, compared to weaker players, expert players did not evidence a superiority in general or logical reasoning ability, nor did they search through more possible moves before selecting one. With regard to reasoning, the main difference between the experts and novices was that the masters spent more time considering good moves, and the novices spent more time exploring poor moves. This pioneering work on chess skills by DeGroot (1965), Chase and Simon (1973), and Charness (1985, 1986) supports the position that component processes become specialized (or encapsulated) with skill acquisition or expertise.

Like experts in chess and other domains, experienced individuals can recall at a glance far more specialized information than novices. Chi, Glaser, and Rees (1982) indicated that a differential ability to categorize problems may also be an important factor distinguishing novices and experts. Compared to novices, experts have better knowledge about which steps to use for problems belonging to particular categories, and they can better recognize into which category different problems should be placed.

In this section we have highlighted the attributes of expert knowledge and the differences between novices and experts by several examples drawn from the domains of medicine and chess. However, it should be noted that similar differences between experts and nonexperts have also been reported in the domains of bridge (Charness, 1979, 1983; Engle & Bukstel, 1978), computer programming (Jeffries, Turner, Polson, & Atwood, 1981; McKeithen, Reitman, Rueter, & Hirtle, 1981), music (Charness, 1986), and physics (Charness, 1986, Larkin, 1981, 1983; Simon & Simon, 1983).

DEVELOPMENTAL IMPLICATIONS OF THE
COGNITIVE SCIENCE PERSPECTIVE

The cognitive science perspective was developed by experimental psychologists who approached the study of cognition in a nondevelopmental manner and by a number of computer scientists who grappled with the issue of artificial intelligence. Nevertheless, the cognitive science orientation has important implications for the developmental analysis of cognitive change. For example, several developmentalists (Chi, 1985; Glaser, 1984; Keil, 1981, 1986) have argued that a major component of the growth of thinking in children is the possession of accessible and usable knowledge. It has been shown that children's developing knowledge structures serve as "schemes" that enable different, more advanced kinds of thinking (Chi & Koeske, 1983). Furthermore, in those studies that have controlled for pre-experimental knowledge differences in evaluating cognitive performance in young adults and old adults, no or only minimal age-related declines in performance are found (Charness, 1985, 1986; Hoyer, 1985; Hultsch & Dixon, 1983). Thus, even though there are age-related deficits in the acquisition and processing of new information (Plude & Hoyer, 1985), most adults continue to use acquired knowledge in an effective and proficient manner throughout their later years.

This leads to the suggestion that knowledge continues to accumulate and to become increasingly refined with age and experience but that the control processes presumed responsible for acquiring new knowledge decline with increasing age (Hoyer, 1985). This leads to the hypothesis that older persons become less skilled at general problem solving, but more skilled, sensitive, and adaptive within specialized areas.

Many older adults, for example, continue to perform competently in everyday cognitive tasks and within skilled domains, even though they may perform poorly compared to younger adults on laboratory measures of ability. Welford (1958) observed that this discrepancy may be due, in part, to a "natural" selective attrition from jobs that require abilities that the older worker no longer has. In one study of work behavior by Sewell and Belbin (in Belbin, 1953; Welford, 1958), it was reported that there were no clear age trends in terms of performance output as a function of job type, but there was a difference in the *age distribution* of workers holding the more time-stressful jobs.

It may also be the case that older adulthood is characterized by the development of a specialized understanding of both intra- and interpersonal relations. Dittmann-Kohli and Baltes (1986), for example, suggested that older adults are likely to acquire expertise within the domain of personal knowledge (i.e., wisdom) and are therefore more likely to resolve those ill-defined interpersonal problems that pervade human relationships.

Thus, we suggest that with age and experience there is a transition from a less organized initial cognitive state to an increasingly more organized steady cognitive state based on the emergence of a self-organizing knowledge-based system. Developmentally, then, knowledge and the domains within which it is represented become increasingly specialized. It may be that individual differences in cognitive function are related to the nature and degree of organization of knowledge and that with the accumulation of experience, effective cognitive function becomes increasingly dependent on the systematicity of the self-organized knowledge framework. Development, in other words, is marked by cumulative learning and knowledge acquisition within the constraints imposed by evolving, self-organizing knowledge structures.

Generally, with aging, people retain much of the information that is organized within previously constructed knowledge domains. Thus, adult cognition is characterized by the continued refinement of knowledge within domains, whereas child cognition is typified by the acquisition of more elementary knowledge within an ever-broadening number of domains.

The processes that generate, transform, interpret, and integrate new input and old information change and decline with *age* (see chapter 5). Although we disagree with the componential assumption that all of the system's capacities can be explained by the efficiency of the relevant subcomponents, clearly the status of such processes contribute in part to the general acquisition efficiency of the system. Older adults may exhibit a reduced efficiency in information processing, but such age-related losses generally do not interfere with cognitive effectiveness in real-world contexts. It can be hypothesized that existing knowledge serves a compensatory function in that cognitive processing becomes increasingly selective with advancing age. Acquired knowledge determines in part the selection of items and elements for inclusion within the problem space (cf. Newell, 1980; Newell & Simon, 1972). That is, acquisition processes are in part dependent on what has already been acquired.

Charness (1985) and Salthouse (1984) have shown that expert knowledge can compensate for general losses in processing speed and working memory. Charness (1985) has reported, for example, that older chess experts do not recall as many chess pieces from a briefly presented display of a game board as do younger chess experts. Thus, older experts seem to have lost the ability to access some of the game-like configurations of chess pieces as quickly as they once could. However, older chess experts were found to be just as competent compared to younger chess experts (and even quicker than younger chess experts) in choosing the best chess move from four possible alternatives. More specifically, these older experts were found to search just as many moves ahead as younger novices, and they were found to entertain fewer possible moves than their younger counterparts. Charness (1985) concluded, therefore, that older chess experts compensate for general processing and memory deficits by bringing to bear elaborate retrieval structures that they have acquired over years of practice that enable them to consolidate complex sequences of moves into higher-order chunks. The growth of these elaborate knowledge structures allows older experts to search for appropriate moves just as deeply and quickly (but even more proficiently) as younger experts.

Similarly, Salthouse (1984) discovered that among typists varying in age and skill level there was a significant positive correlation between age and reaction time, tapping speed, and digit symbol substitution. Yet, for these same groups of subjects, typing speed was uncorrelated with age. Through a set of ingenious experiments, Salthouse was able to determine that older expert typists compensate for age-related declines in speed and reaction time by looking farther ahead at printed text and thereby giving themselves more time to plan what their next keystroke should be. Furthermore, Salthouse's findings illustrate the domain-specific nature of the older adults compensatory mechanisms (i.e., these subjects did not employ the "look ahead" strategy on any of the other tasks he administered, such as digit symbol substitution, although the implementation of this strategy would have certainly improved their performance).

Finally, it should be noted that expertise probably cannot compensate for decrements in the fluid abilities and physical prowess that underlie performance in some content areas. For example, performance in such sporting activities as golf, tennis, and basketball declines with age even among individuals who manifest expert performance during young adulthood. But performance within those content areas that allow more time for planning and reflection and demand less snap decisions and physical exertion (e.g., musical composition, visual art) may actually improve because of the cumulative effects of age and experience. In connection with this point, Charness (1985) has commented that

> when people can draw upon domain-specific knowledge and when they have developed appropriate compensatory mechanisms they can treat us to a memorable performance, whether on the keyboard of a typewriter, a piano, or on the podium of an orchestral stage. When the task environment does not afford the same predictability or opportunity to plan ahead, however, as is the case in fast-moving sports environments, degradation in hardware cannot be compensated for by more efficient software. Thus it is not surprising that athletes may no longer be at their primes past the thirties in some sports, though I think it is only fair to note that many of them can also still give memorable performances. (p. 23)

CRITIQUE OF CONTEMPORARY PERSPECTIVES ON ADULT COGNITION

We have considered four basic views of adult cognition: genetic–epistemological, psychometric, information processing, and cognitive science. Each of these perspectives provides valuable information about the nature of adult cognitive development, yet each has major limitations. No single one of these contemporary views offers an integrated, comprehensive account of the course of adult cognitive development. In the following section we will review the basic strengths and limitations of each of these four views.

In earlier chapters (2, 3, and 4) we presented evidence that suggests that adults frequently display postformal *styles* of thinking that predispose them to conceptualize reality, as well as their knowledge of reality, in open-ended, relativistic, and dialectical terms. Theoreticians and researchers working within the context of genetic–epistemological theory have provided developmentalists with important insights about the qualitative differences that exist between adolescent and adult styles of thinking. The genetic–epistemological approach to the study of adult cognition, however, has several limitations. Piagetian theorists, for example, have: (a) regarded postformal thinking as all-pervasive rather than as domain specific, (b) relegated such basic cognitive processes as attention and memory to the status of mere performance variables, (c) disregarded the role played by knowledge in adult cognitive activity, and (d) subordinated the content of cognition, knowledge itself, to the structural characteristics of cognition (i.e., generalizable, logical–mathematical thought structures).

We have also presented evidence in chapter 5 that suggests that general mental abilities (i.e., fluid intelligence) and information-control processes (e.g., attention, memory) show age-related declines. Researchers working within the context of psychometric and information-processing theory have concluded that adults display increasing difficulty in adaptive problem solving because they usually acquire less information and process it in a slower and less efficient manner. Research and theory within these traditions, however, are limited in several ways. Psychometricians and advocates of the information-processing point of view, for example, have: (a) failed to recognize the emergence of qualitatively new styles of thinking during the adult years, (b) displayed an overreliance on the construction of experimental tasks and measuring instruments that lack ecological validity, and (c) failed to acknowledge the growth of domain-specific knowledge systems and the role played by extant knowledge on the acquisition of new information and the solution of ecologically relevant problems.

In the present chapter, the cognitive science position has been presented. This position describes intelligent problem solving as dependent on the application of highly specialized knowledge systems, rather than the result of generalized, fluid mental abilities. As such, adulthood is characterized by the growth of expert knowledge systems within specific domains. Research and theory within the cognitive science framework, however, is limited in a number of ways. For example, cognitive scientists have: (a) failed to recognize the styles of thinking unique to adulthood (i.e., adults have the capacity to understand knowledge as relativistic, dialectic, and self-constructed), (b) ignored the development of what may be termed *metaknowledge* during the adult years (i.e., how adults acquire a perspective of both the growth and meaning of their knowledge systems), (c) focused their attention on the means by which expert knowledge aids in the process of problem solving but neglected the role played by expert knowledge in the process of problem finding, (d) disregarded the manner in which basic psychological processes become committed to the growth of domain-related knowledge, and (e) avoided identifying the processes responsible for the shift from novice to expert.

See Table 6.2 for a summary of the strengths and weaknesses associated with the genetic–epistemological, cognitive science, psychometric, and information-processing perspectives on adult cognition.

THE ENCAPSULATION MODEL

We conceptualize cognition as consisting of three interrelated dimensions: *processing*, *knowing*, and *thinking*. These dimensions, unfortunately, have each been studied in relative isolation from each other by contemporary cognitive psychologists. Processing, for example, has been explored by adherents of the information-processing and psychometric approaches. Psychologists in these traditions have studied the way in which general problem-solving skills operate in controlled testing situations and have examined the speed and efficiency of the processes by which the human cognitive system encodes, stores, and retrieves information. In general, researchers working within the psychometric and information-processing traditions have viewed adulthood as a period of *negative* developmental change. They have concluded that adults become less adept at general problem solving and process reduced amounts of information in progressively less efficient manner.

Developmental changes in thinking have been the focus of theory and research within the genetic–epistemological framework. The predominant emphasis has been on the description of qualitatively unique styles of thinking that emerge during adulthood. Researchers working within the genetic-epistemological tradition have viewed adulthood as a period of *positive* developmental change. Adulthood, from their perspective, is marked by the transition from formal to postformal styles of thinking. These postformal styles of thinking, which predispose adults to view reality in relativistic and dialectical terms, provide the necessary basis for: (a) the solution of both closed (i.e., well-defined) and open (i.e., ill-defined) problems, and (b) the discovery of new perspectives from which new problems may be identified.

The cognitive science framework focuses attention on the dimension of knowing. The predominant concern has been with the nature and representation of expert knowledge systems. Theory and research within the cognitive science orientation, we have noted, is inherently nondevelopmental. In fact, proponents of the cognitive science approach seem to be more interested in the production of computer models of artificial intelligence than with an explication of age-related changes in human expertise. We have argued, however, that research conducted within the context of the cogni-

TABLE 6.2. Perspectives on Adult Cognition

PERSPECTIVE	FOCAL POINT	NATURE OF DEVELOPMENTAL CHANGE	MAJOR SHORTCOMINGS
Genetic-Epistemological	The development of postformal styles of thinking; styles of thinking that predispose the adult to conceptualize reality (as well as his/her knowledge of reality) in open, relativistic, and dialectical terms.	*Positive*: adulthood is characterized by the growth of styles of thinking (i.e., postformal thinking) that are qualitatively different from and more sophisticated than adolescent styles of thought (i.e., formal operational thinking). Adults are capable of dealing with well-defined and ill-defined problems. Adults become capable of problem finding as well as problem solving.	Regards postformal thinking as all-pervasive rather than domain-specific. Disregards the role of knowledge per se in adult cognitive activity (i.e., the content of cognition is subordinated to the general/structural characteristics of cognition). Views basic cognitive processes, such as memory, attention, etc., as mere performance variables rather than as central, important features of the adult cognitive system.
Cognitive Science	The growth, elaboration, and specialization of domain-specific knowledge systems. Specific knowledge systems, rather than generalized mental abilities, provide the basis for intelligent, adaptive problem solving.	*Positive*: adulthood is characterized by the novice/expert shift. Expert knowledge systems are domain specific and contain the declarative and procedural knowledge necessary to solve complex problems. Expert knowledge systems become highly automatized and intuitive and do not draw upon central, uncommitted cognitive processes. Also, expert knowledge within a domain allows for the efficient acquisition of new information within that domain.	No mention of the means by which basic cognitive processes become dedicated to the establishment of domain-specific knowledge. Disregards the manner by which adults use postformal thinking styles in order to develop a perspective on the knowledge they possess and use. Does not specify the processes and/or mechanisms responsible for the novice/expert shift. Does not address the role of expert knowledge in the problem-finding process.

118

Psychometric	Examines changes in the nature of generalized problem-solving skills and cognitive abilities (i.e., fluid intelligence; changes in the amount of specific information (i.e., crystallized intelligence) accumulated over time and experience.	*Multidirectional*: fluid intelligence, the "g" factor, decreases with age. Crystallized intelligence increases (or remains stable) with age. Adults, therefore, are viewed as less capable of solving novel problems and acquiring new information; they must rely on previously acquired information (i.e., crystallized intelligence) to adapt to environmental demands.	No acknowledgement of the growth of qualitatively different styles of thinking and reasoning (e.g., postformal thinking). An overemphasis on the quantitative changes in adult reasoning, and a total disregard for the qualitative changes which characterize adult thinking and reasoning. An over-reliance on tasks and measuring instruments that lack ecological validity (i.e., tasks and instruments which do not tap the expert knowledge systems and real-life experiences of the typical adult). Crystallized forms of intelligence are not viewed as organized in a domain-specific manner.
Information Processing	Examines the basic cognitive processes responsible for the encoding, storage, and retrieval of environmental information. Examines the rate at which information is processed, seeks to determine the amount of basic cognitive resources necessary for successful problem solving.	*Negative*: the information control processes (e.g., attention, memory, etc.) that are responsible for encoding, storing, and retrieving information are assumed to diminish with age. Furthermore, the rate at which information is processed is assumed to diminish with age. Therefore, with increases in age, adults are viewed as capable of processing less information in a slower and less efficient manner.	No acknowledgement of the growth of qualitatively different and more powerful styles of thinking (i.e., postformal styles of thinking) during the adult years. No acknowledgement of the growth of domain-specific knowledge systems and the role played by existing knowledge systems on the acquisition and utilization of new information. An overreliance on artificial, highly structured laboratory tasks which lack ecological validity. No explanation of the processes implicated in problem finding and/or creativity.

tive science approach suggests that adulthood is a period characterized by *positive* developmental change. During the adult years, knowledge is more likely to become expert, intuitive, and domain specific. Armed with a rich network of domain-specific expert systems, adults remain capable of solving real-life, personally meaningful tasks. We have warned, however, that adulthood is more likely to be characterized by the refinement and broadening of extant knowledge systems than by the acquisition of new forms of domain-specific expertise.

Our Encapsulation Model integrates and extends the three dominant strands of adult cognition: processing, knowing, and thinking. This view of adult cognitive development has its roots in all of the previously mentioned approaches: genetic epistemological, psychometric, information processing, and cognitive science. Specifically, we suggest that both speeded mental processes and fluid mental abilities become increasingly dedicated to and encapsulated within particular representations of knowledge (i.e., domains) throughout adult development. As information control processes and fluid mental abilities become encapsulated within the parameters of domain-ordered knowledge systems, extant knowledge becomes more differentiated, automatized, accessible, usable, and "expert" in nature. The loss of fluid abilities and control processes identified in psychometric and information-processing research, therefore, has little functional significance for most adults in most situations. Basic psychological resources become increasingly dedicated to and encapsulated within the form of domain-specific knowledge. Thus, the process of encapsulation represents a necessary and adaptive feature of adult cognitive development. This is *not* to say that we argue that there are no losses in the component processes and fluid abilities that comprise the cognitive system. We realize that there are "real" age-related declines in cognitive "hardware" that occur independent of the process of encapsulation. To argue that there are no age-related losses in the component processes of cognition independent of encapsulation would seem to be untenable. Such an extreme position would lead to the conclusion that:

> If there are no changes in a person's cognitive machinery with age, you would expect monotonic increasing functions in performance with age, if only because people would be expected to increase their knowledge base over a lifetime of working in a professional domain. (Charness, 1985, p. 7)

Thus, we argue that observed declines in basic mental abilities may be viewed in both a positive/adaptive manner as well as a negative/maladaptive manner. These declines are positive/adaptive to the extent that the general pool of mental abilities must necessarily decrease in size as those abilities become encapsulated within domain-specific representations of knowledge. Alternatively, these declines are negative/maladaptive to the extent that they also reflect, to a certain extent, a bio-maturationally determined decrease in the pool of available mental processes and the speed at which these processes operate.

With age and experience there is an accumulation of domain-specific knowledge. However, the acquisition of new knowledge (i.e., information that is *unrelated* to that already encapsulated in specific domains) becomes increasingly difficult with advances in age. Adults do not seem to be ideal learning machines. Childhood and adolescence may represent epochs of the life span that are characterized by the rapid acquisition of new knowledge in a variety of ever-expanding domains, whereas adulthood is a time during which individuals refine and develop a perspective on their knowledge. Furthermore, adults' reduced capacity to acquire new knowledge may be compensated for by the ability to develop expertise within existing knowledge representations and the development of a postformal perspective on that expert knowledge. Once adults conceptualize their domain-specific knowledge in a relativistic, dialectic, and open-ended manner, they become capable of: (a) solving the ill-defined problems characteristic of real life, (b) finding and identifying new problems and new perspectives from which they may be solved (e.g., problem finding), and (c) producing creative and sophisticated works within defined areas of expertise. Furthermore, we propose that the emergence of postformal styles of thinking is also dependent on the encapsulation of basic psychological resources such as fluid abilities and control processes.

Our view concerning the nature of encapsulation addresses an important issue that was raised in chapter 1. Namely, the need to construct a "performance" rather than a "competence" viewpoint of adult cognition. Competence theories tend to fragment cognition into a number of independent components and assign these components differential amounts of importance. Genetic–epistemological theory, for example, stresses the importance of internal cognitive competencies (i.e., thought structures) and downplays the role of cognitive processes such as memory and attention, which only serve to determine if the competence is manifest in an individual's performance. At the other extreme, information-processing theory focuses on the age-related decline in the mental processes that directly control the acquisition (and integration) of new information and the application of old information. But they pay little attention to the importance of the forms of knowing and styles of thinking (i.e., the competencies) that are acquired, accessed, and applied over time.

Alternatively, we suggest that cognition has a functional, adaptive, and goal-directed quality that is most apparent when adults are confronted with the problems of everyday life. Throughout the chapters of this text, we have presented evidence that suggests that adults most successfully negotiate real-life problems via the implementation of domain-specific styles of postformal thinking and domain-specific forms of expert knowledge. Most importantly, we proposed that such basic cognitive processes as attention, memory, and reasoning, through the process of encapsulation, lay the foundation upon which domain-specific thought and knowledge will ultimately emerge. Therefore, our position is that basic cognitive processes manifest themselves in forms of knowing and thinking and that encapsulation is the mechanism by which the processes of cognition become the products of cognition. For example, we consider memory as a cognitive process that is always tied to cognitive *entity* (i.e., knowledge), and we view knowledge as a cognitive *process* (i.e., encapsulation) by which memory takes on a specific form. Our viewpoint most clearly suggests a holistic approach to adult cognition. Cognitive processes, styles of thinking, and forms of knowing all take on equal status and importance in our view. It is impossible, therefore, to separate knowledge and thought from the domains within which they are represented and from the basic psychological abilities that are responsible for their creation.

Given the tenets of the Encapsulation Model, it is futile to continue to examine the cognitive performance of older adults via a singular assessment of their fluid or unencapsulated mental abilities. Assessments of cognitive functioning should emphasize the forms of *knowing* and the style of *thinking* that a person uses to create and resolve the problems of everyday life. The frequently reported age-related declines in fluid abilities may, to a large extent, be due to the practice of assessing mental processes apart from the domains in which they have become encapsulated. We strongly believe that age differences in the component processes of cognition cannot be meaningfully assessed or fully understood without taking into account the individual's level of knowledge and thought within the domain within which these processes are assessed.

Knowledge Domains as Conceptual Entities

The Encapsulation Model proposes that adult thought and knowledge are domain specific. The concept of domain, however, is extremely difficult to define. What, exactly, is meant by domain? Are domains relatively large, like one's language system, or are they relatively small, like the knowledge involved in tying one's shoelaces? Baddeley (1982) defined a domain as an area of memory in which there are extensive associative links and connections. The rich associative links that characterize particular domains of highly skilled individuals may be connected to other domains and divided into subdomains. The structure of a particular domain is not necessarily uniform across individuals who possess knowledge in this area. Information-processing skills are often specific to particular kinds of knowledge. We suggested that knowledge and thought are best represented as the encapsulation of mental processes. That is, fluid abilities become dedicated to the construction and maintenance of individual domains. The efficiency of processing incoming information and the actions and decisions that are made in accordance with this information are influenced by existing domain-ordered knowledge. Domains are refined and enlarged as necessary, and new categories and domains evolve.

Recently, Gardner (1983) proposed that there are at least seven natural categories, modules, or frames of intelligence within which information is encoded and organized. Gardner suggested that each frame roughly corresponds to a predetermined location in the neocortex which is a function of genetic hard-wiring. Gardner fails to explain how these innate modules may be blended into specific knowledge domains, and he neglects to explicate the mechanisms by which general/uncommitted cognitive processes become transformed into specific knowledge domains.

Our position is distinct from Gardner's theory of multiple intelligences, in that individuals are presumed to *construct* unique domains of knowledge. Thus the number and types of domains cannot be specified *a priori*. People build, via the encapsulation process, an organization of cognition based on the use of their mental capacities. From this functional perspective, domains are acquired representations of different areas of cognitive involvement. Although there may be some innateness to the development of some domains of knowledge (e.g., language is a likely candidate), and although the knowledge itself constrains its organization (Keil, 1981, 1986), it is suggested here that the developing organism is relatively self-organizing with regard to the number and nature of domains.

Fodor (1983, 1985) also suggested that human intellect primarily consists of an array of pre-formed cognitive modules. Even though Fodor has also argued for the coexistence of a central, uncommitted cognitive system, he downplayed the importance of this central system and neglected the process by which components of this system become encapsulated in the form of knowledge domains. It is important to distinguish between Fodor's use of the term *modules* and our use of the term *domains*. Modules may be regarded as hard-wired, autonomous, and impenetrable. In fact, genetic factors probably account for individual differences in the size, breadth, and power of specific modules. Modules, for example, provide a musician with the ability to discriminate various pitches, melodies, and rhythms. By themselves, however, modules are not sufficient for the creation and performance of musical composition. Alternatively, domains represent knowledge structures that are self-constructed and cognitively accessible to the individual (i.e., individuals can think about the nature, meaning, and development of their domain-specific knowledge and determine how and when domain-specific knowledge leads to action). A musician's ability to create and perform musical compositions is dependent, to a great extent, on the gradual development of domain-specific musical knowledge, as well as the domain-specific ability to think about this musical knowledge in a sophisticated way. The development (i.e., encapsulation) of this domain-specific musical knowledge is primarily dependent on experience, practice, and motivation. However, we recognize that the power and breadth of some modules may possibly influence the type and nature of the knowledge domains a person chooses to construct. We argue, therefore, that modularity theorists such as Fodor have missed the essence of adult cognition. They have neglected the processes involved in creating, developing, modifying, and enriching knowledge domains in adult development. See Table 6.3 for a summary of the different characteristics of modules and domains. An inspection of Table 6.3 reveals the relationship between hard-wired cognitive modules and self-

TABLE 6.3. A Comparison of Modules and Domains

DIMENSIONS	MODULES	DOMAINS
Basic Characteristics	Hard-wired via genetic mechanisms (i.e., analogous computer hardware)	Self-constructed through experience and encapsulation (i.e., analogous to computer software)
	Static	Dynamic
	Permanent	Evolving
	Impenetrable (i.e., impervious to introspective awareness)	Penetrable (i.e., susceptible to introspective awareness)
	Autonomous and independent	Nonautomomous and potentially interdependent
Basic Functions	To get information into the human cognitive system	To give meaning and expression to the information that has been brought into the human cognitive system
Developmental Trajectory	The number of modules remains fixed over the course of development (note: some decrements may occur due to physical trauma, accident and/or disease)	The number of domains increases over the course of development
	Remain equally important across all developmental eras	Take on increasing importance and significance over the course of development
Relationship Between Modules and Domains	The number and importance of modules is not influenced by number and strength of extant domains	The number and importance of domains is directly influenced by the number of extant modules
Generalized View of the Human Cognitive System*	Bottom–Up	Top–Down

*Cognition involves the interplay of modules and domains, thus cognition is, to a certain extent, both Bottom–Up and Top–Down.

constructed knowledge domains. This table suggests that cognition is necessarily both "bottom–up" (i.e., modular) and "top–down" (i.e., knowledge based and domain-specific). More specifically, our Encapsulation Model proposes that knowledge domains primarily result from the encapsulation of general/central mental abilities. Of course, the types of knowledge domains a person chooses to construct are influenced, in part, by the relative strength and power of the modules that he/she possesses. The Encapsulation Model, therefore, addresses the comments recently expressed by Gardner (1985):

> While current debate pits the generalists against the modularists . . . it may be that both the modularists and the central processors have hit upon important truths. The modularists may be right in thinking that many domains operate by their own laws; the centralists, in believing in another, synthetic intellectual realm where modular processes prove inadequate, and where horizontal processes prove necessary. Debate might then come to center on whether any of the modular realms can be subsumed under some aspect of a central-processing view. (p. 133)

Generality of Domain-Specific Knowledge

When knowledge structures of wide application, such as measurement and assessment systems, number concepts, and arithmetic problem-solving schemas become available to the developing individual, learning and thinking in many areas can be influenced. Thinking about one kind of problem can indeed aid problem solving and the conceptualization of problems in other domains. For example, knowing mathematics can enhance one's approach to musical composition, visual design, the analysis of economic theory, or the interpretation of statistical computations or psychological data. Although some symbol and number manipulation systems may show a high degree of generality across domains, other knowledge systems may be specialized and not applicable and generalizable across situations and tasks. Thus, knowledge-based models of cognition and cognitive development are constrained by the specific properties and characteristics of the knowledge domains through which they are defined (Keil, 1981, 1986).

Unique integrations of knowledge domains emerge through an individual's particular blending of ideas from different areas. Unique blendings of disciplines and ideas are evident in most if not all intelligent adults. Sociocultural factors determine the extent to which a particular blending is considered as creative or exceptional.

The Encapsulation Model: A Summary

The major aspects of the Encapsulation Model are as follows:
1. Processing, knowing, and thinking are the three dimensions of cogni-

tion that must be addressed and unified in any comprehensive theory of adult cognitive development.

2. Fluid mental abilities and information control processes are the foundations upon which the growth of knowledge and thinking are based.

3. The continued encapsulation of fluid mental abilities and information-control processes represents an adaptive and necessary function in the development of expert knowledge and postformal thinking. Fluid abilities and control processes appear to decline with age as they become encapsulated within domain-specific knowledge representations.

4. Adult styles of thinking and forms of knowing are the end result of the encapsulation process.

5. Knowledge and thought in adulthood are primarily domain-specific, not domain general.

6. The reduced capacity to acquire new knowledge in adulthood (due to the "real" bio-maturational declines in the hardware systems that support the human cognitive system) may be compensated for by the specialization and differentiation of extant knowledge and thought.

7. The products of adult cognitive development are the growth of expert knowledge and the emergence of postformal styles of thought. These hallmarks of adult cognition are dependent on the process of encapsulation.

SUMMARY

In this chapter, we proposed the Encapsulation Model of adult cognitive development. This model complements, integrates, and extends the work of those psychologists who have aligned themselves with several contrasting approaches to the study of cognition: the cognitive science approach, which emphasizes the growth of knowing, the genetic–epistemological, which emphasizes the growth of thinking, and the information-processing and psychometric approaches, which focus on the processing of stimulus input.

We have suggested that a unified theory of adult cognition must recognize and integrate the changes in processing, knowing, and thinking that occur throughout development. The continued growth of domain-ordered knowledge is basic to cognitive development throughout the life span and occurs most typically during adulthood. The growth of domain-specific postformal styles of thinking that stress the open, dialectic, and relativistic nature of knowledge also emerge in adulthood. The expansion of thought and the refinement of knowledge result from the encapsulation of central processes and fluid abilities.

Our integrative model is capable of explaining both the results of research studies that have identified the cognitive competencies of older adults as well as those that have revealed patterns of cognitive decline in adulthood.

7

Cognitive Functioning in Everyday Life: Personal Adaptation and Coping

The person will cope if he can, defend if he must and fragment if he is forced, but whichever mode he uses, it is still in the service of his attempt to maintain organization.

N. Haan
Coping and Defending

Human cognition has a functional, instrumental, and goal directed quality that is easier to observe within the context of real-life, personally meaningful problems than in highly structured tasks administered under controlled laboratory conditions (Dittmann-Kohli & Baltes, 1986; Eckensberger & Meacham, 1984; Hacker, 1985; Volpert, 1984). Consistent with this action-theoretic perspective, a comprehensive model of cognition should be able to explicate the means by which adults successfully adapt to the ecologically relevant and personally meaningful problems encountered in everyday life. Previous researchers have generally neglected real-world cognitive functioning. All too often, they have investigated adult cognition through the use of ecologically limited and personally noninvolving laboratory problems.

Several researchers (Kramer, 1983; Sternberg & Berg, 1986) have recently noted the importance of the social context in which intelligence occurs. They suggest that with advancing age, adults are more likely to conceptualize intelligence within the context of personal problem solving. Adults seem to view intelligence, therefore, as the ability to cope and adapt to those salient interpersonal and intrapersonal problems that characterize everyday life. Thus, with increases in age, adults' implicit understanding of intelligence becomes more social in orientation.

In this chapter, we consider how basic cognitive processes become encapsulated in the form of unique styles of thought and specific knowledge systems. The styles of thinking and forms of knowing that result from the encapsulation of basic cognitive processes help adults to adapt to real-life social/personal problems and stressors. More specifically, we argue that adults bring to bear postformal styles of thinking upon their accumulated knowledge in the domain of personal knowledge in order to effortfully evaluate, master, and control the most stressful of real-life problems. Also, we show how life's "daily hassles" are often managed by the mindless and effortless application of well-established heuristics within the domain of personal knowledge. Because knowledge of self is a central component of the personal domain, we also discuss the role of self-representations in the adaptation process. Finally, we argue that mature forms of personal knowledge give rise to a mode of adaptation that may integrate and unify the cognitive and affective realms of experience.

EARLY VIEWS OF ADAPTATION

We begin with a discussion of older and more recent conceptualizations of adaptation. As we shall see, these views have become more cognitive in their orientation. However, even contemporary views have neglected, for the most part, the importance of developmental or age-related changes in the application of cognitive resources to the process of adaptation.

Initial interest in adaptation among psychologists stemmed from clinical investigations of stress and the physiological consequences of the general adaptation syndrome (Selye 1956, 1974). Life events, if stressful enough, were thought to tax our adaptative ability to the point of producing physical health problems and specific diseases and illnesses. Furthermore, the etiology of aging/deterioration as well as a number of specific diseases and life-threatening illnesses was assumed to be related to the number or severity of major life stresses (Braukmann, Filipp, Angleitner, & Olbrich, 1981). Consistent with this viewpoint, Seligman (1975) suggested that individuals experience the greatest degree of stress and have the most difficulty in adapting to events that are neither predictable nor controllable. Under such situations, individuals display the behavioral manifestations of depression, which Seligman termed learned helplessness.

Based on this early conceptualization, investigators began to search for those stressors that were either most likely to produce anxiety, arousal, and psychosomatic problems or were most difficult to predict and control. Holmes and Rahe (1967) developed the Social Readjustment Rating Scale, which ranked the amount of stress associated with specific life events (see Table 7.1). This instrument, widely used in research investigations over the

TABLE 7.1. The Amount of Stress Contained in Several Different Life Events

RANK	LIFE EVENT	STRESS VALUE
1	Death of spouse	100
2	Divorce	73
3	Marital separation	65
4	Jail term	63
5	Death of close family member	63
6	Personal injury or illness	53
7	Marriage	50
8	Fired at work	47
9	Marital reconciliation	45
10	Retirement	45
11	Change in health of family member	44
12	Pregnancy	40
13	Sex difficulties	39
14	Gain of new family member	39
15	Business readjustment	39
16	Change in financial state	38
17	Death of close friend	37
18	Change to different line of work	36
19	Change in number of arguments with spouse	35
20	Mortgage over $10,000	31
21	Foreclosure of mortgage or loan	30
22	Change in responsibilities at work	29
23	Son or daughter leaving home	29
24	Trouble with in-laws	29
25	Outstanding personal achievement	28
26	Wife begins or stops work	26
27	Begin or end school	26
28	Change in living conditions	25
29	Revision of personal habits	24
30	Trouble with boss	23
31	Change in work hours or conditions	20
32	Change in residence	20
33	Change in schools	20
34	Change in recreation	19
35	Change in church activities	19
36	Change in social activities	18
37	Mortgage or loan less than $10,000	17
38	Change in sleeping habits	16
39	Change in number of family get-togethers	15
40	Change in eating habits	15
41	Vacation	13
42	Christmas	12
43	Minor violations of the law	11

Source: From Holmes, T.H., & Rahe, R.H. (1967). The social readjustment rating scale. *Journal of Psychosomatic Research*, 11, 213-218. Copyright 1967 by Pergamon Press. Reprinted with permission.

past decade, ignored the important role of subjectivity and failed to recognize individual differences in the cognitive appraisal of similar life experiences. Lazarus (1981) noted these problems and suggested the futility of defining in advance the degree of stress within any life event.

CURRENT VIEWS OF ADAPTATION:
THE LAZARUS POSITION

Lazarus and his colleagues (Folkman & Lazarus, 1980; Lazarus, 1966, 1981; Lazarus & DeLongis, 1983; Lazarus & Folkman, 1984, Lazarus & Launier, 1978) have examined the way in which the individual subjectively represents and perceives potentially stressful events. Subjective cognitive appraisals are judgments of threats, challenges, or neutrality to one's personal sense of well-being (Whitbourne, 1985). Once appraisals have been made, they provide an inextricable link between the person and the environment. Cognitive appraisal, which plays the critical role in understanding how individuals perceive and manage stressful life events, consists of two components: primary and secondary appraisal.

Primary Appraisal

The initial process of cognitive evaluation, primary appraisal, allows individuals to determine the potential threat of an event. Thus, events are stressful only if they are subjectively interpreted as such. Subjective cognitive constructions are said to be primary because they precede any emotional or affective reaction to an event. The process of primary appraisal and the cognitive interpretation of the subjective meaning of the event determine the emotional reaction of the individual to the event. Those events that are deemed stressful produce emotional reactions of tension, anxiety, and dread, whereas those events that are seen as opportunities for challenge and growth lead to reactions of hope, excitement, and joy (Lazarus & Folkman, 1984; Lazarus, Kanner, & Folkman, 1980).

Secondary Appraisal

Following the initial cognitive assessment and subsequent emotional reaction to the primary appraisal process, secondary appraisal begins. Secondary appraisal also is cognitive in character and involves the exhaustive search for potential resources (within the individual *and* within the larger environment) to assist with coping. Secondary cognitive appraisal also entails an understanding of the "costs" of coping—what new problems may emerge if a particular course of action is followed (Whitbourne, 1985). Thus, individuals determine both their own coping resources and the range of potential environmental resources. Potential resources that may help with a particular stressful event are identified and categorized relative to those that are available but not relevant to the particular situation. Consider, for example, clergy, who are among the first persons selected in helping to cope with the death of a family member, yet who are rarely identified or chosen in helping to cope with on-the-job stress.

The secondary appraisal process seems descriptively isomorphic with the properties of formal operational styles of thinking. Individuals generate as many solutions to their problems as possible (both personal and environmental) and then logically evaluate which, in their judgment, will prove most successful in promoting effective coping.

The process of secondary appraisal includes both cognitive appraisal and cognitive decision making. However, secondary appraisal and the ultimate selection of an effective coping strategy is bound by the manner in which the individual has previously defined the nature of the threat in the initial primary appraisal process. That is, from the primary appraisal process and the subjective definition of threat or stress, persons evaluate the nature of the event and determine what form of coping needs to be done. It is clear from Lazarus' position that coping and adaptation is a lengthy process with recursive feedback at many levels.

Reappraisal

Lazarus and DeLongis (1983) have recently highlighted the notion that coping is indeed an ongoing process rather than a single activity or event. They argued that individuals continually reevaluate the methods and resources they have chosen to help them adapt to the subjectively defined stressors that threaten their sense of well-being. When changes occur in how the individual structures the problem in the environment, and when the problem changes the individual, both the situation and the person's coping mechanisms are reassessed and altered.

Styles of Coping:
Problem-Focused and Emotion-Focused

Folkman and Lazarus (1980) have suggested two general ways in which individuals attempt to adapt: problem-focused coping and emotion-focused coping. Problem-focused coping strategies refer to attempts by individuals to obtain additional information for more effective cognitive problem solving or to actively change the stressful situation or event. Emotion-focused coping is a strategy that emphasizes behavioral and cognitive techniques that have as their goal the management of emotional tension produced by the stressful life situation or event (Braukmann et al., 1981). This strategy does not necessarily remove the perceived stress but rather helps in managing or reducing the emotional distress (Folkman & Lazarus, 1980).

According to Lazarus (Folkman & Lazarus, 1980; Lazarus & Folkman, 1984), these two alternatives (problem-focused versus emotion-focused coping) are functions of the subjective appraisal process. Lazarus suggests that choices between these alternative strategies are made in a careful and systematic fashion. The process of selection is said to be deliberate, logical, and rational not only for deciding between emotion-focused and problem-focused alternatives, but also for choosing resources within these categories. Support for Lazarus' position comes from several sources. When situations are deemed to be beyond one's control, for example, individuals employ emotion-focused coping behaviors. Rather than try to change themselves or the situation, individuals try to change the way they feel about the situation (Folkman & Lazarus, 1980; Lazarus, 1980; Pearlin & Schooler, 1978). Alternatively, Lazarus and Folkman (1980) have reported that more problem-focused coping was evident among adults who perceived that situations could indeed be changed.

It should be emphasized that Lazarus and his associates (Folkman & Lazarus, 1980) did *not* regard problem-focused and emotion-focused coping as *stable* styles or traits that define individual differences in the management of stress. Instead, Lazarus regarded problem-focused and emotion-focused coping as qualitatively different strategies that adults select to manage stress depending on their subjective appraisal of the source of the stress, the intensity of the stress, and the physical, personal, and social resources they have at their disposal. Lazarus suggests, therefore, that: (a) the same individual may employ an emotion-focused strategy to control certain stressors and a problem-focused strategy to master other kinds of stressful events; and (b) problem-focused coping strategies may not be regarded as more effective than emotion-focused coping strategies or vice versa.

Problems with the Lazarus Model

We agree that adaptation involves cognitive activity that is designed to bring about successful mastery and control over stressful life events. On the other hand, we feel there are problems with Lazarus' viewpoint. First, Lazarus overemphasizes the role of cognition to the detriment of affect and emphasizes the primacy of the former over the latter. Second, we disagree with Lazarus' contention that problem-focused and emotion-focused coping strategies are equally effective forms of adaptation. Third, his view of appraisal is nondevelopmental and ignores the role of domain-specific knowledge and domain-specific thought in helping adults to cope and adapt. In the rest of this chapter we articulate our view of adaptation by addressing these problems.

ADAPTATION, COGNITION, AND EMOTION

Controversy over the role of emotion in coping has produced several contrasting positions. The first, advocated by Lazarus and his colleagues, fits the cognitive appraisal model. Until a problem or stressor is perceived and validated cognitively, there is no emotional reaction or response. The primacy of cognition over affective responding is clear.

There is strong counterargument, however, from a position developed by Zajonc (1980), who suggested that affective evaluations precede cognitively based evaluations. The primacy of affect over cognition is based on the supposition that affect is a more basic, rapid, and permanent process (Zajonc, 1980). Considerable evidence is identified by Zajonc to support this hypothesis. For example, first impressions are found to be primarily affective in character and difficult to alter despite the subsequent presentation of cognitively relevant information. Affective processing, it is speculated, involves mainly the right hemisphere, results in rapid judgments without the need for autonomic feedback, and generally follows a neurophysiological mechanism of excitation like that involved in activation (Zajonc, 1980). Although not "pure" or distinct, the excitation connected with affective processing appears to be largely cholinergic (Callaway, 1981) and is associated with a major brain site of norepinephrine, the *locus coeruleus* (Zajonc, 1980). Zajonc's model offers a bottom-up approach to processing major life events and stressors. Events are received by our senses and are then moved directly to affective levels of processing. Only after affective processing do we enter into cognitive modes of analysis. Life events and stresses thus would be seen as initially processed in an affective context.

Two other alternatives, which need to be explored, question the basic validity of the primacy issue. First, just as theorists suggest that there are parallel and partially separable processing and representational systems of cognition, there may be analogous processing of life stressors. Adults may process stressful life events in such a way as to simultaneously permit *both* cognitive and affective processing. Paivio's dual coding hypothesis (Paivio & Csapo, 1973), for instance, suggests the existence of discriminably different systems for the processing of pictures versus words. If stressful life events can also be processed simultaneously from both an emotional and a cognitive framework, then the issue of primacy becomes moot.

Second, Basseches' (1980, 1984a, 1984b) model of dialectic thinking argues for the interdependence and nonseparability of cognition and affect. In Basseches' terminology, the parts and the whole of a system have a *constitutive* relationship with one another. Thus, it is the nature of the relationship that gives meaning to the elements of the relationship. It is the dynamic, evolving relationship between the parts and the whole that makes the parts and the whole what they are, rather than the fixed and stable characteristics of the parts and the whole that makes the relationship what it is.

Following Basseches, we suggest that affect and cognition may have a constitutive relationship with regard to knowledge structures within the domain of personal knowledge (Roodin, Rybash, & Hoyer, 1984; Rybash & Roodin, 1986; Rybash, Roodin, & Hoyer, 1986). It may be the schematic representations within the domain of personal knowledge that give rise to both the thoughts (cognition) and feelings (affect) that accompany critical life events and experiences. If thoughts and feelings are constituted by their relationship to personal knowledge schemata, it becomes meaningless to view thoughts and feelings as existing independent of one another and trivial to raise the question of whether thoughts have primacy over emotions or vice versa. This position is somewhat similar to the one advocated by Kegan, Noam, and Rogers (1982). They argued that the question, "What is the relationship between cognition and affect?" should be recast in the form: "What relationship *has* both affect and cognition?" (p. 105).

ADAPTATION, MASTERY, AND COGNITIVE RESTRUCTURING

Bandura (1982) and his colleagues (Bandura, Adams, Hardy, & Howell, 1982) have emphasized the important link between adaptation and notions of personal efficacy. Individuals with higher levels of self-efficacy will more easily establish positive coping behaviors, develop the sense of self as a coping resource, and benefit from sources of stress in everyday life. Having a component of self-efficacy in one's judgment and cognitive appraisal leads individuals to plan, to control, and to "take charge" of their own lives (Bandura, 1982; Krantz, 1983; Lachman, 1986; Lefebvre-Pinard, 1984). The internal reorganization or cognitive transformation characteristic of problem-focused coping is itself a form of *direct* action and control. Moreover, it is in adulthood that one becomes more capable of planning, controlling, taking charge, and maintaining a degree of mastery in dealing with both the cognitive and emotional components of coping. This cognitive capability has been explored most often within the context of metacognition (Flavell, 1981). Recently, metacognition has been linked with the concept of self-control (Lefebvre-Pinard, 1984), so that mature coping integrates both metacognitive knowledge with the self-selection of appropriate strategic problem-solving behaviors. Even Piaget and Vygotsky (see Lefebvre-Pinard, 1984) became enamored with a description of cognitive development that included the growth in conscious awareness of one's own problem-solving abilities.

Recent work (Taylor, 1983; Wood, Taylor, & Lichtman, 1985) on adaptation to life-threatening illness (i.e., breast cancer) has revealed the complex interrelationship between adaptation, mastery, and cognitive restructuring. Clearly, the diagnosis of cancer poses a major threat to the person—a threat in which mastery, control, self-esteem, and personal efficacy are difficult to retain. This personal tragedy promotes the need for major cognitive restructuring of both the event and one's own perception of control. Restructuring is designed to enhance the person's well-being rather than undermine it, while at the same time allowing the person to maintain a veridical understanding of the problem to be faced. For example, one theme identified by participants in Taylor's research was the need to understand why the cancer occurred and the creation of special, personal techniques to manage the disease. Among the 78 women interviewed, 95% attempted to search for a causal explanation for their cancer. Also, these women were found to actively search for meaning in their experience, to derive new-found elements of self-knowledge ("I was very happy to find out that I am a very strong person"), and to reevaluate life priorities ("What you do is put things into perspective").

A second theme identifiable in adapting to the cancer was attempting to gain a sense of control or *mastery* over it. The threatening event needed to be managed so that women could feel that it would never occur again. Although it may seem a somewhat "magical" belief, nearly 67% of the women felt that they had a considerable degree of control over the course or reoccurrence of cancer. In fact, those with this magical belief made overall more positive adjustments. A common belief was that of maintaining a positive mental attitude. ("I believe that if you're a positive person, your attitude has a lot to do with it. I definitely feel I will never get it again.") Women not only felt in control of the cancer mentally and attitudinally, but nearly half actually changed behaviors that they hypothesized would reduce the probability of the cancer reoccurring. For example, a common reaction was that of changing diet or reducing unnecessary forms of medications.

The final theme identified by Taylor and her colleagues (Taylor, 1983; Wood, Taylor, & Lichtman, 1985) was the attempt to regain feelings of self-esteem. A common method was to choose a reference group against which to compare oneself, which allowed for a favorable comparison. Thus, older women felt better off than younger women, married women felt sorry for unmarried women, and those who were in very difficult straits consoled themselves by acknowledging that they were still alive. The cognitive comparison process allows for a degree of self-enhancement: Relative to others, things are not that bad. Women chose relevant dimensions on which to make these comparisons. This process of constructive social comparisons allowed the women to identify those who were worse off and yet still doing well. Moreover, such reference groups seemed to motivate or inspire women to cope, because their own condition was not as bad.

The most successful of Taylor's subjects "took charge" of their lives, actively searched for meaning, and thus preserved their sense of personal well-being. Their sense of mastery and cognitive control is similar to the concept of problem-focused coping. Haan (1962, 1977) and Vaillant (1971, 1977) have referred to this successful form of adaptation as having its basis in mature, reality-oriented mechanisms that lead to direct, positive action. At the same time, however, Taylor's data give new meaning to the phrase reality oriented. The successful copers in Taylor's research were aware of the severity of their illness, yet cognitively enhanced their evaluation of themselves and optimized their chances of survival.

Thus, the sense of control, competence, and mastery sometimes proceeds through cognitive restructuring, which is functionally adaptive. In order to take charge of their lives, adults cognitively reconstruct the meaning, significance, and overall impact of significant life events and personal problems. Greenwald (1980) suggests that three forms of cognitive restructuring help to preserve our sense of mastery and our feelings of self-efficacy: egocentrism, beneffectance, and cognitive conservativism. The first process ensures a positive view of self and distorts our personal contributions, perception of direct control, and the locus of responsibility for outcomes. The second process considers success to be the result of personal effort and shifts responsibility to external causes in cases of failure. The third process provides protection against threatening new information. Because personal knowledge is largely positive in tone, adults discount the source and the credibility of even minimally negative information.

This viewpoint suggests that adults are not the logical, efficient, and rational problem solvers suggested by many cognitive psychologists. Kahneman and Tversky (1984) and Tversky and Kahneman (1971, 1974, 1981, 1983), for example, have shown just how much adult thinking is influenced by illusion, distortion, and subjective perception. And Nisbett and Ross (1980) suggest that personal knowledge systems permit the differential evaluation of negative outcomes of self and others. Negative outcomes in others are understood as the result of stable personal characteristics such as effort or ability, whereas our own failures are more often attributed to environmental factors beyond our control. Thus, the tendency to identify causal explanations is as much a human frailty as it is a source of successful adaptation.

Thus far, we have presented theoretical arguments and empirical data that suggest that individuals successfully adapt to stressful life events by cognitively restructuring and taking charge of these situations. Despite previous emphasis on the cognitive underpinnings of adaptation, however, there has been no investigation of the relationship between successful adaptation and unique styles of adult thinking and unique forms of domain-specific knowledge.

ADAPTATION, POSTFORMAL THINKING, AND PERSONAL KNOWLEDGE

In a recent study, Kaus, Lenhart, Roodin, and Lonky (1982) investigated the relationship between adaptation and two forms of moral reasoning: conventional and postconventional (Gibbs, 1977, 1979; Kohlberg, 1973, 1976). They discovered that adults who were postconventional moral reasoners (i.e., self-reflective, meta-ethically aware) tended to employ more problem-solving resources in coping with significant personal loss (e.g., death of a parent, divorce) than those who displayed conventional moral reasoning (i.e., maintaining social norms and interpersonal role expectations). Further support for the relationship between adaptation and moral reasoning was found in a series of studies by Lonky, Kaus, and Roodin (1984). These researchers found that the single best predictor of the use of cognitively oriented (i.e., problem-focused) coping strategies was the presence of post-conventional moral reasoning. More specifically, adult women who had coped with a significant personal loss in an affirmative rather than an abortive fashion (cf. Gibbs, 1979) were predominantly postconventional in their moral reasoning. These affirmative styles of problem-focused coping seemed to represent a "constructive" balance between the cognitive *and* affective dimensions of the loss experience (Roodin, Rybash, & Hoyer, 1984). Furthermore, those adults who evidenced postconventional moral reasoning and a cognitively oriented coping strategy displayed a reality-oriented mode of adaptation. This mode of adaptation allowed them to objectively evaluate the complete impact of the loss and cognitively transform the negative loss event into a growth-inducing experience. Those adults who evidenced conventional moral reasoning skills and a reliance on emotion-focused adaptation techniques, however, seemed to distort cognitively the loss experience in a functionally nonadaptive manner and adopt a passive, nonaction-oriented mode of adaptation. These subjects were characterized by their inability to control, master, and profit from the loss experience.

It should be noted that the affirmative and abortive copers identified by Kaus et al. (1982) and Lonky et al. (1984) displayed styles of adaptation that may be analogous to Haan's constructs of *coping* and *defending* (Haan, 1962, 1977). Haan regarded coping as a reality-oriented process that is goal oriented, objective, and flexible, operating as an open system that enhances intra- and intersubjective reality and communication. Defending, on the other hand, was conceptualized as a reality-distorting process that has its roots in denial, repression and projection; it operates as a semiopen system that impairs intra- and intersubjective reality and communication.

Recent research (Cornelius, Caspi, & Hannum, 1983) has identified a link between modes of adaptation and cognitive ability. Having administered Haan's (1977) trait scales of coping and defending to 116 adults, Cornelius et al. found that coping was positively correlated with both fluid and crystallized intelligence. Defending, however, was negatively related to both of these forms of intelligence. Despite these relationships, the specific way in which fluid and crystallized abilities promote effective adaptation or encourage defending is unclear. For example, why should the psychometrically defined components of fluid and crystallized intelligence (e.g., memory span, relational thinking; vocabulary, general information) be related to either coping or defending?

There is another perspective from which to view the relationship between adaptation and cognition. Consider, for example, the observed relationship between reality-orienting, functionally adaptive modes of coping and post-conventional moral reasoning, vis-à-vis reality-distorting, functionally nonadaptive modes of coping and conventional moral reasoning. In a series of recent papers (Roodin, Rybash, & Hoyer, 1984, 1985; Rybash & Roodin, 1986; Rybash, Roodin, & Hoyer, 1986) we have argued that postconventional moral reasoning is characterized by the presence of postformal thinking within the domain of personal knowledge. Personal knowledge (see Gardner, 1983) has been conceptualized as: (a) the coordination of interpersonal understanding (knowledge of *self*) and intrapersonal understanding (knowledge of *others*), and (b) having its roots in the interactions that take place between the self and other selves, rather than between the self and physical objects.

To Gardner's (1983) generalized description of personal knowledge, we would add that personal knowledge has a developmental history that is characterized by the gradual evolution of the abilities to: (a) differentiate the concerns, motivations, and emotions of self from other, (b) coordinate one's understanding of the differential concerns, motivations, and emotions that characterize both self and other, (c) conceive of both self and other as dynamic, self-reflective systems that change and evolve other time, (d) realize that the psychological existence of self is tied to other just as the existence of other is tied to self, and (e) envision both self and other as components of a social/cultural system that has the capacity to change both self and other as well as the tendency to be changed by both self and other.

Developmental psychologists have focused considerable attention on the acquisition and representation of personal knowledge (Broughton, 1978; Edelstein & Noam, 1982; Kegan, 1982; Selman, 1980). Several writers have argued, for example, that mature representations of self are characterized by a postformal rather than a formal style of thought. Kegan suggested that "'full formal operations' may not be the fullest picture of maturity in the domain of the person" (1982, p. 228). He envisioned formal operations as giving rise to purely dualistic, closed, and polarized representations of self and other. Postformal thought, he noted, allows adults to see themselves as constituted by their relationships to others—there is no closed boundary between self and other; self and other are open, mutually interdependent systems that evolve and change over time. Broughton (1978) has also seen the importance of maintaining a dynamic, materialist dialectic position on mature self-representations. He noted that it is only through direct activity and experience that we evolve a "transpersonal" understanding of self.

An individual who displays formalized thinking strategies within the domain of personal knowledge is likely to view a problem-in-living as a closed system problem that is composed of a finite number of separable variables. The individual's subjective definition of the problem may become polarized into independent cognitive and affective dimensions. Affect is viewed as secondary to cognition and only clouds or impairs cognition. Thus, the formal reasoner is predisposed to engage in a logical, rational search for the one philosophically abstract and absolutistically true principle or problem-solving strategy that will help in dealing with a stressful life event. The continued search for the one correct, logical solution may lead the formal reasoner to feel overwhelmed by the contradictory thoughts and feelings that frame the problem. It becomes easier and more efficient for the formal thinker to distort reality than to attempt to resolve a seemingly unresolvable problem. Thus, formal thinking may give rise to defensive modes of adaptation marked by feelings of passivity and instances of maladaptive distortion.

Alternatively, those adults who display postformal thinking within the domain of personal knowledge adopt a radically different perspective. For example, a postformal thinker views a problem-in-living as an "open-system" problem. A problem is regarded as open, in that it is viewed as consisting of a set of potentially infinite, dynamic, and interdependent variables. Similarly, one's subjective experience of the problem is unified in the sense that it cannot be separated into independent cognitive and affective components. Because the postformal thinker envisions an open problem as having no "single correct solution," he/she searches for a solution that is relativistically true. Relativistic solutions are derived from the current context in which the problem is perceived.

Consistent with this argument, previous investigators (Gilligan & Murphy, 1979; Murphy & Gilligan, 1980; Perry, 1970) have found that conventional moral reasoners evidenced a formalized understanding of self, others, and problems-in-living, whereas postconventional moral reasoners brought to bear a form of thought that reunited self with other and cognition with affect in the resolution of concrete, personally meaningful problems. Broughton (1978) has also commented that with growth in the domain of personal knowledge, adults integrate the purely theoretical knowledge derived from formal levels of thinking with the constraints of practical or concrete reality. Adult personal knowledge is marked, therefore, by a passage from epistemology to being and from ideas to life (Longergan, 1967).

Postformal thought within the domain of personal knowledge allows adults to be reality oriented because it permits them to understand the self-constructed nature of personal knowledge and social reality. Furthermore, postformal reasoning within the domain of personal knowledge gives rise to a relativistic brand of knowledge, a conceptualization of self and other as open, interdependent, and dynamic systems and the capacity to synthesize contradictory feelings and thoughts in a meaningful way. Therefore, postformal thinkers are not so readily overwhelmed by the demands of everyday life, feel a strong sense of mastery and personal control, and unify the thoughts and feelings that define their experience.

The above-mentioned theme has also been expressed by Dittmann-Kohli and Baltes (1986). They argued that the adult who possesses wisdom within the personal domain and is capable of dealing with moral/interpersonal problems in an affirmative, reality-oriented manner, displays several characteristics of postformal thought (e.g., relativism in judgment, acceptance of contradiction, conception of problems as open). Refer to Table 7.2 for a summary of the comparisons of formal and postformal styles of resolving personal problems. These two different styles are compared in four different dimensions: representation of self and other, personal problems concepts, the relationship between cognition and affect, and mode of adaptation.

In adult development within the domain of personal knowledge, there are not only changes in the style of thinking (formal to postformal), but also accumulated increases in personal knowledge. Atchley (1983), for example, suggested that most adults believe that they know more about themselves than others do. They typically maintain positively biased beliefs and perceptions of self and successfully dismiss most contradictory information from others. These biases are effective, efficient, and adaptive. For example, despite the prevalence of negative stereotypes of the elderly (ageism), research has revealed that self-esteem is generally positive and becomes increasingly so with advances in chronological age (Atchley, 1983). Lowenthal (1977) additionally suggested that older adults carry forward a view of personal knowledge and self-efficacy that is largely derived from success experiences in middle age. The past seems to become a greater resource for interpreting the present with increased age (Boden & Bielby, 1983). Lachman (1986), Bandura (1977), and Kuypers and Bengston (1973) suggest the importance of maintaining a sense of personal efficacy throughout adult development despite the apparent reality of reduced control in certain domains. Lachman (1986) reported declines in personal efficacy, beginning in early

TABLE 7.2. Resolving Personal Problems: Two Different Styles

RELEVANT DIMENSIONS	FORMAL STYLE	POSTFORMAL STYLE
Representation of self and other	Dualistic, independent static entities.	Integrated, interdependent, dynamic systems.
Concepts of personal problems	Closed problems resolved only through logical analysis.	Open problems resolved through an understanding of the limits of logical analysis.
Relationship between cognition and affect	Personal reasoning is viewed as "rational thinking" that may be clouded and/or impaired by emotion. Cognition takes precedence over emotion.	Personal reasoning represents the recognition and integration of cognition and emotion. Neither cognition nor emotion takes precedence over the other.
Mode of adaptation	Reality-distortive, passive (defensive).	Reality-accepting, active-mastery (coping).

middle age, leveling off in the forties and fifties, and increasing in later life (e.g., the sixties). Higher personal efficacy in later life may be the result of a lowering of aspirations with age and fewer role responsibilities (Veroff, Douvan, & Kulka, 1981). Lachman (1986) suggested that increases in efficacy in later life are related to the ease of managing fewer life goals and tasks. This reflects the accumulated experience and sense of inner mastery characteristic of the elderly, who are aware of both their capabilities and limitations.

Dittmann-Kohli and Baltes (1986) also suggest that with increasing age there is a corresponding growth in personal knowledge. They have argued that expert knowledge within the personal domain lays the foundation for wisdom. Specifically, they commented that

> wisdom is an ability and process involving a highly developed form of abstract as well as specific factual and procedural knowledge. This definition is similar to the treatment of expertise in other areas such as physics, the arts, or chess (Chi et al., 1983) as it involves long-time experience and a particular quality of the knowledge system that enables superior problem definition and solution and optimal judgment. Thus the expertise of wisdom is not limited to proficiency in the use of formal logic. (p. 35)

Stylistic changes in thinking about personal knowledge and the development of expertise within the domain of personal knowledge can only occur through the encapsulation process. Through the encapsulation process, cognitive resources such as attention, memory, and perceptual processes are employed to construct the domain of personal knowledge. The increasing tendency to encapsulate cognitive processes within the domain of personal knowledge arises because the unique experiences that constitute adult life (cf. Baltes, Reese, & Lipsitt, 1980) increasingly demand coping and adaptation. Thus, the interwoven nature of processing, thinking, and knowing within the personal domain via the encapsulation process is central to understanding adult cognition.

We have presented a perspective on adult adaptation to critical life events. However, it should be emphasized that knowledge within the personal domain also enables us to cope with those minor problems or daily hassles that characterize everyday life. Individuals appear to construct a set of scripts and schemata (Schank & Abelson, 1977) that are designed to help them to cope with those "irritating, frustrating, distressing demands and troubled relationships that plague us day in and day out" (Lazarus & DeLongis, 1983, p. 247). These schemata, once constructed, allow for somewhat mindless (Langer, 1978) coping—free from the many descriptions of an intense, demanding, and effortful enterprise. Automatized (Shiffrin & Schneider, 1977) aspects of coping allow for "top–down" processing economy with mundane stressors such as a rush-hour traffic jam and free the individual from having to spend time, effort, or cognitive resources on these problems.

In many instances, individuals apply basic scripts, schemata, and heuristics to new situations rather than developing new ones. Mischel (1981) has applied the term *cognitive economics* to this attempt to minimize the need for change. In order to permit efficiency of operation, personal knowledge schemas and heuristics are preserved if at all possible. They provide the individual with a sense of mastery and control. Thus, one of the hallmarks of adult cognitive functioning is to come to terms as efficiently and effectively as possible with environmental demands.

The problem with an overreliance on automatized styles of adaptation, however, is that metacognitive processes (Brown, 1978; Flavell, 1979), potentially accessible and functional for most adults, may be largely ignored. This may lead to inefficient and erroneous adaptation as well as reduced personal efficacy (cf. Langer & Imber, 1980; Lefebvre-Pinard, 1983). Individuals, for example, may so automatize their coping strategies that they fail to engage in the minimal levels of conscious activity necessary for personal survival (Langer, 1981, Langer & Rodin, 1976). In contrast, Lefebvre-Pinard (1983) has argued that individuals who implement coping strategies through effortful, conscious activity have more effective social adaptations and a greater sense of subjective well-being. Thus, successful adaptation and mastery are linked to behaviors that are grounded in effortful, conscious activity.

ADAPTATION, COMMITMENT, AND THE SELF

The preservation and enhancement of personal knowledge, especially self-representations, pervade nearly all cognitive activity in adulthood (Roodin & Rybash, 1985). Individuals maintain a commitment to their self-representations in the face of both major and minor life stresses that demand either effortful or automatic adaptation. This commitment ensures the maintenance of a coherent, consistent internal organization and provides a degree of stability, continuity, and identity across developmental periods.

Although adults at times appear to "disengage" from some formal roles and social demands, individuals maintain a consistent representation of self. It is indeed rare that events are so stressful and affectively charged that they challenge us to forego our commitment to self.

The concept of commitment may be framed, we suggest, in terms of motivation and ideology. In Dember's classic paper, "Motivation and the Cognitive Revolution," it is clear that behavior derived from an ideology is intense, emotionally charged, dramatic, and able to exist despite the presence of competing motives and even negative social sanctions (Dember, 1981). A similar type of ideological self-commitment is the apparent basis of adult coping—a strong motivation to preserve and enhance what we have come to recognize and value in ourselves. In the face of numerous threats, life stresses, and challenges, it appears that we strive to maintain consistency in our own "personal agendas" and subjectively defined sense of self. Self-system and ideology are synonomous. We may find excess in both, sometimes leading to maladaptive behavior, distortion of reality, and great personal risk to the individual. Dember (1981) notes Koestler's comment that "man's tragedy is not an excess of aggression, but an excess of devotion" (p. 2). Devotion or commitment to self is a necessary facet of adult cognition.

Action theory (Chapman, 1984; Eckensberger & Meacham, 1984) provides a means for integrating the relationship between adaptation, self, and commitment. This theory, emerging in European psychology, stresses the intentional, purposeful, goal-directed, conscious, and voluntary nature of human beings and human behavior. Individuals' *intentional* actions are viewed as: future oriented, freely chosen, and potentially guided by conscious control. Furthermore, action theorists assume that knowledge can only acquire meaning and value if it is realized in direct relationship with the material world; that is, in the context of the person's actions (Eckensberger & Meacham, 1984; Kossakowski & Otto, 1977; Mehan, 1981). The person, his/her knowledge, and the material environment are seen as linked through the individual's activity. If one adopts an action theory point of view:

> it follows that . . . intelligence has an instrumental character and that its development occurs in the context of human activity (Boesch, 1976; Kossakowski & Otto, 1977). Goals, plans, processes of regulation, outcomes, and transition to subsequent actions are the central factors determining cognitive activity and problem-solving. In action theory, problem-solving and thought processes are inherently interwoven with the task of human activity in everyday life, its planning, execution, and evaluation. Thus, for intelligence to be understood it is imperative to analyze its structure and function in the context of real-life activities and the respective goal-structures and ecologies of individuals. (Dittmann-Kohli & Baltes, 1986, p. 20)

The relationship between knowledge, cognition, and behavior has also been described by Lefebvre-Pinard (1983) within an action-theoretic context:

> If cognition indeed has some relevance for an individual's life one should assume that there is some relationship between the way the individual thinks about his physical and social environment and the way he acts in it. . . . Traditional models of cognition have in fact aimed at explanations of how knowledge develops and how it is organized rather than how this knowledge is used to regulate behavior in everyday life. (p. 25)

Adaptation, within the context of action theory, can be viewed as an activity that has as its goal the preservation and enhancement of self-knowledge and self-representation. Thus, the "self" may be viewed as a representation that is created, preserved, and enhanced through activity. This is consistent with Kegan's (1982) viewpoint, which suggests that the self is both an activity and a fixed entity: "We are not the self who hangs in the balance at this moment in our evolution. We are the activity of this evolution. We compose our stages and we experience this composing" (1982, p. 169). Thus, the self should not be regarded as the primary initiator of all activity, nor as an overarching, integrative entity (cf. Edelstein & Noam, 1982, Loevinger, 1976).

SUMMARY

In this chapter we have described how adults use postformal styles of thinking and expert knowledge within the domain of personal knowledge to help them master and adapt to real-life, social/personal tasks and problems. Thus, by examining how adults cope with real-life problems we paint a different portrait of adult cognition than the irreversible decrement model developed from affectively neutral and ecologically irrelevant laboratory studies of componential processes. Our integrated perspective suggests that human cognition is a functional, instrumental, and goal-oriented activity that ably assists adults to adapt effectively and efficiently to real-life social/personal problems. We discussed the role played by the self in the adaptation process. Furthermore, we suggested that the self operates as both entity and process.

The integration of cognition and affect, the recognition that social/personal problems are open not closed, and the interdependent nature of self and other are all seen as critical to successful adaptation in adulthood. Recognition of this interdependent reality is best accomplished by those adults who possess postformal styles of thinking and expert knowledge structures within the personal domain.

8

Synthesis: Processing, Knowing, and Thinking

There is no absolute knowledge. And those who claim it, whether they are scientists or dogmatists, open the door to tragedy. All information is imperfect, we have to treat it with humility. That is the human condition . . . .

J. Bronowski
The Ascent of Man

We divide this concluding chapter into four sections. In the first section, we offer brief summaries of the modes of processing, forms of knowing, and styles of thinking that are unique to adult cognition and have been discussed in greater detail in previous chapters. In the second section, we review the basic features of our *Encapsulation Model*, a model that integrates and extends the extant theory and research regarding adult cognition, and we point out the uniqueness and comprehensiveness of this model. In the third section, we discuss the impact of the Encapsulation Model on the direction of future research within the area of adult cognition. In the fourth section, we provide a critique of the Encapsulation Model.

PROCESSING

We recognize the reality of age-related declines in the componential processes of cognition that have been so carefully documented by adherents of the information-processing and psychometric paradigms. With increasing age, adults seem to process less information in a progressively slower, less efficient manner. This general conclusion seems most valid, however, when information-processing abilities are studied outside of the domains within which adults have developed cognitive expertise.

We have shown that research on attentional processes may be viewed from two rather different perspectives. On the one hand, age-related deficits in attentional performance are most evident under capacity-limited conditions. However, practice, experience, or familiarity with the task may facilitate performance of older adults to a level comparable to that of younger ones.

A similar pattern of divergent results is obtained when memory is studied. Information that is related to our rich personal history appears to suffer far less than information that is isolated, factual, and not part of an organized knowledge structure. Thus, despite the laboratory data suggesting memory decline in middle and old age, knowledge that is integrated within a specific-domain manner remains relatively permanent, accessible, and fixed in long-term memory. Consistent with Perlmutter's suggestion (1980, 1986), it seems as if acquired knowledge about our own cognitive system can compensate for losses in the mechanics of memory and other information-processing functions.

In general, research conducted within the information-processing paradigm indeed suggests demonstrable decline in the control processes of memory and attention with advancing age. However, it should be realized that much of the research in this area takes place in laboratory contexts and employs tasks that lack ecological validity. On the other hand, we have argued that when memory and attention are assessed under domain-specific, real-life contexts, there is little evidence for negative developmental change. This is because much of adult cognitive performance may be occurring in a top–down fashion, rather than from the bottom–up or data-driven model assumed in the information-processing paradigm. As this paradigm is examined, it appears to be unable to explain how the application of extant knowledge structures directs cognitive processing. Psychologists working within the confines of the information-processing approach have used ecologically irrelevant tasks to study the performance of the elderly and have constructed "loss" models of aging. These models contribute little to our understanding of the developmental processes that enable older adults to continue to function adequately in most settings.

A similar set of criticisms may be directed at the research conducted within the framework of the psychometric model. It has been argued that intelligence is a multidimensional construct and that some of the components of intelligence decline over time (i.e., fluid mental abilities), while other components seem to remain stable or even evidence positive developmental growth (i.e., crystallized mental abilities). We have suggested that observed declines in fluid intelligence (i.e., generalized mental ability) are more apparent than real. Fluid measures of intelligence, from our point of view, fail to take into account the actual contexts within which adults think. Thus, the significance of the finding that fluid intelligence declines with age may *not* be that intelligence declines, but that with age much of everyday cognitive performance depends less on fluid abilities and increasingly more on contextual and domain-related factors.

Caution is also in order in interpreting the finding that crystallized forms of intelligence may increase with age. For example, many of the test questions used to assess crystallized skills (e.g., "How far is the distance from New York to Paris?") seem to measure a knowledge base that is somewhat trivial and outside of most adults' areas of expertise. It is difficult, if not impossible, to see how such knowledge is used in the solution of personally meaningful tasks. Furthermore, there seems to be no acknowledgement by psychometricians concerning the organization or domain-specific nature of accumulated knowledge (i.e., crystallized intelligence).

Information-processing and psychometric models attempt to explain developmental changes in adult cognition by exploring individual subprocesses. However, *all of a system's capacities cannot be explained by the efficiency of the components.* Older adults, despite reductions in efficiency and speed of processing with advances in age, may not display comparable reductions in cognitive effectiveness in any of the familiar domains of specialized expertise that they have developed throughout their lifetime. Thus, it appears far too limiting to focus purely on the processes and abilities that define the components of the cognitive system. An integrative viewpoint must address the manner by which the processes of cognition become the products of cognition.

KNOWING

Adult forms of knowledge are represented within specific domains. These knowledge structures arise through the process of encapsulation, in which fluid mental abilities and information-control processes become increasingly dedicated to the representation of specific information. Furthermore, adult knowledge structures are not uniformly developed in all domains. And assessments of generalized logical thinking skills and psychometrically defined fluid intelligence are not functionally related to adults' uniquely developed knowledge systems. Therefore, we have strongly emphasized that the *growth and encapsulation of domain-specific knowledge* is the most salient feature of adult cognition.

We have seen that knowledge not only becomes encapsulated and domain-specific during adulthood, but it also can be characterized as increasingly:

1. expert
2. automatized
3. intuitive
4. self-constructed
5. active

The shift from novice to expert is one that is characterized by highly skilled problem solving within a particular domain and most typically occurs in adult life. Although no generally agreed upon taxonomy exists for identifying experts from novices, there appear to be fundamental differences in the way in which these individuals represent, apply, and become introspectively aware of their knowledge systems. In highly structured domains, expertise seems to be rule based and procedural, whereas in less structured domains, expertise is most likely based on a blend of different skills: rapid and efficient integration coupled with inductive processes. Highly skilled older adults, we have argued, typically continue to function as experts in domains that they have mastered despite apparent losses in component abilities or control processes such as memory or attention. We have also proposed that due to the continued allocation (i.e., encapsulation) of fluid mental abilities to previously constructed domains, coupled with reductions in component processes, older adults are less likely, compared with younger adults, to develop new knowledge in domains outside of their area(s) of expertise. Furthermore, it often appears that within certain types of domains, older adults are better able to maintain and even extend the expertise that they developed earlier. Dittmann-Kohli and Baltes (1986), for example, have characterized older adulthood by the growth of expertise within the domain of personal knowledge (e.g., wisdom). Similarly, in those domains that foster artistic, literary, and philosophical expression, older adults may draw upon an ever-expanding knowledge base in order to produce their work (e.g., the visual art of Pablo Picasso and Georgia O'Keefe).

Research suggests that despite highly developed knowledge systems, most adult experts are not conscious of the processes and rules that enable them to perform competently (Lesgold, 1983). This suggests that an *intuitive* approach to problem solving is characteristic of expertise within domains. Therefore, although expert problem solving seems firmly rooted in highly developed forms of declarative and procedural knowledge, these knowledge bases are not *consciously* brought to bear during the problem-solving process. Furthermore, experts may not necessarily be able to describe how they arrive at a decision. In fact, experts have great difficulty understanding how novices, who are accessing the same information as themselves, arrive at a different decision or outcome. It seems that expertise within any domain gives rise to a set of intuitions that are derived from the automatic, unconscious processing of relevant information.

The use of the term *intuitive* in the above instance contrasts with Tversky and Kahneman's notion of intuitive heuristics. Kahneman and Tversky (1984) and Tversky and Kahneman (1981, 1983) have suggested that adults are extremely likely to make irrational and illogical decisions in both personal and impersonal matters because they apply their knowledge in an intuitive (i.e., unconscious, biased, unscientific, and nonrational) manner. We suggest, however, that these intuitive heuristics (except for their unconscious quality) are more likely to be descriptive of the judgments and decisions of novices than of experts.

Adults, we have also argued, actively participate in the construction of the domains in which they develop expertise. This contrasts sharply with recent views of modularity suggested by Gardner (1983) and Fodor (1983, 1985), who provided a neurophysiological basis to their respective hard-wired models. In their view, domain-specific modes of knowing (i.e., modules) exist *a priori*, independent of experience and individual choice. Alternatively, we emphasize that personal and experiential factors in development help to create the neurophysiological correlates of domain-specific knowledge identified most notably by Gardner (1983). We suggest that over the course of time and development, the effects of experience on an undifferentiated central nervous system provide the major impetus for the modularity of the mind. The data supportive of the modularity position (e.g., Gardner's observations, 1978, 1982, 1983, of adult stroke patients who have suffered localized neurological damage) have been derived from minds that, in our opinion, were already modularized through considerable past experience.

THINKING

There is a growing sentiment that adults represent and conceptualize knowledge in a developmentally unique manner. Consistent with this position, we have presented evidence that adults think about their accumulated knowledge in a postformal manner. We have also argued that postformal reasoning represents a number of specific styles of thinking rather than a structural stage of cognitive development. We suggested that postformal thinking styles lead adults to conceptualize knowledge as dynamic and active both in its construction and in its continued refinement. Moreover, there is also the recognition of the dialectical in postformal styles of adult thought. Individuals come to appreciate and accept contradiction as a basic facet of physical and social reality. They develop a sense of the holistic and constitutive nature of their knowledge systems, and they conceptualize reality, as well as their knowledge of reality, within an open, self-evolving framework. Given this intuitive grasp of reality, the postformal thinker perceives less of a need for problem solving within closed systems and a greater need for problem finding within and between open systems. Finally, there is the growing appreciation by postformal thinkers of the inseparable relationship between themselves and the knowledge that they create. Postformal thinking leads adults to conceptualize their knowledge as a *relationship* between subject and object. Thus, knowledge becomes personalized and is increasingly cast within a contextual and relativistic framework. The following comments made by Scarr (1985) concerning the ultimate nature of the "knowledge" gleaned from scientific research studies seem to have their basis in a postformal style of thinking:

If one adopts, as I do, a constructionist position on epistemology, then knowledge of all kinds, including scientific knowledge, is a construction of the human mind. Sensory data are filtered through the knowing apparatus of the human senses and made into perceptions and cognitions. The human mind is also constructed in a social context, and its knowledge is in part created by the social and cultural context in which it comes to know the world. Knowledge of the world is therefore always constructed by the human mind in the working models of reality in the sciences. (p. 499)

Further, she goes on to argue:

The admission that reality is a construction of the human mind does not deny the heuristic value of the construction. Indeed, we get around in the world and invent knowledge that is admirably useful. But the claim that science and reality are human constructions denies that there is any one set of facts that is real and absolute. Instead, it asserts that there are many sets of "facts" that arise from different theory-guided perceptions. (p. 501)

Postformal styles of thinking may also be seen in the creative accomplishments of adults across a wide range of fields and disciplines (e.g., art, music, literature, philosophy, science). Hofstadter (1979, 1982, 1984), for example, who is not typically identified with the postformal movement in developmental psychology, has inadvertently used several of the characteristics of postformal thinking in order to describe the creative works of several adults. For example, Hofstadter (1979) noticed that the creative accomplishments of many adults are typified by the presence of *strange loops*. He used the notion of strange loops to indicate that in some instances "by moving upwards (or downwards) through the levels of some hierarchical system, we unexpectedly find ourselves right back where we started" (Hofstadter, 1979, p. 10). Thus, what often appears to be a linear, irreversible, and continuous change, is often found to emerge as a dramatic, cyclic, and reversible pattern. Examples of the strange loop phenomenon are to be found, according to Hofstadter (1979), in the visual art of Escher, the mathematical theorems of Goedel, and the musical compositions of J. S. Bach. The most interesting component of these strange loops, we believe, lies in their apparent dialectical and contradictory qualities. In fact, Hofstadter (1979) suggested that dual tendencies to invent and savor contradiction are the most exciting, powerful, and beautiful characteristics of human cognition. We suggest that postformal styles of thought, with their attendant emphasis on the dialectical and the contradictory, allow adults to: (a) welcome the strange loops that have been constructed by others, and (b) actively construct new strange loops of their own.

Hofstadter has focused his attention on the strange loops created by others. However, we have discovered a most interesting strange loop in Hofstadter's own work. Hofstadter (1982) has suggested that psychologists have typically conceptualized cognition as a process in which a central processor (e.g., self or mind) manipulates a set of passive symbols (i.e., static bits or chunks of knowledge or information) through the implementation of various rule systems. Hofstadter argued, however, that symbols as well as the knowledge they represent are essentially active, *not* passive. In fact, Hofstadter (1982) maintained that "not only are we not symbol manipulators . . . we are manipulated by our symbols" (p. 16). These speculations give new meaning to the nature of human knowledge and the human self. Traditionally, the self has been viewed as the central agent, or processor, which intentionally coordinates stored bits of information with newly available information via the application of specific rules of thought in order to solve problems and make decisions. There are several problems associated with this position (e.g., "What accounts for the self's willfulness, autonomy, and prowess?", etc.). Hofstadter's (1982) arguments suggest that the self is the emergent awareness of the active symbols and knowledge structures that define the cognitive experience, *not* the creator and manipulator of those symbols and structures. The strange loop, of course, is that the realization of the active nature of knowledge leads to a realization of the nonactive nature of the self (i.e., the self is *not* the prime mover that creates and manipulates its accumulated knowledge). But such a realization depends on the self's ability to actively examine, via a postformal thinking style, its knowledge in order to ascertain the inherent activity and autonomy of that knowledge!

The above-mentioned argument, we suggest, is consistent with the manner in which we have conceptualized human development and human knowledge (chapters 1 and 6) and the self-representations (chapter 7). Most specifically, we have regarded self and knowledge as both entities and processes that may only be revealed through behavior sequences that have some functional/utilitarian goal or purpose.

THE ENCAPSULATION MODEL

We have proposed a model of adult cognition that represents and integrates the emerging data and theoretical advances within the genetic-epistemological, cognitive science, psychometric, and information-processing traditions. Our integrated approach focuses on the encapsulation of fluid mental abilities and the concomitant growth of sophisticated knowledge structures. Furthermore, our model explains the simultaneous presence of age-related declines in the component processes of the human cognitive system, the emergence of postformal styles of thinking, and the growth of expert, domain-specific knowledge systems. The utility of this integrative model was illustrated in the area of adaptation and coping. Our model provides a framework from which to view the competence and success that is characteristic of much of adult cognitive functioning, as well as the inevitable losses and declines that emerge with age.

Most importantly, we have highlighted the growth of domain-specific knowledge during the adult years. Constructed through direct experience, such knowledge is not necessarily diminished nor lost as a function of advanced age. It remains extant, whole, and accessible, rarely undergoing major deficit unless pathological degeneration of the nervous system occurs. Adults maintain and enhance their knowledge domains, such that encapsulated knowledge becomes more sophisticated, automated, and intuitive with advances in chronological age. Furthermore, adults seem to be able to conceptualize some of their knowledge systems in relativistic/dialectic terms and are also capable of applying their knowledge to ill-defined problems. We suggest that in those selective knowledge domains that are functionally adaptive, cognitive performance remains to be characterized by expertise throughout development. These domains of expertise are a product of the individual's unique personal history, accumulated experience, and perceived mastery, control, and competence. Thus, the encapsulation and preservation of knowledge structures within self-constructed domains are important features of adult cognitive development.

Expertise typically emerges during the adult years. Once present and characteristic of particular domains, expertise remains a hallmark of cognitive functioning throughout the remainder of adult life. The ability to allocate an apparently dwindling amount of cognitive resources for the purpose of maintaining domain-specific expert systems is another important feature of adult cognitive functioning. By channeling a seemingly limited pool of cognitive resources into previously constructed and functionally adaptive knowledge domains, the adult's personal sense of competence and self-efficacy is enhanced. Such a position suggests that: (a) the acquisition of new information as well as the concomitant construction of new knowledge domains become increasingly difficult in later adulthood, and (b) if already established knowledge domains may become less personally meaningful and important with increasing age, these domains will exhibit decay through disuse, self-chosen disinterest, and functionally defined irrelevance (not because of age per se).

Although we have highlighted the role of knowledge in adult cognition, we have also related the growth of domain-related expertise to changes in the stylistic qualities of adult thinking. And we have argued that the growth of domain-specific knowledge systems and postformal thinking styles is best conceptualized as resulting from the encapsulation of general, uncommitted cognitive resources and processes. Thus, we have constructed an integrative position that is consistent with the remarks recently made by Sternberg (1985b):

> If there is a generalization to be made about domain-general processes and domain-specific knowledge it is this: Processes of various degrees of domain generality are critical to the acquisition and utilization of domain-specific

knowledge, just as domain-specific knowledge is critical to the acquisition and utilization of further domain-specific knowledge. Both processes and knowledge must be fully and jointly considered in any theory in the psychology of learning and instruction. (p. 572)

Importance of the Encapsulation Model

Our Encapsulation Model captures the functional/adaptive nature of much of everyday cognitive performance across the adult life span. It suggests that adults may display superior levels of problem solving and problem finding when they draw upon domain-specific knowledge as well as domain-specific thought. It also recognizes the realities of associated age-related decline in those nonencapsulated areas of cognitive functioning.

Our model highlights the need for expanding beyond the narrowly circumscribed conceptualizations of adult cognition, such as the growth of logical abilities (e.g., the genetic–epistemological approach) or the loss of information-control processes (e.g., the information-processing and psychometric approaches). Our viewpoint leads to the conclusion that a description of the particular knowledge systems and stylistic features indicative of mature cognition is not necessarily specifiable in advance nor independent of the particular domains of specialization that individuals self-select. Moreover, there appear to be adult developmental trajectories that remain largely experiential, individually self-determined, and irreversible. These provide a sharp contrast to the assumptions of previous developmental periods in which biological–maturational processes are said to provide a relatively universal program of organism–environmental exchange with inherently predictable outcomes. Thus, adult cognitive development reflects individual differences in structure and content to a degree not found in childhood and adolescence.

Most certainly, we have assigned a critical role to knowledge in the development of adult cognition. It is the accumulation of knowledge that acts as a catalyst in the formation of the domains within which that knowledge will ultimately be represented. And it is the establishment and maintenance of these domains that facilitate the utilization of old knowledge as well as the acquisition of new knowledge. A great deal of previous research within the information-processing and psychometric traditions has supported the notion that adulthood is largely characterized by diminished cognitive ability. We suggest that these apparent losses are, in part, an artifact of the failure to measure domain-specific knowledge systems within which adults have developed some expertise. The greater the level of expertise within a domain (i.e., the more the encapsulation), the lesser the probability that domain-related fluid abilities will be found to decrease with age.

The domains of knowledge should *not* be conceptualized as pre-formed or hard-wired. The reemergence of the nativist position can most easily be seen in the writings of Chomsky (1975) as well as in the more current works of Fodor (1983, 1985), Gazzaniga (1985), and Gardner (1983). From our perspective, pre-formed modules seem to play a supporting role (not a leading role) in adult cognition. There are several reasons for our position.

First, knowledge domains are qualitatively different than the pre-formed faculties or modules advocated by the nativists. We suggest that adult cognition is typified by the self-construction of knowledge domains. Specifically, we agree with Charness (1985) that it is primarily the growth of knowledge and the push of motivation that account for individual differences in the growth of specific domains. For example, pre-formists could argue that language acquisition is a hard-wired skill in the vast majority of human children and that lesions in certain areas of the left hemisphere lead to specific forms of language disorders in most adults. But how are we able to explain from a strict pre-formist position why two adults (e.g., a poet and an essayist) who are both "expert" at using language nevertheless manifest their expertise in different ways. Could it be said that these individual differences are solely due to the fact that one person is more pre-wired for poetry than prose, whereas the other person possesses a different neural circuitry? We think not! No matter how hard-wired poetry could be (if it is hard-wired at all), could its hard-wired component be more important than the knowledge the developing poet seeks to accumulate about the nature, meaning, and relationship of words to other words, and of words to ideas and images? Put differently, the pre-formist/modularity view primarily attributes the development of cognitive expertise during the adult years to the vagaries of genetic inheritance. We disagree with this generalized view despite our belief that specific domains within specific individuals may have their genesis, in part, in some type of genetically based system. From our perspective, for example, we would suggest that although Mozart may have been more pre-wired than most with regard to his ability to discriminate pitches and rhythms, we would also suggest that his compositions arose from what he "knew" about music and the time and effort he chose to channel into musical activity.

Second, the differences in the quality of adult cognitive performance, both intraindividually and interindividually, are extensive. They seem to arise from mature decisions in adulthood as to how one displays competence and self-efficacy within self-selected domains of knowledge that are created by direct action and experience with the real world. Thus, we find it increasingly difficult to work from an innate position suggesting that the types of domains of knowledge are hard-wired in advance. Increasing numbers of psychologists suggest that it is the "construction" of knowledge categories and domains that focuses adult cognition in selected areas (Chi, 1985; Keil, 1981, 1986). It is clear that one cannot specify the domains of expertise for any adult on an *a priori* basis. Without this appreciation for each individual's contribution to the growth of their domain-specific styles of thinking and forms of knowing (Lerner, 1982), no account of adult cognition will be complete.

Comprehensiveness of the Encapsulation Model

Our Encapsulation Model is distinctly more comprehensive than previous models of adult cognition. We have integrated the three major dimensions of cognition: processing, knowing, and thinking. Traditionally most of the work in the area of adult cognition has been directed at an analysis of thinking (the genetic–epistemological approach) and processing (the information processing and psychometric approaches). More recently, the cognitive science approach has examined the question of *knowing* and has focused attention on knowledge, knowledge representation, knowledge structures, and expert knowledge systems. None of these previous approaches, however, has yielded the necessary integrative perspective necessary to account for the complexities of adult cognition.

Some contemporary developmentalists have tried to conceptualize adult cognition by integrating two of these dimensions. Dittmann-Kohli and Baltes (1986), for example, have reexamined the concept of wisdom by synthesizing thinking and knowing. Wisdom, they argued, is best understood as the construction of expert knowledge within the domain of social or practical intelligence. Furthermore, they maintained that the accumulated knowledge within this domain is conceptualized by the wise person in a relativistic, dialectical, and open-ended (i.e., postformal) manner. This storehouse of expert knowledge cast within a postformal framework allows the wise adult to offer pragmatic solutions to the ill-defined problems that characterize everyday life. The dimension of adult cognition omitted in this formulation is that of processing. There is limited, if any, mention of how adults allocate and use psychological resources such as attention and memory in order to maintain the expert knowledge and postformal thought that have become encapsulated within specific domains. Furthermore, Dittmann-Kohli and Baltes (1986) seem to confuse bio-maturationally determined, age-related declines in fluid intelligence with age-related declines in basic psychological processes and resources that result from the encapsulation process. They view fluid intelligence as a generalized mental ability that is independent of domain-specific knowledge structures and declines with age. Alternatively, we suggest that fluid abilities become increasingly encapsulated over time within specific knowledge domains and that basic mental abilities cannot be viewed in isolation from specific representations of knowledge. Therefore, the continued growth and elaboration of specific knowledge domains demands the continual commitment (i.e., encapsulation) of uncommitted cognitive abilities and resources. This gradual encapsulation of uncommitted, generalized mental abilities and cognitive processes is a necessary and adaptive feature of adult cognition.

Sternberg (1984, 1985a) has presented an integrative view of cognition that has links to all of the three dimensions that were identified earlier: processing, knowing, and thinking. Briefly summarizing this triarchic theory of intellectual development, Sternberg suggested three major divisions to intelligence: (a) a contextual subtheory that relates intelligence to the external world of the individual, (b) a componential subtheory that relates intelligence to the internal world of the individual, and (c) a 2-factor subtheory that describes links between intelligence and *both* internal and external worlds. The integrative framework provided by Sternberg assumes that intelligent behavior is purposive, adaptive, and selective in shaping the real-world environments with which individuals have to contend. The mental mechanisms or processes needed for planning, execution, and evaluation of intelligent behavior are also included under component processes. Context is another major dimension that overrides the application of intelligence. Sternberg relates context to two factors. One is the perception of the need for adaptation to novelty, and the second is the use of automatized information processing.

When we consider our framework in comparison to Sternberg's, we identify commonalities as well as basic differences. On the one hand, we agree that the functional adaptive character of intellectual processes is basic to the concept of adult cognitive activity. We also agree that there is a goal directedness and action–theoretic nature to cognitive activity in adulthood. However, we suggest that there are vastly different processes involved in the construction of adult cognitive competence. First, although Sternberg suggests that adaptation to novelty or the application of previously acquired patterns of automatized strategies makes up the essential component of intelligence, we remain committed to a developmental view that considers the importance of age-related change in the available pool of uncommitted control processes and the growth of domain-specific expert knowledge.

Second, Sternberg is committed to the use of "mental mechanisms" to allow individuals to plan and execute cognitive activity. We interpret these to be similar to the notions of meta-cognitive awareness, meta-reflective self-awareness, and executive processes such as those associated with taking charge of one's own activity, self-efficacy, and personal competence. Although Sternberg's theory assumes that these mental mechanisms are equally applicable to all contexts, we argue that these mechanisms are manifested most adaptively in those encapsulated domains that the individual has articulated and developed through experience. Thus, we do not find support for his general model in all of adult cognitive processing, but only in those self-constructed domains of personally relevant knowledge.

Third, Sternberg has not fully recognized the unique changes in adult development that moderate his triarchic theory. For example, a developmental theory of intelligence must account for age-related declines in control processes as well as age-related increases in expert knowledge and age-related changes in the stylistic qualities of thinking.

Our Encapsulation Model attempts to provide a full accounting of all three facets of the development of adult cognition: processing, thinking, and knowing. It is both integrative and developmental and offers important insights into the functional significance of adult cognitive functioning.

DIRECTIONS FOR FUTURE RESEARCH

Given the tenets of the Encapsulation Model, we suggest that future investigators will need to redirect their research efforts in several different ways. Therefore, we briefly outline what we feel are some of the most important research questions that follow from our viewpoint on adult cognition.

First, we have strongly emphasized the important role of knowledge in adult cognition — how knowledge systems become encapsulated within domains, and how domain-specific knowledge systems contribute to the phenomenon of cognitive expertise. Given this orientation, we see the need for a variety of longitudinal studies that explore the question of how domain-specific expertise arises over the course of development. All too often, cognitive expertise has been studied by proponents of the cognitive science orientation after it has already been developed (e.g., knowledge engineering). Research studies within the cognitive science approach had the goal of determining the heuristics used by expert problem solvers for the purpose of constructing expert software packages — a pragmatic but *not* basic research goal. This issue has also been addressed by Sternberg (1985b):

> Of course, experts differ in knowledge from nonexperts in levels of knowledge, almost by definition, and they differ as well in the ways they organize knowledge. But the fundamental question may be why they become experts whereas others, even after equally long hours of study, do not. It is at least as important to understand the acquisition of expertise as it is to understand the results of this acquisition. Views that heavily emphasize knowledge essentially begin their story at the end: They do not always take adequate account of learning. (p. 572)

A related set of questions involves defining the nature of expertise. "Does expertise consist of quantitative increases in the amount of accessible information?" "Is expert knowledge conceptualized in a different way from nonexpert knowledge?"

Second, there is also a need for further study of processing strategies among novices and experts within various knowledge domains. The ability of some older adults to maintain their processing skills needs examination. Not only is it important to study their abilities, but it is also important to study the continuity of these strategies throughout development. Consider, for example, a comparison between adult chess masters and emerging child prodigies. Are the processing strategies of these two disparate groups identical (or different)? Just as there are many alternative ways of representing expert knowledge, there may also be a variety of different processing approaches that vary developmentally. A related question involves an analysis of the means by which cognitive processes and resources are allocated for the purpose of acquiring new information during adulthood, especially older adulthood. As we have already mentioned, older adulthood is generally characterized by the maintenance of pre-existing knowledge structures, not the accumulation of new ones. Does the acquisition of new information require the dissolution of already established domains, or can knowledge be simultaneously present in new and old domains? For example, due to the rapid technological changes that occur on a societal wide basis (e.g., the influx of computers) and the unique events of one's life (e.g., retirement, grandparenthood, death of a spouse), an older adult may need to acquire new skills. An older working physician, for example, may be called upon to learn how to use computer programs as diagnostic aids, whereas a retired physician may find more enjoyment in his mastering those hobbies and interests (e.g., sailing, photography) that were of secondary interest during the working years. How might these two older persons compare to each other in their ability to learn new skills? The working physician might have a relatively difficult time learning the fine points of computer-assisted diagnosis because he still needs to invest psychological resources in order to maintain the expert medical knowledge he already possesses. The retired physician, on the other hand, may have an easier time learning about the intricacies of photography because he can afford to rechannel those psychological processes that have supported his knowledge of medicine — knowledge that he no longer needs to maintain at an expert level.

Third, it is important to determine how novices and experts *think* about the knowledge systems they possess. It may be found, for example, that the novice/expert shift is accompanied by a parallel change in the way in which the attendant knowledge is conceptualized in an epistemological sense. Novices may be found to conceptualize their knowledge systems, as well as the problems to which their knowledge is applied, in an absolute, static, and formal manner, whereas experts may be more likely to conceptualize knowledge systems and problem spaces in a relativistic and open-ended manner (i.e., in a postformal style). Or, it may be discovered that changes in thinking and knowing may emerge independently of one another.

Fourth, it may be that the extent to which experts conceptualize knowledge in a postformal manner is constrained by the nature of the knowledge domain in question. For example, philosophers interested in the study of metaphysics or ethics may be more likely to regard philosophical knowledge in a postformal manner compared to physicists who are interested in the problems of motion in the laboratory. There is some evidence to suggest that postformal thinking seems to be, in part, domain specific. Adults who evidence postformal styles of thinking when evaluating moral/personal problems may not manifest the same thought characteristics when evaluating problems that are more physicalistic/mathematical in nature.

Fifth, it seems of foremost importance to determine if formal versus postformal styles of thinking determine the manner in which novices and experts actually employ their knowledge in real-life settings. For example, expert physicians who view their accumulated medical knowledge (e.g., how disease is caused and treated) and their accumulated personal knowledge (e.g., how they view their obligations to themselves, their profession, and their patients) in a postformal manner will treat their patients (both medically and interpersonally) in a very different way than physicians who conceptualize their knowledge in a formal manner.

Sixth, if styles of thinking (formal versus postformal) are found to be related to forms of knowing (novice versus expert), it is important to determine whether changes in thinking cause changes in knowing or vice versa and whether changes in thinking and knowing are related in a purely non-causal manner. Glaser (1984) has made the point that one difference between individuals who display more or less ability in thinking and problem solving is the possession of knowledge. Specifically, Glaser (1984) has argued that:

> Much recent work emphasizes a new dimension of difference between individuals who display more or less ability in thinking and problem solving. This dimension is the possession and utilization of an organized body of conceptual and procedural knowledge, and a major component of thinking is seen to be the possession of accessible and usable knowledge. (1984, p. 97)

Seventh, the relationship between the problem-finding component of postformal thought and degree of knowledge deserves further investigation. It seems that many of the greatest discoveries and theoretical reformulations in scientific disciplines have been made by those who possess expertise within the discipline. However, Sternberg (1985b) has recently argued that:

> There is no evidence to support the view that the really great contributors to any field of endeavor are the ones who know the most about the field. If anything, many of the greatest contributors simply do not have time to read about everything that happens in their (or others') fields. A solidly knowledge-based point of view may well predict who will do better in academic achievement tests. . . . But this point of view will not account for the much more interesting aspects of expertise—the ability to find important problems, the ability to think creatively, the knack for studying problems in a tractable but interesting way, and so on. (p. 572)

Eighth, it is important to investigate the interrelationships among knowledge domains as they exist and develop intraindividually. How does an individual draw upon information in one domain in order to solve problems in other domains? Is such an ability related to some form of generic reasoning ability such as analogical reasoning (see Holyoak, 1984)? A combination of quantitative and qualitative research methods employing large N's and small n's would be useful for the investigation of these issues. For example, the relationship between styles of thinking (formal versus postformal) and forms of knowing (novice versus expert) within particular domains might be studied by examining the "talk aloud" protocols of experts and novices during the problem-solving process as well as having these different types of individuals "introspect" about the nature of their knowledge and the means by which they use it during problem solving (see Ericsson & Simon, 1984).

Ninth, it is important to determine those domains within which expert knowledge can (and cannot) play a compensatory role as the older individual experiences age-related declines in the component processes of cognition. For example, it was noted in chapter 6 that with increasing age there is a performance decrement in sports-related activities (e.g., golf) even among expert players, but there are many instances of enhanced expert-like performance in other domains (e.g., music, art) that accompany the aging process. Therefore, more attention needs to be given to the manner by which domain-specific knowledge structures and thinking styles can compensate for the loss of componential mental processes and physical abilities across a wide range of domains. This research would have an important impact on many of the decisions that surround work-related activities (e.g., forced retirement) of older adults.

CRITIQUE OF THE ENCAPSULATION MODEL

We have proposed a model of adult cognition that integrates and expands upon the various theoretical traditions within developmental psychology and the cognitive sciences. We believe that the Encapsulation Model provides a breadth of coverage and a range of application that far exceeds the extant perspectives from which adult cognition has been conceptualized. Despite the many positive features associated with our viewpoint, we feel that our position may be questioned on a number of different dimensions and at a variety of different levels of analysis. Therefore, we offer the following criticisms of our perspective.

Overinclusiveness

In an attempt to provide a description of cognitive functioning in adulthood, we have provided a synthesis that includes many phenomena that are not typically linked to the study of cognition. For example, we suggest that self-selected domains of encapsulated knowledge remain intact, functionally invariant, and characterized by expertise in mature adult development. Thus, the importance of motivation, self-efficacy, and goal directedness become inexorably linked within our Encapsulation Model. When we add to this synthesis the corresponding contributions of the self-system, commitment, affect, individual choice of domains of expertise, and action theoretic contexts, we find the focus of adult cognitive functioning broadened along a wide variety of dimensions. This breadth, however, presents challenges as our synthesis begins to encompass divergent traditions (e.g., motivation, personality, self, emotion, etc.). The potential linkages across these traditions have not yet been adequately described theoretically and are difficult to assess empirically. The comprehension of cognitive development becomes more confusing.

Vagueness

Our integrated account of adult cognitive functioning lacks some of the precision and clarity necessary for empirical verification. The conceptual links across the many dimensions we have related to cognitive functioning in adulthood are difficult to define operationally and suffer from a lack of precision both conceptually and psychometrically. Such general notions as goal directedness or individual commitment are difficult to define in an *a priori* fashion. In other words, predictive tests of the relationship of these divergent factors to adult cognitive functioning are difficult to derive. We are left with many vague operational definitions that are created idiosyncratically and defined *a posteriori*. Consequently, future researchers may need to adopt qualitative research methods in order to investigate some of the questions raised by our position.

Contextualism

An understanding of the development of knowledge domains and cognitive expertise in adulthood requires a contextualist framework. The contextual framework suggests that knowledge systems are constructed uniquely by each adult. There are basic questions as to how this idiosyncratic process is initiated and maintained. For example, there may be common processes, given adult similarities in biological hardware, but are all domains of expertise created through the same mix of biologically given processes? Furthermore, while our Encapsulation Model posits the growth of domain-specific knowledge systems as a *universal* phenomenon, our model does not identify the salient factors that account for the growth of expertise within various cultures. For example, formal education may play a significant role in the development of expert knowledge systems in Western culture, but a minimal role in more traditional cultures. Also, even those knowledge domains that are equally valued in both traditional and industrial cultures (e.g., personal knowledge, wisdom, etc.) may develop through different pathways that represent different blends of experience and meta-reflective opportunity.

Process of Knowledge Encapsulation

The breadth of our integration notwithstanding, the methods used to identify how component processes build domains of expertise remain largely unspecified. This is not to say that in principle the processes are unspecifiable but that psychologists have not yet fully explored this important question.

In this same regard, Anderson (1983) suggested that there is a progression from declarative knowledge to procedural knowledge to compiled knowledge of the type that produces expertise. His conceptual framework, however, remains difficult to assess experimentally, and verification is sorely needed. Furthermore, the mechanisms by which proceduralization occurs need to be described in order to have a full accounting of the process of knowledge encapsulation and its attendant expertise emerging in later adulthood. Without this information, the functional description of adult cognition remains incomplete.

Individual Differences

Our synthesis has suggested that it is in the realm of individual differences that psychologists attempting to describe adult cognitive functioning need to be more concerned. Adults uniquely choose to construct domains from which expertise evolves. The process of selecting and constructing domains of expertise from the range of potential alternatives is not sufficiently detailed. For example, what accounts for individual differences in the rate at which knowledge domains are selected and constructed?

A similar question needs to be raised regarding the factors responsible for individual differences in the manifestation of postformal styles of thinking. For example, on one hand, certain cultural/environmental opportunities and Western educational experiences may be needed in order to attain a postformal style of thinking. On the other hand, it is obvious that not all of the adults who have these opportunities and experiences develop qualitatively unique postformal styles of thinking.

Functional Conceptualization of Cognition

In examining our functional perspective, it is clear that we disagree with "faculty" psychologists such as Gardner (1983) and Fodor (1983). Although often neglected during the cognitive revolution of the 1960s and early 1970s, L. S. Vygotsky (1956, 1960, 1962, 1978) argued against this position for many years. Vygotsky and his contemporary in Russia, A. R. Luria (1975), both suggested that

> psychological processes are not elementary and inborn faculties, but are, rather, formed during life in the process of reflection of the world of reality, that they have a complex structure, utilizing different methods for achieving their goal, which change from one stage of development to the next. (Luria, 1975, p. 341)

Our functional approach, therefore, views cognition as a complex, *adaptive* activity that is goal oriented and purposive rather than aimless.

A major difficulty with this conceptualization, however, lies in the lack of specification of the goals of mature cognition apart from that of the cognition of younger individuals. Further, the functional approach suggests that common goals may be arrived at by more than a single trajectory. Complex functional systems such as those proposed for adult cognition may produce expertise via a number of alternative pathways. Thus, tests of this model become extremely difficult to design and evaluate.

Processes of Developmental Change

Our integrative approach does not promote the empirical identification of the process of developmental change. We have argued, at the most general of levels, that the human cognitive system must be regarded as both an open self-transforming *entity* and a *process* engaged in the continual transformation of "itself" and the "objects" that constitute its environment. The tendency to view the relationship between the cognitive system and the environment within which it operates (and is operated upon) in this dialectic manner makes philosophical sense. But, empirically minded investigators may be hard pressed to develop adequate research designs that capture the mutual continual transformations that typify the knower–known relationship.

Life Span or Adult Theory of Cognition

We have written this book for the purpose of explicating the dynamics of adult cognition. However, it may be argued that any theoretical account of cognitive functioning must do more than merely address itself to simply one epoch of the human life span. How can cognition during the adult years *not* be related in an intimate way to the changes that take place in processing, knowing, and thinking during the epochs of infancy, childhood, and adolescence. Therefore, our notions concerning adult cognition need to be grounded in a more all-encompassing, life-span perspective.

Related to the above-mentioned criticism, a theory of cognition that focuses a great deal of attention on the growth of expert knowledge during the adult years should also recognize and explain how such expertise develops (although very rarely) during the era of childhood. Although we have not devoted a great deal of attention to this topic, we have suggested that there may be individual differences with regard to the genetic mechanisms that allow for skilled behavior. But we have also suggested that skilled behavior and expert knowledge have their roots in knowledge domains that are self-constructed and not pre-wired. For example, although Mozart may have been more genetically predisposed to perform and create musical compositions than the vast majority of individuals, we would attribute Mozart's expertise to the knowledge he gained about music via his experiences in the world, as well as his motivation to pursue and create such knowledge systems. In a related matter, we also object to those theorists who have argued that adult knowledge systems are the primary result of a hard-wired system that has a genetic basis. These theorists, in our opinion, have made the error of viewing gifted, atypical children as if they were modal, typical adults; a similar error was made by a previous generation of developmentalists who viewed older adulthood as an unwelcomed return to childhood.

SUMMARY

Our perspective on adult cognitive development represents an integration and extension of the cognitive science, genetic–epistemological, psychometric, and information-processing points of view. This perspective, termed the Encapsulation Model: (a) recognizes the adaptive/functional nature of everyday cognition, (b) conceptualizes the refinement of knowledge and the expansion of thought as having their basis in the encapsulation of componential processes and fluid abilities, and (c) regards the human mind and the knowledge it constructs as both an *entity* and a *process*.

We have strongly emphasized that the continued growth of domain-specific knowledge and thought is basic to cognitive development throughout the life span, but occurs most typically during adulthood. Although there may be some innateness to the development of some domains, we suggested that the developing organism is relatively self-organizing with regard to the number and nature of domains. Thus, adults build a functionally adaptive and personally meaningful cognitive system by purposefully "taking charge" of their cognitive activity.

References

Abelson, R. P. (1981). Psychological status of the script concept. *American Psychologist*, *36*, 715–729.

Abrahams, J. P., Hoyer, W. J., Elias, M. F., & Bradigan, B. (1975). Gerontological research in psychology published in the *Journal of Gerontology*, 1963–1974: Perspectives and progress. *Journal of Gerontology*, *30*, 668–673.

Allport, G. (1968). *The person in psychology: Selected essays*. Boston: Beacon Press.

Anders, T. R., & Fozard, J. L. (1973). Effects of age upon retrieval from primary and secondary memory. *Developmental Psychology*, *9*, 411–415.

Anders, T. R., Fozard, J. L., & Lillyquist, T. D. (1972). Effects of age upon retrieval from short-term memory. *Developmental Psychology*, *6*, 214–217.

Anderson, J. R. (1982). Acquisition of cognitive skill. *Psychological Review*, *89*, 369–406.

Anderson, J. R. (1983). *The architecture of cognition*. Cambridge, MA: Harvard University Press.

Arlin, P. K. (1975). Cognitive development in adulthood: A fifth stage? *Developmental Psychology*, *11*, 602–606.

Arlin, P. K. (1977). Piagetian operations in problem finding. *Developmental Psychology*, *13*, 297–298.

Arlin, P. K. (1984). Adolescent and adult thought: A structural interpretation. In M. L. Commons, F. A. Richards, & C. Armon (Eds.), *Beyond formal operations: Late adolescent and adult cognitive development* (pp. 258–271). New York: Praeger.

Armon, C. (1982). *Philosophical and psychological theories of the good: An initial synthesis*. Unpublished paper, Harvard Graduate School of Education, Cambridge, MA.

Armon, C. (1984). Ideals of the good life and moral judgment: Ethical reasoning across the lifespan. In M. L. Commons, F. A. Richards, & C. Armon (Eds.), *Beyond formal operations: Late adolescent and adult cognitive development* (pp. 357–380). New York: Praeger.

Atchley, R. C. (1983). *Aging: Continuity and change*. Belmont, CA: Wadsworth.

Baddeley, A. D. (1982). Domains of recollection. *Psychological Review*, *89*, 708–729.

Baddeley, A. D., & Hitch, G. (1974). Working memory. In G. H. Bower (Ed.), *The psychology of learning and motivation* (Vol. 8, pp. 67–89). New York: Academic Press.

Bahrick, H. P. (1984). Semantic memory content in permastore: Fifty years of memory for Spanish learned in school. *Journal of Experimental Psychology: General*, *113*, 1–29.

Baltes, P. B., Cornelius, S., & Nesselroade, J. R. (1979). Cohort effects in developmental psychology. In J. R. Nesselroade & P. B. Baltes (Eds.), *Longitudinal research in the study of behavior and development* (pp. 61–88). New York: Academic Press.

Baltes, P. B., & Kliegl, R. (1986). On the dynamics between growth and decline in the aging of intelligence and memory. In K. Poeck (Ed.), *Proceedings of the thirteenth world conference of neurology*. Heidelberg, FR Germany: Springer.

Baltes, P. B., & Nesselroade, J. R. (1973). Developmental analysis of individual differences on multiple measures. In J. R. Nesselroade & H. W. Reese (Eds.), *Lifespan developmental psychology: Methodological issues* (pp. 218–252). New York: Academic Press.

Baltes, P. B., Reese, H. W., & Lipsitt, L. P. (1980). Life-span developmental psychology. *Annual Review of Psychology, 31*, 65–110.

Baltes, P. B., & Schaie, K. W. (1976). On the plasticity of intelligence in adulthood and old age: Where Horn and Donaldson fail. *American Psychologist, 31*, 720–723.

Baltes, P. B., & Willis, S. F. (1979). Life-span developmental psychology, cognitive functioning, and social policy. In M. W. Riley (Ed.), *Aging from birth to death: Interdisciplinary perspectives* (pp. 15–46). Boulder, CO: Westview Press.

Baltes, P. B., & Willis, S. F. (1982). Plasticity and enhancement of intellectual functioning in old age: Penn State's Adult Development and Enrichment Project (ADEPT). In F. I. M. Craik & S. E. Trehub (Eds.), *Aging and cognitive processes* (pp. 353–389). New York: Plenum Press.

Bandura, A. (1977). Self-efficacy: Toward a unifying theory of behavioral change. *Psychological Review, 84*, 191–215.

Bandura, A. (1982). Self-efficacy in human agency. *American Psychologist, 37*, 122–137.

Bandura, A., Adams, N. E., Hardy, A. B., & Howell, G. N. (1980). Tests of the generality of self-efficacy theory. *Cognitive Therapy and Research, 4*, 39–66.

Basseches, M. (1980). Dialectical schemata: A framework for the empirical study of dialectical thinking. *Human Development, 23*, 400–421.

Basseches, M. (1984a). Dialectical thinking as metasystematic form of cognitive organization. In M. L. Commons, F. A. Richards, & C. Armon (Eds.), *Beyond formal operations: Late adolescent and adult cognitive development* (pp. 216–238). New York: Praeger.

Basseches, M. (1984b). *Dialectical thinking*. Norwood, NJ: Ablex.

Belbin, R. M. (1953). Difficulties of older people in industry. *Occupational Psychology, 27*, 177–190.

Benack, S. (1984). Postformal epistemologies and the growth of empathy. In M. L. Commons, F. A. Richards, & C. Armon (Eds.), *Beyond formal operations: Late adolescent and adult development* (pp. 340–356). New York: Praeger.

Bertalanffy, L. von. (1968). *General systems theory*. New York: George Braziller.

Berzonsky, M. D. (1978). Formal reasoning in adolescence: An alternative view. *Adolescence, 13*, 279–290.

Berzonsky, M. D., & Barclay, C. R. (1982). Formal reasoning and identity formation: A re-conceptualization. In J. A. Meacham & N. R. Santilli (Eds.), *Social development in youth: Structure and content* (pp. 64–87). Basel: Karger.

Berzonsky, M. D., Weiner, A. S., & Raphael, D. (1975). Interdependence of formal reasoning. *Developmental Psychology, 11*, 258.

Birren, J. E. (1965). Age changes in speed of behavior: Its central nature and physiological correlates. In A. T. Welford and J. E. Birren (Eds.), *Behavior, aging and the nervous system* (pp. 191–216). Springfield, IL: Charles C Thomas.

Birren, J. E. (1974). Translations in gerontology—from lab to life: Psychophysiology and speed of response. *American Psychologist, 29*, 808-815.

Birren, J. E., Woods, A. M., & Williams, M. V. (1980). Behavioral slowing with age: Causes, organization, and consequences. In L. W. Poon (Ed.), *Aging in the 1980s: Psychological issues* (pp. 293-308). Washington, DC: American Psychological Association.

Blackburne-Stover, G., Belenky, M. F., & Gilligan, C. (1982). Moral development and reconstructive memory: Recalling a decision to terminate an unwanted pregnancy. *Developmental Psychology, 18*, 862-870.

Blieszner, R., Willis, S. L., & Baltes, P. B. (1981). Training research in aging on the fluid ability of induction. *Journal of Applied Developmental Psychology, 2*, 247-265.

Boden, D., & Bielby, D. D. (1983). The past as resource: A conversational analysis of elderly talk. *Human Development, 26*, 308-319.

Boesch, E. E. (1976). *Psychopathologie des alltags: Zur okopsychologie des handelns und seiner storungen.* Bern, Switzerland: Huber.

Boesch, E. E. (1984). The development of affective schemata. *Human Development, 27*, 173-183.

Bondareff, W. (1985). The neural basis of aging. In J. E. Birren & K. W. Schaie (Eds.), *Handbook of the psychology of aging* (2nd ed., pp. 95-112). New York: Van Nostrand Reinhold.

Botwinick, J. (1984). *Aging and behavior* (3rd ed.). New York: Springer.

Botwinick, J., & Storandt, M. (1974). *Memory, related functions, and age.* Springfield, IL: Charles C Thomas.

Bower, G. H., Black, J. B., & Turner, T. J. (1979). Scripts in memory for text. *Cognitive Psychology, 10*, 177-220.

Bower, G. H., & Reitmen, J. S. (1972). Mnemonic elaboration in multilist learning. *Journal of Verbal Learning and Verbal Behavior, 11*, 478-485.

Bowles, N. L., Obler, L. K., & Poon, L. W. (1985). *Aging and word retrieval: Naturalistic, clinical, and laboratory data.* Paper presented at the George A. Talland Conference on Memory and Aging, Cape Cod, MA.

Brainerd, C. J. (1978). The stage question in cognitive development theory. *Behavioral and Brain Sciences, 1*, 173-214.

Brainerd, C. J. (1979). *Piaget's theory of intelligence.* Englewood Cliffs, NJ: Prentice-Hall.

Bransford, J. D., Barclay, J. R., & Franks, J. J. (1972). Sentence memory: A constructive versus interpretive approach. *Cognitive Psychology, 3*, 193-209.

Bransford, J. D., & Franks, J. J. (1971). The abstraction of linguistic ideas. *Cognitive Psychology, 2*, 331-350.

Braukmann, W., Filipp, S. H., Angleitner, A., & Olbrich, E. (1981). *Problem-solving and coping with critical life events: A developmental study.* Paper presented at first European Meeting on Cognitive-Behavioral Therapy, Lisbon, Portugal.

Brent, S. B. (1978). Individual specialization, collective adaptation, and rate of environmental change. *Human Development, 21*, 21-33.

Brent, S. B. (1984). *The nature and development of psychological structures.* New York: Springer.

Broadbent, D. E., & Heron, A. (1962). Effects of a subsidiary task on performance involving immediate memory by younger and older men. *British Journal of Psychology, 53*, 189-198.

Bronowski, J. (1973). *The ascent of man.* Boston: Little, Brown.

Broughton, J. M. (1978). Development of concepts of self, mind, reality, and knowledge. In W. Damon (Ed.), *New directions for child development* (Vol. 1, pp. 75–100). San Francisco: Jossey Bass.

Broughton, J. M. (1984). Not beyond formal operations but beyond Piaget. In M. L. Commons, F. A. Richards, & C. Armon (Eds.), *Beyond formal operations: Late adolescent and adult cognitive development* (pp. 395–412). New York: Praeger.

Brown, A. L. (1975). The development of memory: Knowing, knowing about knowing, and knowing how to know. In H. W. Reese (Ed.), *Advances in child development and behavior* (Vol. 10, pp. 104–153). New York: Academic Press.

Brown, A. L. (1978). Knowing when, where, and how to remember: a problem of metacognition. In R. Glaser (Ed.), *Advances in instructional psychology*. Hillsdale, NJ: Erlbaum.

Burke, D. M., & Light, L. L. (1981). Memory and aging: The role of retrieval processes. *Psychological Bulletin, 90,* 513–546.

Callaway, E. (1981). Can the decomposition of attention clarify some clinical issues? *Behavioral and Brain Sciences, 4,* 477–479.

Camp, C. J. (1985). *Utilization of world knowledge systems.* Unpublished manuscript, University of New Orleans.

Caplan, D., & Chomsky, N. (1982). Linguistic perspectives on language development. In D. Caplan (Ed.), *Biological studies of mental processes* (pp. 97–105). Cambridge, MA: MIT Press.

Carey, T. (1982). Maturational factors in human development. In D. Caplan (Ed.), *Biological studies of mental processes* (pp. 1–7). Cambridge, MA: MIT Press.

Carroll, J. B. (1984). An artful perspective on talents. *Contemporary Psychology, 29,* 864–866.

Cattell, R. B. (1971). *Abilities: Their structure, growth, and action.* Champaign, IL: IPAT.

Cattell, R. B., & Horn, J. L. (1978). A cross-social check on the theory of fluid and crystallized intelligence with discovery of new valid subtests. *Journal of Educational Measurement, 15,* 139–164.

Cavanaugh, J. C., & Perlmutter, M. (1982). Metamemory: A critical examination. *Child Development, 53,* 11–28.

Cerella, J. (1985a). Age decline in extrafoveal letter perception. *Journal of Gerontology, 40,* 727–736.

Cerella, J. (1985b). Information processing rates in the elderly. *Psychological Bulletin, 98,* 67–83.

Cerella, J., Poon, L. W., & Williams, D. M. (1980). Age and the complexity hypothesis. In L. W. Poon (Ed.), *Aging in the 1980s: Psychological issues.* Washington, DC: American Psychological Association.

Chapman, M. (1984). Intentional action as a paradigm for developmental psychology: Conclusion; action, intention, and intersubjectivity. *Human Development, 27,* 139–144.

Charness, N. (1979). Components of skill in bridge. *Canadian Journal of Psychology, 33,* 1–16.

Charness, N. (1981). Aging and skilled problem solving. *Journal of Experimental Psychology: General, 110,* 21–38.

Charness, N. (1983). Age, skill, and bridge bidding: A chronometric analysis. *Journal of Verbal Learning and Verbal Behavior, 22,* 146–416.

Charness, N. (1985). *Age and expertise: Responding to Talland's challenge.* Paper presented at the third George A. Talland Memorial Conference on Aging and Memory. Cape Cod, MA.

Charness, N. (1986). Expertise in chess, music, and physics: A cognitive perspective.

In L. K. Obler & D. A. Fein (Eds.), *The neuropsychology of talent and special abilities*. New York: Guilford Press.

Chase, W. G., & Ericsson, K. A. (1982). Skill and working memory. In G. H. Bower (Ed.), *The psychology of learning and motivation* (Vol. 16, pp. 1–58). New York: Academic Press.

Chase, W. G., & Simon, H. A. (1973). Perception in chess. *Cognitive Psychology*, *4*, 55–81.

Chi, M. T. H. (1983). *Trends in memory development research*. Basel, Switzerland: Karger.

Chi, M. T. H. (1985). Changing conception of sources of memory development. *Human Development*, *28*, 50–56.

Chi, M. T. H., Glaser, R., & Rees, E. (1982). Expertise in problem solving. In R. J. Sternberg (Ed.), *Advances in the psychology of human intelligence* (Vol. 1, pp. 7–75). Hillsdale, NJ: Erlbaum.

Chi, M. T. H., & Koeske, R. D. (1983). Network representation of a child's dinosaur knowledge. *Developmental Psychology*, *19*, 29–39.

Chiarello, C., Church, K. L., & Hoyer, W. J. (1985). Automatic and controlled semantic priming: Accuracy, response bias, and aging. *Journal of Gerontology*, *40*, 593–600.

Chomsky, N. (1965). *Aspects of a theory of syntax*. Cambridge, MA: MIT Press.

Chomsky, N. (1966). *Cartesian linguistics*. New York: Harper & Row.

Chomsky, N. (1968). *Language and mind*. New York: Harcourt, Brace, and Jovanovich.

Chomsky, N. (1975). *Reflections on language*. New York: Pantheon.

Chomsky, N. (1979). *Language and responsibility*. New York: Pantheon.

Chomsky, N. (1980). Rules and representations. *Behavioral and Brain Sciences, 3*, 1–15.

Clayton, V., & Birren, J. E. (1980). Age and wisdom across the life-span: Theoretical perspectives. In P. B. Baltes & O. G. Brim, Jr. (Eds.), *Life-span development and behavior* (Vol. 3, pp. 103–135). New York: Academic Press.

Coates, G. D., & Kirby, R. H. (1982). Organismic factors and individual differences in human performance and productivity. In E. A. Alluisi & E. A. Fleishman (Eds.), *Human performance and productivity: Stress and performance effectiveness* (pp. 91–140). New York: Academic Press.

Cohler, B. J. (1982). Personal narrative and the life course. In P. B. Baltes & O. G. Brim, Jr. (Eds.), *Life-span development and behavior* (Vol. 4, pp. 205–241). New York: Academic Press.

Colby, A., Kohlberg, L., Gibbs, J., & Lieberman, M. (1983). A longitudinal study of moral judgment. *Monographs of the Society for Research in Child Development, 48*, 1–124.

Cole, S. (1979). Age and scientific performance. *American Journal of Sociology, 84*, 958–977.

Commons, M. L., & Richards, F. A. (1984). Applying the general stage model. In M. L. Commons, F. A. Richards, & C. Armon (Eds.), *Beyond formal operations: Late adolescent and adult cognitive development* (pp. 141–157). New York: Praeger.

Commons, M. L., Richards, F. A., & Armon, C. (Eds.). (1984). *Beyond formal operations: Late adolescent and adult cognitive development*. New York: Praeger.

Commons, M. L, Richards, F. A., & Kuhn, D. (1982). Systematic metasystematic, and cross paradigmatic reasoning: A case for stages of reasoning beyond Piaget's stage of formal operations. *Child Development, 53*, 1058–1068.

Cornelius, S. W., Caspi, A., & Hannum, J. (1983). *Intelligence and adaptation*.

Paper presented at the meetings of the Gerontological Society of America, San Francisco, CA.

Craik, F. I. M. (1977). Age differences in human memory. In J. E. Birren & K. W. Schaie (Eds.), *Handbook of the psychology of aging* (pp. 384–420). New York: Van Nostrand Reinhold.

Craik, F. I. M., & Byrd, M. (1982). Aging and cognitive deficits: The role of attentional resources. In F. I. M. Craik & S. E. Trehub (Eds.), *Aging and cognitive processes* (pp. 191–211). New York: Plenum.

Cunningham, W. R. (1980). Speed, age, and qualitative differences in cognitive functioning. In L. W. Poon (Ed.), *Aging in the 1980s: Psychological issues* (pp. 327–331). Washington, DC: American Psychological Association.

Cunningham, W. R. (1982). Factorial invariance: A methodological issue in the study of psychological development. *Experimental Aging Research, 8*, 61–66.

Day, M. C. (1975). Developmental trends in visual scanning. In H. W. Reese (Ed.), *Advances in child development* (Vol. 10, pp. 154–195). New York: Academic Press.

Day, M. C. (1978). *Adolescent thought: Theory, research, and educational implications.* Report prepared for the National Institute of Education.

DeGroot, A. (1965). *Thought and choice in chess.* The Hague: Mouton.

Dember, W. (1981). *Cognition, complexity, confusion, closure, commitment, and conversion.* Paper presented at the meetings of the American Psychological Association, Los Angeles, CA.

Denney, N. W. (1979). Problem solving in later adulthood: Intervention research. In P. B. Baltes & O. G. Brim, Jr. (Eds.), *Life-span development and behavior* (pp. 38–67). New York: Academic Press.

Denney, N. W. (1984). A model of cognitive development across the life span. *Developmental Review, 4*, 171–191.

DiLollo, V., Arnett, J. L., & Kruk, R. V. (1982). Age-related changes in rate of visual information processing. *Journal of Experimental Psychology: Human Perception and Performance, 8*, 225–237.

Dittmann-Kohli, F., & Baltes, P. B. (1986). Towards a neo-functionalist conception of adult intellectual development: Wisdom as a prototypical case of intellectual growth. In C. Alexander & E. Langer (Eds.), *Beyond formal operations: Alternative endpoints to human development.* New York: Oxford University Press.

Dittmann-Kohli, F., & Kramer, D. A. (1985). *Task analysis in cognitive aging research: Comparison of traditional and real life approaches.* Paper presented at the International Society for the Study of Behavioural Development Meetings, Tours, France.

Dixon, R. H., & Hultsch, D. F. (1983). Structure and development of metamemory in adulthood. *Journal of Gerontology, 38*, 682–688.

Dixon, R. H., Kramer, D. A., & Baltes, P. B. (1984). Intelligence: Its life-span development. In B. B. Wolman (Ed.), *Handbook of intelligence: Theories, measurements, and applications* (pp. 469–518). New York: John Wiley and Sons.

Donaldson, M. (1978). *Children's minds.* New York: Norton.

Duda, R. O., & Shortliffe, E. H. (1983). Expert systems research. *Science, 220*, 261–268.

Dulit, E. (1972). Adolescent thinking a la Piaget: The formal stage. *Journal of Youth and Adolescence, 1*, 281–301.

Ebbesson, S. O. E. (1984). Evolution and ontogeny of neural circuits. *Behavioral and Brain Sciences, 7*, 321–366.

Eckensberger, L. H., & Meacham, J. (1984). The essentials of action theory: A framework for discussion. *Human Development, 27*, 166–172.

Edelstein, W., & Noam, G. (1982). Regulatory structures of the self and postformal stages in adulthood. *Human Development*, *25*, 407-422.

Ekstrom, R. B., French, J. W., & Harman, M. H. (1979). Cognitive factors: Their identification and replication. *Multivariate Behavior Research Monographs*, No. 79.2.

Ekstrom, R. B., French, J. W., Harman, M. H., & Derman, D. (1976). *Kit of factor-referenced cognitive tests*. Princeton, NJ: Educational Testing Service.

Elkind, D. (1967). Egocentrism in adolescence. *Child Development*, *38*, 1025-1034.

Elstein, A. S. , Shulman, L. S., & Sprafka, S. A. (1978). *Medical problem solving: An analysis of clinical reasoning*. Cambridge, MA: Harvard University Press.

Engle, R. W., & Bukstel, L. (1978). Memory processes among bridge players of different expertise. *American Journal of Psychology*, *91*, 673-689.

Ericsson, K. A., & Simon, H. (1984). *Protocol analysis*. Cambridge, MA: Bradford.

Erikson, C. W., Hamlin, R. M., & Daye, C. (1973). Aging adults and rate of memory scan. *Bulletin of the Psychonomic Society*, *1*, 259-260.

Farkas, M. S., & Hoyer, W. J. (1980). Processing consequences of perceptual grouping in selective attention. *Journal of Gerontology*, *35*, 207-216.

Fiske, S. T., & Kinder, D. R. (1981). Involvement, expertise, and schema uses: Evidence from political cognition. In N. Cantor & J. F. Kihlstrom (Eds.), *Personality, cognition, and social interaction* (pp. 171-190). Hillsdale, NJ: Erlbaum.

Fitzgerald, J. M., & Lawrence, R. (1984). Autobiographical memory across the lifespan. *Journal of Gerontology*, *39*, 692-698.

Flavell, J. H. (1977). *Cognitive development*. Englewood Cliffs, NJ: Prentice-Hall.

Flavell, J. H. (1979). Metacognition and cognitive monitoring: A new area of cognitive-development inquiry. *American Psychologist*, *35*, 906-911.

Flavell, J. H. (1981). Cognitive monitoring. In W. P. Dickson (Ed.), *Children's oral communication skills*. New York: Academic Press.

Fodor, J. (1965). *Psychological explanation*. New York: Random House.

Fodor, J. (1975). *The language of thought*. New York: Thomas Y. Crowell.

Fodor, J. (1979). *The language of thought*. Cambridge, MA: Harvard University Press.

Fodor, J. (1983). *The modularity of mind*. Cambridge, MA: MIT Press.

Fodor, J. (1985). Precis of: *The modularity of mind*. *Behavioral and Brain Sciences*, *8*, 1-42.

Folkman, S., & Lazarus, R. S. (1980). An analysis of coping in a middle-aged community sample. *Journal of Health and Social Behavior*, *21*, 219-239.

Fozard, J. L. (1980). The time for remembering. In L. W. Poon (Ed.), *Aging in the 1980s: Psychological issues* (pp. 273-287). Washington, DC: American Psychological Association.

Fozard, J. L. (1981). Speed of mental performance and aging: Costs of age and benefits of wisdom. In F. J. Pirozzolo & G. J. Maletta (Eds.), *Behavioral assessment and psychopharmacology*, (Vol. 2, pp. 59-94). New York: Praeger.

Fozard, J. L., & Popkin, S. (1978). Optimizing adult development: Ends and means of an applied psychology of aging. *American Psychologist*, *33*, 975-989.

Franklin, H. C., & Holding, D. H. (1977). Personal memories at different ages. *Quarterly Journal of Experimental Psychology*, *29*, 527-532.

Fullerton, A. M. (1983). Age differences in the use of imagery in integrating new and old information in memory. *Journal of Gerontology*, *38*, 326-332.

Furth, H. G. (1969). *Piaget and knowledge: Theoretical foundations* (1st ed.). Chicago: University of Chicago Press.

Galton, F. (1879). Psychometric experiments. *Brain*, *2*, 148-162.

Gardner, E. F., & Monge, R. H. (1977). Adult age differences in cognitive abilities and educational background. *Experimental Aging Research, 3,* 337-383.

Gardner, H. (1973). *The quest for mind.* New York: Knopf.

Gardner, H. (1978). *Developmental psychology* (1st ed.). Boston: Little, Brown.

Gardner, H. (1979). Getting acquainted with Piaget. *New York Times,* January 16.

Gardner, H. (1982). *Art, mind, and brain: A cognitive approach to creativity.* New York: Basic Books.

Gardner, H. (1983). *Frames of mind: The theory of multiple intelligences.* New York: Basic Books.

Gardner, H. (1985). *The mind's new science.* New York: Basic Books.

Garrett, H. E. (1946). A developmental theory of intelligence. *American Psychologist, 1,* 372-378.

Gazzaniga, M. A. (1985). *The social brain.* New York: Basic Books.

Gelman, R. (1979). Preschool thought. *American Psychologist, 34,* 900-904.

Getzels, J. W., & Csikszentmihalyi, M. (1976). *The creative vision: A longitudinal study of problem finding in art.* New York: John Wiley.

Gibbs, J. C. (1977). Kohlberg's stages of moral judgment: A constructivist critique. *Harvard Educational Review, 47,* 42-61.

Gibbs, J. C. (1979). Kohlberg's moral stage theory: A Piagetian revision. *Human Development, 22,* 89-112.

Gick, M. L., & Holyoak, K. J. (1983). Schema induction and analogical transfer. *Cognitive Psychology, 15,* 1-38.

Gilbert, J. C., & Levee, R. F. (1971). Patterns of declining memory. *Journal of Gerontology, 26,* 70-75.

Gilligan, C., & Murphy, J. M. (1979). Development from adolescence to adulthood: The philosopher and the dilemma of the fact. In W. Damon (Ed.), *New directions for child development* (Vol. 5, pp. 85-100). San Francisco: Jossey-Bass.

Ginsburg, H., & Opper, S. (1969). *Piaget's theory of intellectual development: An introduction.* Englewood Cliffs, NJ: Prentice Hall.

Glaser, R. (1984). Education and thinking: The role of knowledge. *American Psychologist, 39,* 93-104.

Glucksberg, S. (1985). *Cognitive aging research: What does it say about cognition? Aging?* Paper presented at American Psychological Association Meetings, Los Angeles, CA.

Goethals, G. R., & Frost, M. (1978). Value change and the recall of earlier values. *Bulletin of the Psychonomic Society, 11,* 73-74.

Goethals, G. R., & Reckman, R. F. (1973). The perception of consistency in attitudes. *Journal of Experimental Social Psychology, 9,* 491-501.

Goldstein, I., & Papert, S. (1977). *Cognitive Science, 1,* 84-123.

Gottsdanker, R. (1980). Aging and the use of advance probability information. *Journal of Motor Behavior, 12,* 133-143.

Greenwald, A. (1980). The totalitarian ego: Fabrication and revision of personal history. *American Psychologist, 35,* 603-618.

Guilford, J. P. (1959). Three faces of intellect. *American Psychologist, 14,* 469-479.

Guilford, J. P. (1966). Intelligence: 1965 Model. *American Psychologist, 21,* 20-26.

Guilford, J. P. (1967). *The nature of human intelligence.* New York: McGraw-Hill.

Guttentag, R. E. (1985). Memory and aging: Implications for theories of memory development during childhood. *Developmental Review, 5,* 56-82.

Haan, N. (1962). Proposed model of ego functioning: Coping and defense mechanisms in relation to IQ changes. *Psychological Monographs, 77,* (8, whole no. 571).

Haan, N. (1977). *Coping and defending: Processes of self-environment organization.* New York: Academic Press.

Hacker, W. (1985). Activity: A fruitful concept in the psychology of work. In M. Frese & J. Sabini (Eds.), *Goal directed behavior: The concept of action in psychology*. Hillsdale, NJ: Erlbaum.

Hartshorne, C., & Weiss, P. (Eds.). (1960). Pragmatism and pragmatics. In *The Collected Papers of Charles Sanders Peirce* (Vol. 5, No. 5.591). Cambridge, MA: Belknap Press.

Hasher, L., & Zacks, R. (1979). Automatic and effortful processes in memory. *Journal of Experimental Psychology: General, 108*, 356–388.

Heglin, H. J. (1956). Problem solving set in different age groups. *Journal of Gerontology, 11*, 310–317.

Hellenbusch, S. J. (1976). On improving learning and memory in the aged: The effects of mnemonics on strategy, transfer, and generalization. (Doctoral dissertation, University of Notre Dame). *Dissertation Abstracts International*, 1459-B. (University Microfilms No. 76-19,496)

Hillman, D. (1985). Artificial intelligence. *Human Factors, 27*, 21–31.

Hofstadter, D. R. (1979). *Goedel, Escher, and Bach: An eternal golden braid*. New York: Vintage Books.

Hofstadter, D. R. (1982). Artificial intelligence: Subcognition as computation. (Tech. Rep. No. 132). Bloomington, IN: Indiana University.

Hofstadter, D. R. (1984). *Metamagical themes*. New York: Basic Books.

Holmes, T. H., & Rahe, R. H. (1967). The social readjustment rating scale. *Journal of Psychosomatic Research, 11*, 213–218.

Holyoak, J. J. (1984). Analogical thinking and human intelligence. In R. J. Sternberg (Ed.), *Advances in the psychology of human intelligence* (Vol. 2, pp. 199–230). Hillsdale, NJ: Erlbaum.

Horn, J. L. (1970). Organization of data on life-span development of human abilities. In L. R. Goulet & P. B. Baltes (Eds.), *Life span developmental psychology: Research and theory* (pp. 423–466). New York: Academic Press.

Horn, J. L. (1982). The aging of human abilities. In B. B. Wolman (Ed.), *Handbook of developmental psychology* (pp. 847–870). Englewood Cliffs, NJ: Prentice-Hall.

Horn, J. L., & Cattell, R. B. (1966). Refinement and test of the theory of fluid and crystallized general intelligences. *Journal of Educational Psychology, 57*, 253–270.

Horn, J. L., & Cattell, R. B. (1967). Age differences in fluid and crystallized intelligence. *Acta Psychologica, 26*, 107–129.

Horn, J. L., & Donaldson, G. (1976). On the myth of intellectual decline in adulthood. *American Psychologist, 31*, 701–719.

Horn, J. L., & Donaldson, G. (1980). Cognitive development II: Adulthood development of human abilities. In O. G. Brim, Jr. & J. Kagan (Eds.), *Constancy and change in human development* (pp. 445–529). Cambridge, MA: Harvard University Press.

Horn, J. L., & McArdle, J. J. (1980). Perspectives on mathematical/statistical model building (MASMOB) in research on aging. In L. W. Poon (Ed.), *Aging in the 1980s: Psychological issues* (pp. 503–541). Washington, DC: American Psychological Association.

Howard, D. V., McAndrews, M. P., & Lasaga, M. I. (1981). Semantic priming of lexical decisions in young and old adults. *Journal of Gerontology, 36*, 707–714.

Howard, D. V., Shaw, R. J., & Heisey, J. G. (1986). Aging and the time course of semantic activiation. *Journal of Gerontology, 41*, 195–203.

Hoyer, W. J. (1985). Aging and the development of expert cognition. In T. M. Shlechter & M. P. Toglia (Eds.), *New directions in cognitive science* (pp. 69–87). Norwood, NJ: Ablex.

Hoyer, W. J. (1986). Toward a knowledge-based conceptualization of adult intellectual development. In C. Schooler & K. W. Schaie (Eds.), *Cognitive functioning and social structures over the life course*. Norwood, NJ: Ablex.

Hoyer, W. J., & Familant, M. E. (1983). *Adult age differences in the use of expectancy information*. Paper presented at the meetings of the American Psychological Association, Anaheim, CA.

Hoyer, W. J., Labouvie, G. V., & Baltes, P. B. (1973). Modification of response speed deficits and intellectual performance in the elderly. *Human Development, 16*, 233–242.

Hoyer, W. J., & Plude, D. J. (1980). Attentional and perceptual processes in the study of cognitive aging. In L. W. Poon (Ed.), *Aging in the 1980s: Psychological issues* (pp. 227–238). Washington, DC: American Psychological Association.

Hoyer, W. J., & Plude, D. J. (1982). Aging and the allocation of attentional resources in visual information processing. In R. Sekuler, D. Kline, & K. Dismukes (Eds.), *Aging and human visual function* (pp. 245–263). New York: Alan R. Liss.

Hoyer, W. J., & Plude, D. J. (1985). Attentional factors in visual function. *Geriatric Ophthalmology, 1*, 32–38.

Hoyer, W. J., Raskind, C., & Abrahams, J. P. (1984). Research practices in the psychology of aging: A survey of research published in the *Journal of Gerontology*, 1975–1982. *Journal of Gerontology, 39*, 44–48

Hoyer, W. J., Rybash, J. M., & Roodin, P. A. (1986). Knowing and thinking in adulthood: A developmental perspective. In M. L. Commons, F. A. Richards, C. Armon, & J. Sinnott (Eds.), *Beyond formal operations 2: The development of adolescent and adult thinking and perception*. New York: Praeger.

Hulicka, I. M., & Grossman, J. L. (1967). Age-group comparisons for the use of mediators in paired associate learning. *Journal of Gerontology, 22*, 46–51.

Hultsch, D. F. (1971). Adult age differences in free classification and free recall. *Developmental Psychology, 4*, 338–342.

Hultsch, D. F., & Dixon, R. A. (1983). The role of pre-experimental knowledge in text processing. *Experimental Aging Research, 9*, 17–22.

Hunt, E. (1978). Mechanics of verbal ability. *Psychological Review, 85*, 109–130.

Inhelder, B. (1962). Some aspects of Piaget's genetic approach to cognition. In W. Kessen & C. Kuhlman (Eds.), *Thought in the young child. Monographs of the Society for Research in Child Development, 27*, (2, Serial No. 83, pp. 19–33).

Inhelder, B., & Piaget, J. (1958). *The growth of logical thinking from childhood to adolescence*. New York: Basic Books.

Intelligence and its measurement: A symposium (1921). *Journal of Educational Psychology, 12*, 123–147, 195–216, 271–275.

James, W. (1890). *Principles of psychology*. New York: Henry Holt & Co.

Jeffries, R., Turner, A. A., Polson, P. G., & Atwood, M. E. (1981). The processes involved in designing software. In J. R. Anderson (Ed.), *Cognitive skills and their acquisition* (pp. 255–283). Hillsdale, NJ: Erlbaum.

Jensen, A. R. (1985). The nature of the Black–White difference on various psychometric tests: Spearman's hypothesis. *Behavioral and Brain Sciences, 8*, 193–263.

Johnson-Laird, P. N. (1983). *Mental models: Towards a cognitive science of language, inference, and consciousness*. Cambridge, MA: Harvard University Press.

Johnson-Laird, P. N., & Wason, P. C. (1970). A theoretical analysis of insight into a reasoning task, *Cognitive Psychology, 1*, 134–148.

Kagan, J. (1984). *The nature of the child*. New York: Basic Books.

Kahneman, D., & Treisman, A. (1984). Changing views of attention and automaticity. In R. Parasuraman & D. R. Davies (Eds.), *Varieties of attention* (pp. 29-61). New York: Academic Press.

Kahneman, D., & Tversky, A. (1984). Choices, values, and frames. *American Psychologist*, *39*, 341-350.

Kaus, C. R., Lenhart, R. E., Roodin, P. A., & Lonky, E. L. (1982). *Coping in adulthood: Moral reasoning and cognitive resources.* Paper presented at American Psychological Association Meetings, Washington, DC.

Kausler, D. H. (1982). *Experimental psychology of human aging.* New York: Wiley.

Keating, D. P. (1980). Adolescent thinking. In J. Adelson (Ed.), *Handbook of adolescent psychology* (pp. 211-246). New York: Wiley.

Kegan, R. (1982). *The evolving self.* Cambridge, MA: Harvard University Press.

Kegan, R., Noam, G. G., & Rogers, L. (1982). The psychologic of emotion: A neo-Piagetian view. In D. Cicchetti & P. Hesse (Eds.), *New directions for child development* (Vol. 16, pp. 105-128). San Francisco: Jossey Bass.

Keil, F. C. (1981). Constraints on knowledge and cognitive development. *Psychological Review*, *88*, 197-227.

Keil, F. C. (1986). On the structure dependent nature of stages of cognitive development. In J. Levin (Ed.), *Stage and structure.* Norwood, NJ: Ablex.

King, P. M., Kitchner, K. S., Davison, M. L., Parker, C. A., & Wood, P. K. (1983). The justification of beliefs in young adults: A longitudinal study. *Human Development*, *26*, 106-116.

Kintsch, W., & Greeno, J. G. (1985). Understanding and solving word arithmetic problems. *Psychological Bulletin*, *92*, 109-129.

Kitchner, K. S., & King, P. M. (1981). Reflective judgment: Concepts of justification and their relationship to age and education. *Journal of Applied Developmental Psychology*, *2*, 89-116.

Klahr, D., & Wallace, J. G. (1976). *Cognitive development: An information-processing view.* Hillsdale, NJ: Erlbaum.

Kliegl, R. (1985). *Acquisition of a memory skill: A paradigm for studying developmental processes.* Paper presented at the Eighth Biennial Meeting of the International Society for the Study of Behavioral Development, Tours, France.

Kliegl, R., Smith, J., & Baltes, P. B. (1986). Testing-the-limits, expertise, and memory in old age. In F. Klix & H. Hagendorf (Eds.), *Proceedings of symposium in memoriam of Hermann Ebbinghaus.* Amsterdam: North Holland.

Kline, D. W., & Schieber, F. (1981). Visual aging: A transient/sustained shift? *Perception and Psychophysics*, *29*, 181-182.

Kline, D. W., & Schieber, F. (1985). Vision and aging. In J. E. Birren & K. W. Schaie (Eds.), *Handbook of the psychology of aging* (2nd ed., pp. 296-331). New York: Van Nostrand Reinhold.

Kline, D. W., Schieber, F., Abusamra, L. C., & Coyne, A. C. (1983). Age and the visual channels: Contrast, sensitivity and response speed. *Journal of Gerontology*, *38*, 211-216.

Kohlberg, L. (1973). Continuities and discontinuities in childhood and adult moral development revisited. In *Collected papers on moral development and moral education.* Moral Education Research Foundation, Cambridge, MA: Harvard University Press.

Kohlberg, L. (1976). Moral stages and moralization: The cognitive-developmental approach. In T. Lickona (Ed.), *Moral development and behavior: Theory, research, and social issues* (pp. 31-53). New York: Holt, Rinehart, and Winston.

Kolers, P. A., & Roediger, H. L., III. (1984). Procedures of mind. *Journal of Verbal Learning and Verbal Behavior*, *23*, 425-449.

Koplowitz, H. (1984). A projection beyond Piaget's formal operations stage: A general system stage and a unitary stage. In M. L. Commons, F. A. Richards, & C. Armon (Eds.), *Beyond formal operations: Late adolescent and adult cognitive development* (pp. 272-295). New York: Praeger.

Kossakowski, A., & Otto, K. (1977). Personlichkeit-tatigkeit-psychische Entwicklung. In A. Kossakowski, A. Kuhn, J. L. Lompscher, & G. Rosenfeld (Eds.), *Psychologische Grundlagen der Personlichkeitsentwicklung im padagogischen prozess.* Köln, FR Germany: Pahl-Rugenstein.

Kramer, D. (1983). Post-formal operations? A need for further conceptualization. *Human Development, 26*, 91-105.

Kramer, D., & Woodruff, D. (1984). Breadth of categorization and metaphoric processing: A study of young and older adults. *Research on Aging, 6*, 271-286.

Kramer, D., & Woodruff, D. (in press). Relativistic and dialectical thought in three adult age groups. *Human Development.*

Krantz, S. E. (1983). Cognitive appraisals and problem-directed coping: A prospective study of stress. *Journal of Personality and Social Psychology, 44*, 638-643.

Kuhn, D., Langer, L., Kohlberg, L. & Haan, N. S. (1977). The development of formal operations in logical and moral judgment. *Genetic Psychology Monographs, 95*, 97-188.

Kuhn, T. (1970). *The structure of scientific revolutions* (2nd ed.). Chicago: University of Chicago Press.

Kuipers, B., & Kassirer, J. P. (1984). Causal reasoning in medicine: Analysis of a protocol. *Cognitive Science, 8*, 363-385.

Kuypers, J. A., & Bengtson, V. L. (1973). Social breakdown and competence. *Human Development, 16*, 181-201.

Labouvie-Vief, G. (1980). Beyond formal operations: Uses and limits of pure logic in life-span development. *Human Development, 23*, 141-161.

Labouvie-Vief, G. (1982a). Growth and aging in life-span perspective. *Human Development, 25*, 65-69.

Labouvie-Vief, G. (1982b). Dynamic development and mature autonomy. *Human Development, 25*, 161-191.

Labouvie-Vief, G. (1984). Logic and self-regulation from youth to maturity. In M. L. Commons, F. A. Richards, & C. Armon (Eds.), *Beyond formal operations: Late adolescent and adult cognitive development* (pp. 158-179). New York: Praeger.

Labouvie-Vief, G. (1985). Intelligence and cognition. In J. E. Birren & K. W. Schaie (Eds.), *Handbook of the psychology of aging* (2nd ed., pp. 500-530). New York: Van Nostrand Reinhold.

Labouvie-Vief, G., & Chandler, M. J. (1978). Cognitive development and lifespan developmental theory: Idealistic versus contextual perspectives. In P. B. Baltes (Ed.), *Life-span development and behavior* (pp. 181-210). New York: Academic Press.

Labouvie-Vief, G., & Schell, D. A. (1982). Learning and memory in later life. In B. B. Wolman (Ed.), *Handbook of developmental psychology* (pp. 828-846). Englewood Cliffs, NJ: Prentice-Hall.

Lachman, J. L., & Lachman, R. (1980). Age and the actualization of world knowledge. In L. W. Poon, J. L Fozard, L. S. Cermak, D. Arenberg, & L. W. Thompson (Eds.), *New directions in memory and aging* (pp. 285-312). Hillsdale, NJ: Erlbaum.

Lachman, M. E. (1986). Personal control in later life: Stability, change, and cognitive correlates. In M. M. Baltes & P. B. Baltes (Eds.), *Aging and the psychology of control.* Hillsdale, NJ: Erlbaum.

Langer, E. J. (1978). Rethinking the role of thought in social interaction. In J. H. Harvey, W. J. Ickes, & R. F. Kidd (Eds.), *New directions in attribution research* (Vol. 2). Hillsdale, NJ: Erlbaum.

Langer, E. J. (1981). Old age: An artifact? In J. L. McGaugh, S. B. Kiesler, & J. G. March (Eds.), *Aging—biology and behavior* (pp. 255–281). New York: Academic Press.

Langer, E. J., & Imber, L. G. (1980). When practice makes imperfect: Debilitating effects of overlearning. *Journal of Personality and Social Psychology, 37,* 2014–2024.

Langer, E. J., & Rodin, J. (1976). The effects of choice and enhanced personal responsibility for the aged: A field experiment in an institutional setting. *Journal of Personality and Social Psychology, 34,* 191–198.

Larkin, J. H. (1981). Enriching formal knowledge: A model for learning to solve problems in physics. In J. R. Anderson (Ed.), *Cognitive skills and their acquisition* (pp. 311–334). Hillsdale, NJ: Erlbaum.

Larkin, J. H. (1983). The role of problem representation in physics. In D. Gentner & A. L. Stevens (Eds.), *Mental models* (pp. 75–98). Hillsdale, NJ: Erlbaum.

Lazarus, R. S. (1966). *Psychological stress and the coping process.* New York: McGraw-Hill.

Lazarus, R. S. (1981). The stress and coping paradigm. In C. Eisdorfer, D. Cohen, A. Kleinman, & P. Maxim (Eds.), *Theoretical bases in psychopathology.* New York: Spectrum.

Lazarus, R. S., & DeLongis, A. (1983). Psychological stress and coping in aging. *American Psychologist, 38,* 245–254.

Lazarus, R. S., & Folkman, S. (1984). *Stress, appraisal, and coping.* New York: Springer.

Lazarus, R. S., Kanner, A., & Folkman, S. (1980). Emotions: A cognitive-phenomenological analysis. In R. Plutchik & H. Kellerman (Eds.), *Theories of emotion.* New York: Academic Press.

Lazarus, R. S., & Launier, R. (1978). Stress-related transactions between person and environment. In L. Pervin & M. Lewis (Eds.), *Perspectives in interactional psychology.* New York: Plenum.

Lefebvre-Pinard, M. (1983). Understanding and auto-control of cognitive functions: Implications for the relationship between cognition and behavior. *International Journal of Behavioural Development, 6,* 15–35.

Lefebvre-Pinard, M. (1984). Taking charge of one's cognitive activity: A moderator of competence. In E. Neimark (Ed.), *Moderators of competence.* Hillsdale, NJ: Erlbaum.

Lerner, R. M., & Bosnagle, N. A. (1981). *Individuals as producers of their development: A life-span perspective.* New York: Academic Press.

Lerner, R. M. (1982). Children and adolescents as producers of their own development. *Developmental Review, 2,* 342–370.

Lesgold, A. M. (1983). *Expert systems.* Paper presented at the Cognitive Science Meetings, Rochester, NY.

Lesgold, A. M., Feltovich, P. J., Glaser, R., & Wang, Y. (1981). *The acquisition of perceptual diagnostic skill in radiology* (Tech. Rep.). Pittsburgh, PA: University of Pittsburgh, Learning Research and Development Center.

Light, L. L., & Anderson, P. A. (1983). Memory for scripts in young and old adults. *Memory and Cognition, 11,* 435–444.

Loevinger, J. (1976). *Ego development.* San Francisco: Jossey-Bass.

Loftus, E. F. (1979). *Eyewitness testimony.* Cambridge, MA: Harvard University Press.

Logan, G. D. (1980). Attention and automaticity in Stroop and priming tasks: Theory and data. *Cognitive Psychology, 12,* 523–553.

Longergan, B.J.F. (1967). Cognitive structure. In B.J.F. Longergan (Ed.), *Collected papers by B.J.F. Longergan.* Montreal: Palm Publishers.

Lonky, E. L., Kaus, C., & Roodin, P. A. (1984). Life experience and mode of coping: Relationships to moral judgment in adulthood. *Developmental Psychology, 20,* 1159–1167.

Lowenthal, M. F. (1977). Toward a sociological theory of change in adulthood and old age. In J. E. Birren & K. W. Schaie (Eds.), *Handbook of the psychology of aging* (pp. 116–127). New York: Van Nostrand Reinhold.

Luria, A. R. (1975). Neuropsychology: Its sources, principles and prospects. In F. G. Worden, J. P. Swazey, & G. Adelman (Eds.), *The neurosciences: Paths of discovery* (pp. 335–361). Cambridge, MA: MIT Press.

Mackworth, N. H. (1965). Originality. *American Psychologist, 20,* 51–66.

Madden, D. J. (1983). Aging and distraction by highly familiar stimuli during visual search. *Developmental Psychology, 19,* 499–507.

Madden, D. J. (1984). Data-driven and memory-driven selective attention in visual search. *Journal of Gerontology, 39,* 72–78.

Madden, D. J. (1985). *Age differences in divided attention.* Paper presented at Gerontological Society of America Meetings, New Orleans.

Madden, D. J., & Nebes, R. D. (1980). Aging and the development of automaticity in visual search. *Developmental Psychology, 16,* 377–384.

Mandler, J. M., & Johnson, N. S. (1977). Remembrance of things parsed: Story structure and recall. *Cognitive Psychology, 13,* 307–325.

McKeithen, K. B., Reitman, J. S., Rueter, H. H., & Hirtle, S. C. (1981). Knowledge organization and skill differences in computer programmers. *Cognitive Psychology, 13,* 307–325.

Mehan, H. (1981). Social constructivism in psychology and sociology. *The Quarterly Newsletter of the Laboratory of Human Cognition, 3,* 71–77.

Mergler, N., & Goldstein, M.D. (1983). Why are there old people? Senescence as biological and cultural preparedness for the transmission of information. *Human Development, 26,* 72–90.

Mischel, W. (1981). Personality and cognition: Something borrowed, something new? In N. Cantor & J. F. Kihlstrom (Eds.), *Personality, cognition, and social interaction.* Hillsdale, NJ: Erlbaum.

Moshman, D. (1982). Exogenous, endogenous, and dialectical constructivism. *Developmental Review, 2,* 371–384.

Murphy, J. M., & Gilligan C. (1980). Moral development in late adolescence and adulthood: A critique and reconstruction of Kohlberg's theory. *Human Development, 23,* 77–104.

Nagel, E. (1957). Determinism and development. In D. B. Harris (Ed.), *Concept of development* (pp. 15–24). Minneapolis: University of Minnesota Press.

Neimark, E. D. (1975). Intellectual development during adolescence. In F. D. Horowitz (Ed.), *Review of child development research* (Vol. 4, pp. 541–594). Chicago: University of Chicago Press.

Neimark, E. D. (1979). Current status of formal operations research. *Human Development, 22,* 60–67.

Neimark, E. D., & Chapman, R. H. (1975). Development of the comprehension of logical quantifiers. In R. J. Falmagne (Ed.), *Reasoning: Representation and process in children and adults* (pp. 135–151). Hillsdale, NJ: Erlbaum.

Neisser, U. (1967). *Cognitive psychology.* New York: Appleton-Century-Crofts.

Neisser, U. (1981). John Dean's memory: A case study. *Cognition, 9,* 1–22.

Neisser, U. (1984). Interpreting Harry Bahrick's discovery: What confers immunity against forgetting? *Journal of Experimental Psychology: General, 113*, 32–35.

Nelson, K., & Gruendel, J. (1981). Generalized event representations: Basic building blocks of cognitive development. In M. E. Lamb & A. L. Brown (Eds.), *Advances in developmental psychology* (Vol. 1, pp. 131–158). Hillsdale, NJ: Erlbaum.

Neves, D. M., & Anderson, J. R. (1981). Knowledge compilation: Mechanisms for the automatization of cognitive skills. In J. R. Anderson (Ed.), *Cognitive skills and their acquisition* (pp. 57–84). Hillsdale, NJ: Erlbaum.

Newell, A. (1980). Reasoning, problem solving, and decision processes: The problem space as a fundamental category. In R. Nickerson (Ed.), *Attention and performance VIII* (pp. 693–718). Hillsdale, NJ: Erlbaum.

Newell, A., & Simon, H. (1972). *Human problem solving.* Englewood Cliffs, NJ: Prentice-Hall.

Nigro, G., & Neisser, U. (1983). Point of view in personal memories. *Cognitive Psychology, 15*, 467–482.

Nisbett, R. E., & Ross, L. (1980). *Human inference: Strategies and shortcomings of social judgment.* Englewood Cliffs, NJ: Prentice-Hall.

Nisbett, R. E., Krantz, D. H., Jepson, C., & Kunda, Z. (1983). The use of statistical heuristics in everyday inductive reasoning. *Psychological Review, 90*, 339–363.

Obler, L. K., & Albert, M. L. (1985). Language skills across adulthood. In J. E. Birren & K. W. Schaie (Eds.), *Handbook of the psychology of aging* (2nd ed., pp. 463–474). New York: Van Nostrand Reinhold.

Olsho, L. W., Harkins, S. W., & Lenhardt, M. L. (1985). Aging and the auditory system. In J. E. Birren & K. W. Schaie (Eds.,), *Handbook of the psychology of aging* (pp. 332–377). New York: Van Nostrand Reinhold.

Overton, W. F. (1976). The active organism in structuralism. *Human Development, 19*, 71–86.

Owsley, C., Sekuler, R., & Siemsen, D. (1983). Contrast sensitivity throughout adulthood. *Vision Research, 23*, 689–699.

Paivio, A., & Csapo, K. (1973). Picture superiority in free recall: Imagery or dual coding. *Cognitive Psychology, 5*, 176–206.

Patel, V., & Groen, G. J. (1986). Knowledge-based solution strategies in medical reasoning. *Cognitive Science, 10*, 91–116.

Pearlin, L. I., & Schooler C. (1978). The structure of coping. *Journal of Health and Social Behavior, 19*, 2–21.

Pepper, S. C. (1942). *World hypotheses: A study in evidence.* Berkeley, CA: University of California Press.

Perkins, D. N. (1981). *The mind's best work.* Cambridge, MA: Harvard University Press.

Perlmutter, M. (1980). An apparent paradox about memory aging. In L. W. Poon, J. L. Fozard, L. S. Cermak, D. Arenberg, & L. W. Thompson (Eds.), *New directions in memory and aging* (pp. 345–353). Hillsdale, NJ: Erlbaum.

Perlmutter, M. (1986). A life span view of memory. In P. B. Baltes, D. Featherman, & R. Lerner (Eds.), *Advances in life-span development and behavior* (Vol. 7). Hillsdale, NJ: Erlbaum.

Perlmutter, M., Metzger, R., Miller, K., & Nezworski, T. (1980). Memory of historical events. *Experimental Aging Research, 6*, 47–60.

Perry, W. B. (1968). *Forms of intellectual and ethical development in the college years: A scheme.* New York: Holt, Rinehart and Winston.

Phenix, P. H. (1964). *Realms of meaning.* New York: McGraw-Hill.

Piaget, J. (1970). Piaget's theory. In P. H. Mussen (Ed.), *Carmichael's manual of child psychology* (3rd ed., Vol. 1, pp. 703–732). New York: Wiley.

Piaget, J. (1971). *Biology and knowledge*. Chicago: University of Chicago Press.

Piaget, J. (1972). Intellectual evolution from adolescence to adulthood. *Human Development, 15,* 1–12.

Piaget, J. (1980). *Experiments in contradiction*. Chicago: University of Chicago Press.

Piaget, J., & Inhelder, B. (1969). *The psychology of the child* (H. Weaver, transl.). New York: Basic Books.

Piattelli-Palmarini, M. (Ed.). (1980). *Language and learning: The debate between Jean Piaget and Noam Chomsky*. Cambridge, MA: Harvard University Press.

Plude, D. J., & Hoyer, W. J. (1981). Adult age differences in visual search as a function of stimulus mapping and information load. *Journal of Gerontology, 36,* 598–604.

Plude, D. J., Cerella, J., & Poon, L. W. (1982). *Shifting attention through visual space: An analysis of age effects*. Paper presented at the meetings of the American Psychological Association, Washington, DC.

Plude, D. J., & Hoyer, W. J. (1985). Attention and performance: Identifying and localizing age deficits. In N. Charness (Ed.), *Aging and performance* (pp. 47–99). London: Wiley.

Plude, D. J., & Hoyer, W. J. (1986). Aging and the selectivity of visual information processing. *Psychology and aging, 1,* 1–16.

Plude, D. J., Kaye, D. B., Hoyer, W. J., Post, T. A., Saynisch, M., & Hahn, M. V. (1983). Aging and visual search under consistent and varied mapping. *Developmental Psychology, 19,* 508–512.

Poon, L. W. (Ed.). (1980). *Aging in the 1980s: Psychological issues*. Washington, DC: American Psychological Association.

Poon, L. W. (1985). Differences in human memory with aging: Nature, causes, and clinical implications. In J. E. Birren & K. W. Schaie (Eds.), *Handbook of the psychology of aging* (2nd ed., pp. 427–462). New York: Van Nostrand Reinhold.

Poon, L. W., & Fozard, J. L. (1978). Speed of retrieval from long-term memory in relation to age, familiarity, and datedness of information. *Journal of Gerontology, 33,* 711–717.

Poon, L. W., & Fozard, J. L. (1980). Age and word frequency effects in continuous recognition memory. *Journal of Gerontology, 35,* 77–86.

Poon, L. W., Walsh-Sweeney, L., & Fozard, J. L. (1980). Memory skill training for the elderly: Salient issues on the use of imagery mnemonics. In L. W. Poon, J. L. Fozard, L. S. Cermak, D. Arenberg, & L. W. Thompson (Eds.), *New directions in memory and aging* (pp. 461–484). Hillsdale, NJ: Erlbaum.

Pople, H. (1977). The formation of composite hypotheses in diagnostic problem solving. *Proceedings of the Fifth International Joint Conference on Artificial Intelligence, 2,* 1030–1037.

Popper, K. R. (1959). *The logic of scientific discovery*. New York: Basic Books.

Quine, W. V. (1953). *From a logical point of view*. Cambridge: Harvard University Press.

Quine, W. V. (1969). Epistemology naturalized. In W. V. Quine (Ed.), *Ontological relativity and other essays* (pp. 69–90). New York: Columbia Press.

Rabbitt, P. M. A., & Vyas, S. M. (1980). Selective anticipation for events in old age. *Journal of Gerontology, 35,* 913–919.

Reese, H. W., & Overton, W. F. (1970). Models of development and theories of development. In L. R. Goulet & P. B. Baltes (Eds.), *Life-span developmental psychology: Research and theory* (pp. 115–145). New York: Academic Press.

Reinert, G. (1970). Comparative factor analytic studies of intelligence throughout the human life-span. In L. R. Goulet & P. B. Baltes (Eds.), *Life-span developmental psychology: Research and theory* (pp. 467–484). New York: Academic Press.

Richards, F. A., & Commons, M. L. (1984). Systematic, metasystematic, and cross paradigmatic reasoning: A case for stages of reasoning beyond formal operations. In M. L. Commons, F. A. Richards, & C. Armon (Eds.), *Beyond formal operations: Late adolescent and adult cognitive development* (pp. 92–119). New York: Praeger.

Riegel, K. F. (1975). Adult life crises: A dialectic interpretation of development. In N. Datan & L. H. Ginsberg (Eds.), *Life-span developmental psychology* (pp. 99–128). New York: Academic Press.

Riegel, K. F. (1976). The dialectics of human development. *American Psychologist, 31*, 689–700.

Robbins, L. C. (1963). The accuracy of parental recall of aspects of child development and of child rearing practices. *Journal of Abnormal and Social Psychology, 66*, 261–270.

Robertson-Tchabo, E. A., Hausman, C. P., and Arenberg, D. (1976). A classical mnemonic for older learners: A trip that works. *Educational Gerontology, 1*, 215–226.

Rock, I. (1983). *The logic of perception.* Cambridge, MA: MIT Press.

Rommetveit, R. (1978). On Piagetian cognitive operations, semantic competence, and message structure in adult–child communication. In I. Markova (Ed.), *The social context of language* (pp. 113–150). Chichester, England: John Wiley.

Roodin, P. A., Rybash, J. M., & Hoyer, W. J. (1984). Affect in adult cognition: A constructivist view of moral thought and action. In C. Malatesta & C. Izard (Eds.), *The role of affect in adult development and aging* (pp. 297–319). Beverley Hills, CA: Sage.

Roodin, P. A., & Rybash, J. M. (1985). Social cognition: A life span perspective. In T. M. Shlechter & M. P. Toglia (Eds.), *New directions in cognitive science.* (pp. 116–134). Norwood, NJ: Ablex.

Roodin, P. A., Rybash, J. M., & Hoyer, W. J. (1985). *Qualitative dimensions of social cognition in adulthood.* Paper presented at Gerontological Society of America Meetings, New Orleans.

Rosch, E., & Mervis, C. B. (1975). Family resemblances: Studies in the internal structure of categories. *Cognitive Psychology, 7*, 573–605.

Rose, R. (1985). The black knight of artificial intelligence. *Science, 6*, 46–53.

Rozin, P. (1976). The evolution of intelligence and access to the cognitive unconscious. *Progress in psychobiology and physiological psychology, 6*, 245–280.

Rubin, D. C. (1985). Autobiographical memory across the lifespan. In D. C. Rubin (Ed.), *Autobiographical memory.* Cambridge, MA: Cambridge University Press.

Rybash, J. M. (1981). *Piagetian dialectics.* Paper presented at the Piaget Society Meetings, Philadelphia, PA.

Rybash, J. M., & Roodin, P. A. (1986). Making decisions about health-care problems: A comparison of formal and post-formal modes of competence. In M. L. Commons, F. A. Richards, C. Armon, & J. Sinnott (Eds.), *Beyond formal operations 2: The development of adolescent and adult thinking and perception.* New York: Praeger.

Rybash, J. M., Roodin, P. A., & Hoyer, W. J. (1983). Expressions of moral thought in late adulthood. *Gerontologist, 23*, 254–260.

Rybash, J. M., Roodin, P. A., & Hoyer, W. J. (1986). Adult morality: A Neo-Piagetian perspective on cognition and affect. *Genetic Epistemologist, 14*, 24–29.

Ryle, G. (1954). *Dilemmas.* New York: Cambridge University Press.

Salthouse, T. A. (1982). *Adult cognition: An experimental psychology of human aging.* New York: Springer-Verlag.

Salthouse, T. A. (1984). Effects of age and skill in typing. *Journal of Experimental Psychology: General, 113,* 345–371.

Salthouse, T. A. (1985). Speed of behavior and its implications for cognition. In J. E. Birren & K. W. Schaie (Eds.), *Handbook of the psychology of aging* (2nd ed., pp. 400–426). New York: Van Nostrand Reinhold.

Salthouse, T. A. (1986). *A theory of cognitive aging.* Amsterdam: North Holland.

Salthouse, T. A., & Somberg, B. L. (1982). Skilled performance: The effects of adult age and experience on elementary processes. *Journal of Experimental Psychology: General, 111,* 176–207.

Scarr, S. (1985). Constructing psychology: Making facts and fables for our times. *American Psychologist, 40,* 499–512.

Schaie, K. W. (1958). Rigidity–flexibility and intelligence: A cross-sectional study of the adult life span from 20 to 70. *Psychological Monographs, 72* (462, Whole No. 9).

Schaie, K. W. (1970). A reinterpretation of age-related changes in cognitive structure and functioning. In P. B. Baltes & L. R. Goulet (Eds.), *Life-span developmental psychology: Research and theory* (pp. 486–507). New York: Academic Press.

Schaie, K. W. (1973). Methodological problems in descriptive developmental research on adulthood and aging. In J. R. Nesselroade & H. W. Reese (Eds.), *Life-span developmental psychology: Methodological issues* (pp. 253–280). New York: Academic Press.

Schaie, K. W. (1977). Toward a stage theory of adult cognitive development. *International Journal of Aging and Human Development, 8,* 129–138.

Schaie, K. W. (1978). External validity in the assessment of intellectual development in adulthood. *Journal of Gerontology, 33,* 695–701.

Schaie, K. W. (1979). The primary mental abilities in adulthood: An exploration in the development of psychometric intelligence. In P. B. Baltes & O. G. Brim, Jr. (Eds.), *Life-span development and behavior* (Vol. 2, pp. 68–117). New York: Academic Press.

Schaie, K. W. (1983). The Seattle Longitudinal Study: A 21 year exploration of psychometric intelligence in adulthood. In K. W. Schaie (Ed.), *Longitudinal studies of adult psychological development* (pp. 64–135). New York: Guilford Press.

Schaie, K. W., & Labouvie-Vief, G. (1974). Generational versus ontogenetic components of change in adult cognitive behavior: A fourteen-year cross sequential study. *Developmental Psychology, 10,* 305–320.

Schaie, K. W., & Strother, C. R. (1968). The effects of time and cohort differences on the interpretation of age changes in cognitive behavior. *Multivariate Behavioral Research, 3,* 259–294.

Schank, R., & Abelson, R. (1977). *Scripts, plans, goals, and understanding: An inquiry into human knowledge structures.* Hillsdale, NJ: Erlbaum.

Scheidt, R. J., & Schaie, K. W. (1978). A taxonomy of situations for an elderly population: Generating situational criteria. *Journal of Gerontology, 33,* 848–857.

Schneider, W., & Shiffrin, R. M. (1977). Controlled and automatic human information processing. *Psychological Review, 84,* 1–66.

Schneirla, T. C. (1957). The concept of development in comparative psychology. In D. B. Harris (Ed.), *The concept of development* (pp. 78–108). Minneapolis: University of Minnesota Press.

Schultz, N. R., Jr., & Hoyer, W. J. (1976). Feedback effects on spatial egocentrism in old age. *Journal of Gerontology, 31,* 72–75.

Schultz, N. R., Jr., Kaye, D. B., & Hoyer, W. J. (1980). Intelligence and spontaneous flexibility in adulthood and old age. *Intelligence, 4,* 219–231.

Seligman, M. E. (1975). *Helplessness.* San Francisco: Freeman.

Selman, R. (1980). *The growth of interpersonal understanding: Developmental and clinical analyses.* New York: Academic Press.

Selye, H. (1956). *The stress of life.* New York: McGraw-Hill.

Selye, H. (1974). *The stress of life* (rev. ed.). New York: McGraw-Hill.

Schaffer, P. (1984, September 2). Paying homage to Mozart. *New York Times Magazine.*

Shiffrin, R. M., & Schneider, W. (1977). Controlled and automatic human information processing: II. Perceptual learning, automatic attending, and a general theory. *Psychological Review, 84,* 127–190.

Shortliffe, E. H. (1976). *Computer-based medical consultations: MYCIN.* New York: American Elsevier.

Simon, H. A. (1981). *The sciences of the artificial* (2nd ed.). Cambridge, MA: MIT Press.

Simon, H. A., & Chase, W. G. (1973). Skill in chess. *American Scientist, 61,* 394–403.

Simon, D. P., & Simon, H. A. (1978). Individual differences in solving physics problems. In R. S. Siegler (Ed.), *Children's thinking: What develops?* (pp. 325–348). Hillsdale, NJ: Erlbaum.

Sinnott, J. D. (1981). The theory of relativity: A metatheory for development? *Human Development, 24,* 293–311.

Sinnott, J. D. (1982). *Do adults use a post-formal "theory of relativity" to solve everyday logical problems.* Paper presented at Gerontological Society of America meetings, Boston.

Sinnott, J. D. (1984). Postformal reasoning: The relativistic stage. In M. L. Commons, F. A. Richards, & C. Armon (Eds.), *Beyond formal operations: Late adolescent and adult cognitive development* (pp. 298–325). New York: Praeger.

Sinnott, J. D., & Guttman, D. (1978). Dialectics of decision-making in older adults. *Human Development, 21,* 190–200.

Smith, J. (July, 1985). *Acquisition of a memory skill by older adults.* Paper presented at the Eighth Biennial Meetings of the International Society for the Study of Behavioural Development, Tours, France.

Solso, R. L. (1979). *Cognitive psychology.* New York: Harcourt.

Spearman, C. (1927). *The abilities of man.* New York: MacMillan.

Sperbeck, D., Whitbourne, S. K., & Hoyer, W. J. (in press). Age, autobiographical memory, and experiential openness. *Experimental Aging Research.*

Sternberg, R. J. (1984). Toward a triarchic theory of human intelligence. *Behavioral and Brain Sciences , 7,* 269–287.

Sternberg, R. J. (1985a). *Beyond IQ.* Cambridge: Cambridge University Press.

Sternberg, R. J. (1985b). All's well that ends well, but it's a sad tale that begins at the end: A reply to Glaser. *American Psychologist, 40,* 571–573.

Sternberg, R. J., & Berg, C. (1986). What are theories of adult intellectual development theories of? In C. Schooler & K. W. Schaie (Eds.), *Cognitive functioning and social structure over the life course.* Norwood, NJ: Ablex.

Sternberg, S. (1969). Memory scanning: Mental processes revealed by reaction time processes. *American Scientist, 57,* 421–457.

Stone, C. A., & Day, M. C. (1980). Competence and performance models and the characterization of formal operational skills. *Human Development, 23,* 323–353.

Storandt, M., Grant, E. A., & Gordon, B. C. (1978). Remote memory as a function of age and sex. *Experimental Aging Research, 4,* 365–375.

Sturr, J. F., Kelly, S., Kobus, D. A., & Taub, H. A. (1982). Age-dependent magnitude and time course of early light adaptation. *Perception and Psychophysics, 31,* 402–404.

Talland, G. A. (1962). The effect of age on speed of simple manual skill. *Journal of Genetic Psychology, 100,* 69–76.

Talland, G. A., & Cairnie, J. (1964). Aging effects on simple, disjunctive, and alerted finger reaction time. *Journal of Gerontology, 19,* 31–38.

Taylor, S. E. (1983). Adjustment to threatening events: A theory of cognitive adaptation. *American Psychologist, 38,* 1161–1173.

Terman, L. M. (1973). *Concept mastery test: Manual.* New York: Psychological Corporation.

Thorndike, E. L. (1926). *Measurement of intelligence.* New York: Teacher's College, Columbia University.

Thurstone, L. L. (1938). *Primary mental abilities.* Chicago: University of Chicago Press.

Tomlinson-Keasey, C., & Keasey, C. B. (1972). Formal operations in females from eleven to fifty years of age. *Developmental Psychology, 6,* 364.

Tulving, E. (1972). Episodic and semantic memory. In E. Tulving & W. Donaldson (Eds.), *Organization of memory* (pp. 381–403). New York: Academic Press.

Tulving, E. (1983). *Elements of episodic memory.* New York: Oxford.

Tversky, A., & Kahneman, D. (1971). Belief in the law of small numbers. *Psychological Bulletin, 76,* 105–110.

Tversky, A., & Kahneman, D. (1973). Availability: A heuristic for judging frequency and probability. *Cognitive Psychology, 5,* 207–232.

Tversky, A., & Kahneman, D. (1974). Judgment under uncertainty: Heuristics and biases. *Science, 185,* 1124–1131.

Tversky, A., & Kahneman, D. (1981). The framing of decisions and the psychology of choice. *Science, 211,* 453–458.

Tversky, A., & Kahneman, D. (1983). Extensional versus intuitive reasoning: The conjunction fallacy in probability judgment. *Psychological Review, 90,* 293–315.

Tyler, S. W., & Voss, J. F. (1982). Attitudes and knowledge effects in prose processing. *Journal of Verbal Learning and Verbal Behavior, 21,* 524–538.

Underwood, G. (1974). Moray vs. the rest: The effect of extended shadowing practice. *Quarterly Journal of Experimental Psychology, 26,* 368–372.

Vaillant, G. E. (1971). Theoretical hierarchy of adaptive ego mechanisms: A 30 year follow-up of men selected for psychological health. *Archives of General Psychiatry, 24,* 107–118.

Vaillant, G. E. (1977). *Adaptation to life.* Boston: Little, Brown.

Veroff, J., Douvan, E., & Kulka, R. A. (1981). *The inner American: A self-portrait from 1957 to 1976.* New York: Basic Books.

Volpert, W. (1980). Psychlogische handlungstheorie—Anmerkungen zu stand und perspektive. In W. Volpert, *Beitrage zur psychologischen handlungstheorie.* Bern, Switzerland: Huber.

Vygotsky, L. S. (1956). *Selected psychological investigations.* Moscow: Izd. Akademii Pedagogicheskhikh Nauk.

Vygotsky, L. S. (1960). *The development of the higher psychological functions.* Moscow: Izd. Akademii Pedagogicheskhikh Nauk.

Vygotsky, L. S. (1962). *Thought and language.* Cambridge, MA: MIT Press.

Vygotsky, L. S. (1978). *Mind in society: The development of higher psychological processes.* Cambridge, MA: Harvard University Press.

Waddington, C. H. (1957). *The strategy of the genes.* London: Allen and Unwin.

Waldrop, M. M. (1984). The necessity of knowledge. *Science, 223*, 1279–1283.

Waldrop, M. M. (1985). Machinations of thought. *Science 85, 6*, 38–45.

Walsh, D. A., & Thompson, L. W. (1978). Age differences in visual sensory memory. *Journal of Gerontology, 33*, 283–297.

Wason, P. C. (1966). Reasoning. In B. Foss (Ed.), *New horizons in psychology* (Vol. 1). Harmondsworth, England: Penguin.

Wason, P. C., & Johnson-Laird, P. N. (1972). *The psychology of reasoning: Structure in content.* Cambridge, MA: Harvard University Press.

Welford, A. T. (1958). *Aging and human skill.* Oxford, England: Oxford University Press for the Nuffield Foundation. (Reprinted, 1973, by Greenwood Press, Westport, CT).

Welford, A. T. (1977). Motor performance. In J. E. Birren & K. W. Schaie (Eds.), *Handbook of the psychology of aging* (pp. 450–496). New York: Van Nostrand Reinhold.

Werner, H. (1957). The concept of development from a comparative and organismic point of view. In D. B. Harris (Ed.), *The concept of development* (pp. 125–148). Minneapolis: University of Minnesota Press.

Wertheimer, M. (1945). *Productive thinking.* New York: Harper & Row.

Whitbourne, S. K. (1985). The psychological construction of the life span. In J. E. Birren & K. W. Schaie (Eds.), *Handbook of the psychology of aging* (2nd ed., pp. 594–618). New York: D. Van Nostrand.

Willis, S. L., & Baltes, P. B. (1980). Intelligence in adulthood and aging: Contemporary issues. In L. W. Poon (Ed.), *Aging in the 1980s: Psychological issues* (pp. 260–272). Washington, DC: American Psychological Association.

Willis, S. L., Blieszner, R., & Baltes, P. B. (1981). Intellectual training research in aging: Modification of performance on the fluid ability of figural relations. *Journal of Educational Psychology, 73*, 41–50.

Willis, S. L., & Schaie, K. W. (1986). Practical intelligence in the elderly. In R. J. Sternberg & R. K. Wagner (Eds.), *Intelligence in the everyday world.* Cambridge, MA: Cambridge University Press.

Wolf, T. (1976). A cognitive model of musical sight-reading. *Journal of Psycholinguistic Research, 5*, 143–171.

Wood, J. V., Taylor, S. E., & Lichtman, R. R. (1985). Social comparison in adjustment to breast cancer. *Journal of Personality and Social Psychology, 49*, 1169–1183.

Wright, L. L, & Elias, J. W. (1979). Age differences in the effects of perceptual noise. *Journal of Gerontology, 34*, 704–708.

Yeasavage, J. A., Rose, T. L., & Bower, G. H. (1983). Interactive imagery and affective judgments improve face-name learning in the elderly. *Journal of Gerontology, 38*, 197–203.

Zajonc, R. B. (1980). A feeling and thinking preferences need no inferences. *American Psychologist, 35*, 151–175.

Zelinski, E. M., Gilewski, M. J., & Thompson, L. W. (1980). Do laboratory tasks relate to self-assessment of memory ability in the young and old? In L. W. Poon, J. L. Fozard, L. S. Cermak, D. Arenberg, & L. W. Thompson (Eds.), *New directions in memory and aging* (pp. 519–544). Hillsdale, NJ: Erlbaum.

AUTHOR INDEX

SUBJECT INDEX

About the Authors

John M. Rybash is Associate Professor of Psychology and Human Services at Mohawk Valley Community College. He received his BA and MA degrees from SUNY College at Oswego in 1970 and 1972, respectively, and his PhD from Syracuse University in 1982. He is the author and/or co-author of over 40 research articles, book chapters, and presentations in the area of life span cognitive development.

William J. Hoyer is Professor of Psychology at Syracuse University. He received his BS degree from Rutgers University in 1967, and his PhD from West Virginia University in 1972. He is the co-author of the text *Adult Development and Aging* (1982, Wadsworth) and author and/or co-author of over 50 research articles and book chapters in the area of cognitive aging. He is on the editorial board of *Psychology and Aging* and is a Fellow in the Gerontological Society of America and the American Psychological Association.

Paul A. Roodin is Professor of Psychology at SUNY College at Oswego. He received his AB degree from Boston University in 1965 and his MS and PhD from Purdue University in 1968 and 1970, respectively. He is the co-author of the text *Developmental Psychology* (1980, Van Nostrand) and author and/or co-author of over 75 research articles, presentations, and book chapters in the area of life span cognitive development. He is on the editorial boards of *Child Development, Perceptual and Motor Skills*, and the *Journal of Mental Imagery*.

Pergamon General Psychology Series

Editors: Arnold P. Goldstein, Syracuse University
Leonard Krasner, SUNY at Stony Brook